A Different Childhood

Iris Johansson

Translated from Swedish by
Karl Nordling

INKWELL PRODUCTIONS.

ISBN: 978-0-9883568-7-0
Library of Congress Control Number: 2012922417

Published by Inkwell Productions
10869 N. Scottsdale Road # 103-128
Scottsdale, AZ 85254-5280

Tel. 480-315-3781
E-mail info@inkwellproductions.com
Website www.inkwellproductions.com

Printed in the United States of America

Thus, every phrasing, practically every word in this book is Iris' own, as they have existed inside her for many, many years. I think it is important to emphasize this because Iris' manner of expressing herself, her phraseology and all the Iriswords (the words she has invented, such as Irisword) add a further dimension to our understanding of autism since it illustrates how an autistic person thinks and expresses herself.

Göran Grip

Table of Contents

Foreword by Göran Grip

Foreword

What is wrong with Iris?

She's just a little late developing said the doctor at the clinic Mjolkdroppen. But that doctor was more interested in appendicitis and other illnesses than in a child's psychic condition.

She is retarded, others said. Or else she is psychotic. Place her in an institution, so she'll learn to behave.

She can provoke gall-fever on a dead horse said her mother.

A good spanking wouldn't hurt said her uncle.

But Iris' father knew she wasn't underdeveloped. Admittedly, she was mostly not contactable, and she was almost totally unteachable. When she spoke it was disconnected, monotonic, and incomprehensible. She wet her pants, refused food, screamed mostly, bit small children, and never did what she was told; in fact she didn't seem to even understand it. She could sit for hours by herself and just rock back and forth.

But why could she in rare short moments solve problems that the grown-ups couldn't, and why did she know so many complicated words she had heard only once? Why did she know to comfort the neighbor lady who just had found out that her son had died? How did she manage with little effort and great precision to provoke gall-fever on her mother, her uncles, and (almost) on dead horses? Why didn't she get hit a single time when she dashed in front of the neighbor's car? And why was she in some ways like an innocent baby, and at the same time a dyed in the wool con artist who developed the most complicated strategies to achieve her devious goals?

No one knew. But Iris' dad didn't give up. Lovingly he protected her from others, from herself. With infinite patience he explained the world to her and showed her time and time again things that other children could understand by themselves.

And when Iris was twelve years old she decided to finally climb out of her autistic, uncommunicative world and be "normal". With great effort she worked her way into "the normal world" and discovered with the total capacity for reflection of an intelligent twelve-year old all the peculiarities of "the normal world", things that for others seemed so self-evident and "natural" but which for Iris were riddles that had to be decoded, behaviors that had to be imitated, strategies that had to be thought out.

At the same time she retained her consciousness of "the primary", about that which counts when nothing else counts – that which counts before our upbringing and all our communication makes us forget it.

In the world of Iris' childhood there was no knowledge about autism, and no good "diagnosis" of her condition was ever found. When she as an adult encountered descriptions of autism and recognized much from her own life she suddenly saw a new dimension in her experiences and got a new understanding of them. She suddenly saw the part of her childhood she describes in the first two chapters, "At home" and "At school", in a new perspective. In the chapter *"About the incomprehensible world Iris lives in"* she formulates the story of her childhood in this light.

When Iris later learned about out-of-body experiences and near-death experiences, she could finally put into words still other aspects of her childhood, experiences that were entirely wordless, and which she as a child thought that every person partook in. One more time she had to reformulate the story of her childhood, and this she describes in the chapter "Outside the ordinary, inside the real".

Iris never succeeded in becoming "normal". But she became so much more. She has adapted to the normal life so well that no one who meets her today can believe that she has had these difficult problems as a child. And so well does she understand what happens inside people and between people when we communicate, that as an adult she has been able to help many youths headed in a bad direction. And during the past twenty years she has worked as a sought-after and successful guide for staff that works with problem-prone people. She also gives presentations and chairs study days and seminars on communications, intuitive pedagogy, majority misunderstandings, misconceptions and much else, not just in Sweden but also in Europe and Russia.

Today we know much more about autism than we did at the end of the nineteen forties. We know that it is something other than either psychosis or development disturbance, and that the level of intelligence can be very high. We know that autism involves reduced communications and social capacity. We know that people with autism may experience visual, aural and emotional inputs in a different and often painful way.

But how do autistic persons themselves perceive their surroundings? Why do they react the way they do? What do they see? What do they comprehend? This we know much less about – precisely because of their difficulty in communication. There are however a number of books written by "so-called" high functioning autistic persons which give insight in the autistic world. And now, here is *A Different Childhood* where Iris Johansson describes her world, eloquently, nuanced, and keen-eyed. With the verbal capacity she has mastered as an adult, she describes her childhood's wordless, concept-less experiences, sometimes with crystal clarity, sometimes with impressionistic expressiveness.

As a child Iris did not realize that people have an inner side. She saw their feelings only as something that "came out in the atmosphere", and which she found very beautiful, especially negative feelings. Consequently she loved provoking others and was pleased when they got angry and enjoyed the beautiful play of color and shapes. As she got a little older she learned to interpret what she saw of other people's feelings – so deeply and precisely that people found it eerie.

Iris also perceived sounds synesthetically. Besides hearing them she saw them as color and shapes.

When Iris sat rocking back and forth it was generally to come "Out", to leave the Iris body and "the ordinary world" and come into "the real world". When she was "Out", she was whole. She understood the world. She could swoop around the people, the animals and the houses on the farm, and she always saw how it all hung together without being able –or willing-- to put it into words. She saw her own body from the outside, sitting in the swing, quiet, absent. That thing was Iris, but it wasn't quite she.

To her father she told of her games and experiences when she was "Out", and he thought of them as her fantasy world.

What I personally noticed when I got to know Iris and heard her tell about her "Out", was that her descriptions resembled those given by many people describing out-of-body experiences, sometimes in the minutest detail. Especially her communications with her two "spirit friends" are remarkably like what is described by one of the foremost authorities on out-of-body experiences, Robert Monroe, in "The Ultimate Journey" and other books. Thus, Iris' Out isn't just her own private fantasy but has many features in common with the experiences of other non-autistic, non-psychotic people. This is not the place to try to interpret what an out-of-body experience is, but Iris' Out has an inner coherence and inner logic, and while she is Out she receives actual, valuable knowledge, both about "the primary" and about "the ordinary world", that she perhaps couldn't have learned any other way.

We also get clear-eyed and humorous insights into life in the nineteen forties and fifties on a Swedish farm with an extended family, with its mix of sham religiousness and unconditional loving, and interesting, gripping life stories that flash by.

To conclude the book, Iris has collected some of the questions she been asked over the years by the parents of autistic children, and which she answers from her unique ability to formulate and describe what it is like to be autistic.

Iris has much to tell us, both about what it's like to be autistic and what it's like to be an "ordinary" person, about how communication works and doesn't work between people, and about how it's possible to transform one's life for the better. It's not for nothing that Iris' calendar for guidance training and seminars is booked two years in advance.

Göran Grip
Physician and author

How this book came about

Iris talked already in the beginning of our friendship about the book she was going to write about her childhood and that would be called *A Different Childhood*. But nothing ever happened with that plan. In 1994 she and I were walking past a book store on Gamla Brogatan in Stockholm. My own book *Allting Finns* (Everything exists) had just come out. I stopped and pointed to the window and said, "Just think Iris when your book is displayed in this window." I noticed that she reacted, but she said nothing. Later she told me that it was in that moment that her thoughts about the book turned into an assignment, something that she actually was going to do.

Two years later I received a couple of diskettes with files for *A Different Childhood,* which she asked me to edit. But immediately thereafter I received counter-instructions. She was going to rework it and do some more writing.

The files were left on my hard drive. The years went by and I thought Iris had abandoned her book project. But ten years later, a few months ago, she came with a CD with new files. "Now it's time for you to edit my book," she said confidently.

I compared the CD to the old files and found that much was word for word the same as earlier, some of it was reworked, and some it was new. When I talked about it on the assumption that she had continued to work with the files I received ten years before she said: "Oh, I thought the old files were lost. I have rewritten the whole thing from beginning to end.

To a large extent word for word – after ten years!

In editing the material to come up with a finished book I have basically just reordered some segments, deleted repetitive parts and chosen the best version between the old and new. I have also asked her to further develop certain parts that I had recorded from her dictation.

Thus, every phrasing, practically every word in this book is Iris' own, as they have existed inside her for many, many years. I think it is important to emphasize this because Iris' manner of expressing herself, her phraseology and all the Iriswords (the words she has invented, such as Irisword) add a further dimension to our understanding of autism since it illustrates how an autistic person thinks and expresses herself.

CHAPTER 1

At Home
(Iris as seen by others)

On a leased parsonage farm in the middle of southern Sweden there lived an extended family. Grandfather, grandmother, mother, father, two brothers, and three uncles were the base around the girl. And also Emma, a distant relative of the mother. There was also Urban, a man with cerebral palsy, who wanted to become a shoemaker and was assisted in achieving this goal. Every summer there were also seven or eight "summer children" from impoverished homes in the big city, often with single parents who were unable take time off for vacation with them. There were also from time to time asocial or delinquent youths who otherwise would have been in some reform school, but instead got to work as farmhands with us. Sometimes there was a girl who had gotten "unsuitably" pregnant and been thrown out by her family. Other times an addict or a developmentally disturbed person who was uncommunicative in some way. Anxiety was a normal feature of the milieu.

The whole thing started with the childhood of my father's maternal grandmother (mormor).

Her parents were farmers and had a large family farm. They

struggled and slaved. Father's mormor had seven siblings, and all were supposed to get married and be set up on their own.

Mormor didn't want to get married to some dumb hick farmer so she asked her father if she couldn't instead stay home and take care of her parents in their old age. He felt that would be a shame because she was beautiful and smart and a good worker, so he knew she would make a good farm wife. But she did not want to be controlled by a man – as a woman she was legally incompetent – and if somebody was going to be her guardian she wanted it to be her father.

Since he had a weak spot for his beautiful daughter he agreed; she would not have to be married off.

Many men came courting but all were turned down and nobody understood why.

Then one day some guest workers came to chop beets. It was a group of young men who worked as day laborers. Among them was one who was a kind of hobo, a dreamer who mostly rested on the hoe and didn't get much done.

The daughter was the supervisor for his team and she saw that he was useless for this work. He couldn't tell the difference between turnips and weeds. She showed him what to do but at the same time was wondering what his mind was full of. He talked about the most surprising thoughts and contemplations he had and she was captivated by him. She worked side by side with him; or rather he walked by her side and talked while she worked.

One day after work she went to her father and asked permission to marry the guest worker. The father was shocked.

This good-for-nothing, this hobo who wasn't good for anything, him his beautiful and accomplished daughter wanted to marry. He didn't understand it at all, but at the same time he had this weakness for his daughter and he couldn't refuse her request even though he knew it would cause a scandal.

She pledged that if they could just live in the little house the parents had built for themselves to live in after they turned over the farm, she would take care of him, their children, and of course mother and father.

After a tough battle with his wife he said yes and the couple was married in a simple ceremony. It caused a scandal and a lot of gossip. They had eight children and they did take care of the parents, and in addition, the husband from time to time brought home some unfortunate person or another that he found along the road, and the wife made a place for them at the table.

That's how the kind of collective I grew up in got started.

One of their daughters, my father's mother and my grandmother (farmor) eventually married a farmer's son and they leased a farm. That farm became similar to farmor's childhood home. They had seven children and they took in and cared for people that came their way. A psychotic man and his sister who cared for him. A young girl who had a child; the child was autistic. An alcoholic who wanted help to become sober. A loner who didn't want to work and who needed help with the every-day things. And from time to time many more. My farmor continued in the tradition of her father without really understanding the point with it. In this way a new collective was brought about on the farm.

Then my father was born. He was the straggler in the group. His six siblings had arrived about a year apart and farmor thought that she was through bearing children, but then he came five years later. Farmor found it difficult, because she was sorely needed in the fields; he was born the sixth of July and she worried about how they would manage the harvest.

Then her mother died and she realized that her father, as the good-for-nothing he had always been, would return to his hobo-ways and this she could not accept. She brought him home to her house and told him: "You haven't been much good at working, but you have been a good father; kids you do take good care of, so now you'll have to take care of this little tyke. "

That's what was done. Father was taken care of by his maternal grandfather (morfar) and they spent a lot of time avoiding my farmor, so they wouldn't get dragged into unnecessary work. Farmor always worried that her beloved father wouldn't make it to heaven because he didn't work "by the sweat of his brow" but spent his time daydreaming and trying to understand life. In her eyes, this was both sinful and ungodly.

Morfar had a great interest in cows so the milking became his assignment. When he went to the barn to milk the cows he took the little grandson with him and afterwards he took the boy into the house so the mother could nurse him.

He pondered about the cows' reluctance to let go of the milk. Sure, they gave milk to their calves but they had so much more to give, and humans needed some of it but the cows resisted, so it was necessary to force the milk out of the cow's udder. The normal procedure was to feed the cow some hay, put on a kick halter so she had to stand on three legs, tie up the tail to the ceiling, or do something else that distracted the cow to make her let go, so you could milk her. Cows can't concentrate on two things at the same time.

But he wanted the cow to give the milk voluntarily through some sort of agreement. He looked at the cow, talked to it, stroked it lovingly on the neck and haunches and kept at it until she was totally satisfied and easy to milk. He proceeded like this with every cow. It took a very long time, but he seemed to have all the time in the world. Besides, he couldn't understand humans very well and often considered them so dumb that he'd rather associate with the cows.

This way, Father found himself in the barn with his morfar and the cows, and became a part of this process. He learned to understand nonverbal communication and to understand that it was the most important thing in the world: to be in connection, to be in contact, in communication and relationship.

When morfar and Father weren't tending the cows they disappeared to a creek and played with fishes and small animals, or were in the woods listening to birds. The grandfather knew a lot about nature's secrets and shared it with father. He had a special confidence in himself, in his ability to be contented and thereby could achieve empathy and communication with everything and everyone. It was only people that morfar couldn't understand. They were, as he said, into so much "extry". He felt that they kept quibbling about right and wrong, about being proper and godly, to sin and forgive, to pray and ask for God's forgiveness. In his eyes it was completely different things that were important. If a person was happy inside, then he could not be mean to anyone. So his goal was to always be happy inside. He tried to convey this to Father by showing him all the nature's phenomena, his love of life and finding meaning from that, that there is value in just being, that the world is beautiful, and that there is so much more to discover than we have time for in a lifetime.

This is the spirit father grew up in until he was twelve years old, when morfar died.

My mother was a welfare child, orphaned and poor. Her mother died when she was two months old. Her dad was a seasonal farm worker from Skåne, and he left the girl to her fate when his wife died. She had TBC, and my mother was infected by it at birth. She developed lupus; skin TB on her face and neck.

As an infant she was nursed by a neighbor who had a baby about the same time. After that she was moved from family to family for a period; later she ended up with her maternal grandfather. He was single but he had a daughter at home who was about twenty. He went to the authorities and pleaded for the little girl to be treated in the hospital. To start with they treated her sores at the local hospital by burning, but when that didn't do any good she was sent to a sanitarium in Halland. There she spent the first six years of her life, and when they came to bring her home she ran into the woods and hid, because she didn't recognize the ones who had come to get her.

Anyway, she came home, shy and scared. Fortunately, Emma was there. Mother could get some moments of comfort from her, but Emma worked and slaved on the estate from early morning to late at night, so it was mostly at night that she could be with Emma, sleeping with her. Everyone else was afraid they would be infected by her sores, but Emma said: "If the Good Lord wishes me well, I'll be ok even if the girl sleeps in my bed." Emma was OK, she did not get infected.

When Father was nine and starting his third year in school, my mother was starting in the first grade. In this little community all the kids knew each other before they started school, but nobody had seen this girl before. She was skinny and pale, and had ugly treatment scars from tuberculosis on her face and neck. She didn't know any of the other kids. She had met her older siblings only after she came home from the sanitarium, and they were ashamed of her because of the big scars and sores on her face. She was scared and got bullied by the other kids. They called her names, excluded her, treated her like a leper and were very nasty. Nobody wanted to sit with her so she was left by herself. She cried and cried and hid her ugly face.

Father became incensed. This is not how you treat a new scared little kid who is like a wounded bird. The girl sat on the stairs hiding her head in her hands. He went between her and the group bullying her and screamed at them to stop. He picked up his wooden clog and started chasing them and screamed if anyone hurt a hair on her head, he would kill the bastard.

Then he went back to her, took her hand and said "From

now on you are with me, stick with me and I will make sure that no one hurts you." She calmed down at once and went quietly with him.

When they came into class and everybody avoided her so they wouldn't have to sit with her, he asked his seat mate to move and went and got her. The teacher protested, since the first graders were supposed to sit at the front, but he challenged her: "If there is someone who will sit with her and be her friend then she can go to the front, otherwise she sits with me for I am her friend." Nobody volunteered so she remained sitting by his side. It had the benefit that she taught him how to read because she had learned that at age four at the sanitarium

That's how my parents met. But after the first two years in the same class they did not see each other until he was twenty and she eighteen.

My farmor could never understand her father, the hobo. She thought him irresponsible and shiftless. He did not believe in education. He considered that people turned out best if they were left alone to experiment and learn from experience and from the grownups telling stories about life. He figured all you needed was to prevent anything dangerous or harmful to others, to explain and let the child continue with trial and error to discover what is useful. In his philosophy there was no evil; evil happened because of ignorance and lack of security.

My father's morfar believed in God, but like he said: "I don't have much respect for God's representatives on earth, they just want to help themselves at God's and other peoples' expense. They use God to get power and have other people crawl at their feet and give their last farthing to the church, and that is not what godliness is about." He was clear on the human yen for the sweetness of power, the need to have domination and control over others, to have them bow and scrape and ask permission. He thought this was abominable and he despised those who practiced that kind of intimidation. He held it sinful to take advantage of people that way.

During the final years of morfar's life he was cared for by my Father. He was doing poorly and had difficulty getting out of bed and outside in nature. Father tended the cows himself and milked them before he went to school, and when he came home he took care of his morfar and had him along in the barn when he was doing his chores. Morfar told him everything he knew. He continued to decline and died just after father turned twelve. It was a great loss, Father was deeply grateful that he had been able to have his friend for twelve years.

Shortly after of morfar's death it was time for father to go to confirmation. He went to his mother and asked to be excused. He had heard about Darwin's teachings and he couldn't reconcile it with the God that the establishment believed in. If there was a god, it wasn't the god that the sham-religious in the congregation worshiped; that he could never believe. He was clear on what his morfar had told him about what real unconditional love was, and if there was a God, that was just how he was, not judging, condemning and punishing. That was the work of humans.

He read the bible and listened attentively to the preachers and asked impertinent questions, and he couldn't make any sense of it. For him it was incomprehensible. If there was a God, the world would not look like it does, with so much suffering. If there is a God, he would have known about human nature and wouldn't have put the tree of knowledge in the Garden of Eden... Anyway, to live in a paradise must be incredibly dull and unstimulating, where no unsolved problem is ever faced and not a single mystery is confronted. Besides, if God exists, the bible can't be right, since that awful, petty, punishing figure is impossible to see as a good and omnipotent God. To be any kind of symbol he would have to be better than ordinary crass human beings.

His mother was horrified and felt that he shamed the whole family. She believed she'd wind up in hell for eternity since she had a son who was such an apostate.

He decided he would go through with the confirmation for her sake and told the minister that he did not want to be asked about faith and participate in communion, but wanted to skip that.

He could see himself genuflecting by the altar in awe of the infinite, but he did not want "the flesh and blood" of Jesus in himself. The minister was a good man who thought it to his credit that he refused to feign. That's the way he was confirmed. The minister thought that God surely saw the doubt in him and let it happen father's way.

The years passed. Father and his brothers took up music. They played the saxophone, accordion and saw. All the young boys and girls in the area gathered in the granary at our house to play and dance. It became a tradition that there was music and dance in the granary every Saturday, from the end of spring planting until the end of fall harvest. It was known far and wide, and people came already in the afternoon on Saturdays and brought with them food and instruments. Oldsters, married folks, and children went home towards the evening, and after that, only young single people and the kids of the house remained.

Wintertime it became like a youth-center in the bunk house. All the young people were there, listening to Radio Luxembourg, playing cards and ping pong, playing live music, and talking. The religious people in the area considered it a den of iniquity, a scandal, but father insisted that it prevented many opportunities for sinning.

Everyone learned to play some instrument and everyone learned to dance, and when Father was sixteen he was allowed to go with his brothers to public dances. Actually, you were supposed to be eighteen, but he was allowed anyway because he was so mature and wise, and never got drunk.

Father had an older brother, Sven, who was sickly his whole life. He was asthmatic already at three weeks, and he hovered between life and death many times. Nobody thought he would even live to be one. He made it past his first birthday, and then they figured he was living on borrowed time. Year after year went by, he was badly afflicted by asthma and supersensitive to almost everything, the weather, seasons, dust, hay. His schooling became very chopped up and inadequate, partly because they thought there wasn't any point for him to learn a lot since he was going to die soon anyway, and partly because he was often absent from class due to illness.

When he was eleven he did not want to live any longer. He gave in to the illness, stopped eating and drinking. Father was then barely four years old. Father crawled into bed with him. Sven told him to leave but he said he would stay until Sven was well. Sven insisted that he leave, but he refused again and again. Sven asked him why he didn't go outside to be with the others or with morfar instead of sitting there being bored in his bed and Father answered: "Because then you plan to die, and I don't want you to die so I am going to sit here until you no longer want to die." Sven couldn't keep from laughing and decided to continue to live as long as life stood him by. A few days later he was up on his feet again.

When the morfar had died, Father devoted himself to Sven. He made sure that Sven made it outside during the day and he fixed up a bike for him so they could go for bike rides. Father was twelve and Sven was nineteen. Father thought that it was time that Sven started to play an instrument. He didn't have the ability to blow any wind instrument, so forget that. He couldn't do anything strenuous, so accordion was also out. But he was very musical so Father got him a saw and a file. Sven became a virtuoso at bending a saw and stroking with a bow to bring out the most beautiful tunes, and also at playing *with spoons.*

Sven got scoliosis in addition to the asthma, and grew a big hump on his back. He had a lot of acne, even in the face. He was shy and timid, and seldom dared to associate with other people; only if somebody came to the house and showed an interest in him would he dare speak to them.

Father thought that Sven should learn to dance. It was difficult, since he was often out of breath, but Father did not give up. They danced to the music from an old wind-up gramophone, and little by little Sven's condition improved and he found it fun. He had a very good sense of rhythm and after a short time he was a good dancer.

When Father was sixteen and was admitted to the dances he took Sven, who was then twenty-three with him, but Sven was too shy to ask anyone to dance. Then Father would dance with somebody and after the dance go with the lady to Sven and introduce them to each other and sneak away. Then Sven couldn't do anything except ask her to dance. This way he got Sven out on the dance floor, and soon there were more and more girls who thought that Sven was pleasant and a good dancer, and he joined the group and became part of the gang.

Sven wanted to get a light motorcycle, because he had so little strength for biking and the distances to the dance places were long. Also, he didn't dare ride alone because he never knew when he would get an attack and need to stop right away and get help with his breathing. Father and Sven each got a motorcycle and they ventured further away from home. This was a new world for Sven and he appreciated it a lot.

Father wondered why Sven didn't fall for some special girl, why he never courted anyone. There were many who cast glances at him. He maintained that he would probably soon die anyway. He didn't want somebody to bind herself with him and maybe have children who would be fatherless. Sven loved children and missed having his own, but as he said, "With death as your travel companion you don't take on family and children."

Once at a dance Father met the brother of the little girl he had sat next to during her first two years in school and asked what became of her. He answered: "She sits at home because she looks so awful that there can't be any sensible man who would be interested in her."

Next Saturday Father rode his bike to her house and invited her to go with him to the dance. She was terrified and said the same as her brother said: "There isn't anyone who wants to dance with me. I would just be a wallflower, and be ashamed, and that I do not want."

"I want to dance with you, and I will dance with you all the dances you wish, and if nobody else asks you I'll book you for all the dances." Mother laughed then and said: "But I don't have anything to wear." That was actually true, since no one had bought anything nice for her. Since she looked so bad, it wasn't worth it to spend any money for nice clothes for her. Father went to a neighbor who had a daughter about the same size and asked if he could borrow a dress and a pair of shoes for the dance. He could, and he came back with the whole outfit and said: "Now you have, so get dressed and let's go." She could offer no more objections and got on the bike rack and they rode off to the dance.

Sven was already there and joined Father and the girl. Then they took turns and danced with mother the whole night and had a lot of fun. Father received a lot of strange questions and many thought it was unpleasant of him to bring such an ugly girl to a public dance. People believed she was contagious, and did not hide their disgust, but Father didn't care, he liked her, that was the important thing for him.

Father was very good looking, and since he was a great dancer, there was great disappointment among those he used to dance with when he started taking mother to the dances. There was much nasty talk behind their backs and mother was even subjected to threats and malice.

Father went to his parents and said he was going to marry mother when the girl turned twenty-one and became of age, and that they would live on the farm.

Father's parents and siblings, except for Sven, got very upset and tried to talk him out of it. It was unthinkable that a farmer's son would marry a welfare kid, on top of it one who was sick, who had been brought up in a sanitarium, and who looked so bad that one was ashamed just to look at her. What a scandal for the family and for the whole area, what would people say?

Father explained that he loved this little person and that it didn't matter to him that she had a couple of scars in her face. She was practical, capable, and reliable, she had a good sense of humor and the gift of gab, laughed easily and became angry the same way, she was a good dancer and they had a lot of fun together. So whatever other people said, he planned to live his life with mother.

"I can't let something like that happen, I can't live under the same roof as that person" Father's mother said. "And where are you planning to move to mother?" he asked her and that ended the discussion.

They got engaged and "went steady" until Father was

twenty-three and mother was twenty-one. They got married in the church and Father had received some money by asking the invited guests for money instead of presents. This also was scandalous. Mother's relatives didn't even have "the salt for the porridge" and could not hold the wedding for her. Plus, they were ashamed of her. But with this unusual arrangement Father made sure she got the necessities.

Mother, who had lost her own mother at two and a half months of age, and grown up in a sanitarium for TB patients, and who had never met her father, knew she could not deal with small children. She got stiff and terrified by their needs and didn't want any because she knew she was unable to care for them.

Father wanted children very much and said if she bore them he would take care of them. He would see to it that she got the help she needed so she didn't need to be afraid. He talked it over with Sven and inquired if he could consider joining our family, not just like the others that lived under the same roof with us, but in another way by bonding with the children that would come in the family. He loved the idea, and that's how it became. His assignment was to always be available to mother as much as he was able and had the strength for. For him it was like having his own family without having to worry about death taking him away from his responsibility.

First my brother was born, completely normal and functional but crying at night. Mother got to sleep and Father walked and carried him until he fell asleep. During his first year he didn't sleep through the night a single time, and when the baby was awake he made arrangements for keeping the baby with him while working in the barn.

Fifteen months later I was born, and I wasn't planned. A child that didn't make a sound. A child who was awake all the time when others were awake, but who did not make contact with her surroundings. Mother has told me that when she was pregnant with me, her TB flared up again and she had to go to the hospital for treatment. When I was to be born she had to lie in the infectious disease ward because they did not know if she was still contagious. She hated hospitals and loathed lying there, but she had no choice. When I was born, my mother couldn't see me or touch me; I was transported immediately by taxi the 80 miles to the regional hospital where I received serum vaccine. I had to stay there for three days so they could make sure that the vaccination took.

Then I came back, and according to my mother I was screaming like stuck pig. She found it terribly upsetting, turned away and said "Oh no-no". Then I quieted she said, and after that I was so well behaved that they didn't notice that I was there. After that I showed no signs of any needs.

When I was grown she told me this story without understanding that there is something wrong with a child that stops making contact just because the mother gets scared by the child's needs. Maybe it was the case that the vaccination had an effect. Maybe it was the case that the three days of separation had an effect. Maybe it was the case that I had a weakness in my system that emerged then. Maybe it was a combination.

A few days later Father came to get us and took over the

responsibility.

He noticed that I didn't do any "hunger-crying"; he had to bring me to the breast every four hours so I could get some nourishment in me. I didn't react to being cold or wet or alone, I didn't sleep like other babies. He went to Mjolkdroppen clinic and saw the doctor and discussed his concerns, but the doctor couldn't find anything wrong, except he thought that it should be the mother who took care of me, not the father.

Father was also scolded by the other mothers that came to Mjolkdroppen; they thought it was outrageous that a father came there with his children. They couldn't understand why the mother didn't come. He explained, but then they figured she couldn't be a normal person. Father used to stay outside with us until it was our turn, and often the nurse would feel bad for him and let us into a special room and allow us to go ahead. This created a lot of resentment and became the subject for gossip in the community.

When I was seven weeks old, my father noticed another odd thing about me. My brother had pushed my crib so my fingers got squeezed between the crib and the wall and turned completely blue, but I didn't scream. "Warning, warning" his head signaled, but he thought it was just a one-time thing.

Some months later I was stung by a bee right between the eyes and dark bruises developed, which we used to consider a sign of blood poisoning, and I didn't scream then either. Father brought out a doctor to look at me and he said that the infection must cause unbearable pain and he couldn't understand why I was so untroubled.

Father realized that there was something not right with me. That I wasn't interested in my surroundings and didn't play, that I didn't cry for my needs, that I didn't make contact with anyone.

In his world it was essential to be connected with others. The most important thing in life was to be in contact. That's what makes you feel alive and gives you your self-worth. That's what allows you to develop naturally: that you are affected by the people around you.

This led Father to observe me closely and he came to the decision that since I wasn't going to make contact with my surroundings, he was going to make sure the surroundings made contact with me.

In the door opening to the kitchen he hung a small hammock where I lay when he wasn't carrying me on his back or could leave me with Emma. Everyone who passed could play with me. They could go under or around the hammock but it was not possible to avoid making contact with me. Even if it wasn't stated explicitly, I believe that Father had instructed everyone to play with me on the way in or out.

When I was bigger he hung a swing at eye-level height there instead. During the coldest part of winter when the door to the entry hall was kept closed he moved the hammock to the door between the kitchen and the bedroom. Most people passed through there also from time to time, so it was equally effective in contacting me and "disturbing" me.

He also made a carrying harness out of an old rucksack that he cut holes in, that he put on his back. In the nineteen forties in Sweden it was not common to carry children in a baby pouch, especially not while working with animals in the barn.

There are two factors about the carrying pouch that I now understand had the greatest impact on my development.

One was that Father suffered from psoriasis which made it difficult for him to have clothes between his skin and mine, which meant that I sat right next to his bare skin on his back. Thus I was in contact with him in a different way than if there had been fabric between us. This has had a great significance for me later in life.

The other factor is that Father had a habit of talking to himself. He would never have admitted this. He claimed he was talking to the cows, the radio, the dog, but in my world he constantly talked aloud to himself. With me resting my head on his back this caused me to constantly follow his word-melody. I have a clear memory of how words sounded, how the word-melody sounded, and I also know that I started sounding during that period. I didn't understand the meaning of the words, but I enjoyed listening.

I sat on his back until I was four and a half years old. If he couldn't take care of me himself, and I wasn't in the house and hanging in the kitchen doorway, he left me with Emma. Emma was more than eighty years old and a remarkable woman. She was a distant relative of my mother's and she lived with us because she didn't want to live in some nursing home. She had poor eyesight and hearing, and only one arm. She was born with one arm out of joint and it never grew out. Under her dress sleeve you could see a small thin white arm with an immobilized hand.

Emma had led a remarkable life. She had a unique way of thinking and understanding people. In her youth she had had two children outside of marriage, a son that was retarded and died at seventeen, and a beautiful little girl that died of appendicitis when she was five. This was a great tragedy for her, since she was very fond of children. Father asked why she never married and she said that nobody wanted to marry a poor, ugly, one-armed girl. You could be rich and ugly and get married, but not poor, ugly, and crippled.

She worked on the estate as a day laborer and did not get to attend school. She started working as a maid's helper when she was seven and worked her whole life. When she was twelve she went to the school teacher and asked if she could clean for him in exchange for him teaching her to read and write, which he agreed to do. She was born in the eighteen sixties, and as a single woman she was in a very vulnerable position.

When the social democratic party was organized in Sweden she was one of the first to join. She also started a women's association, and was the initiator of a library in the local *Folkets Hus* (People's House).

At one occasion she saved the estate owner's son from drowning and received a cow as thanks. She couldn't keep the cow, since she had neither a barn nor feed, so she went to the big city with the cow. This took a few days. She sold the cow at the market place, and then stayed in the city a few months with relatives and saw every movie that was being shown. It was the only excursion she made in her life and it enriched here enormously. She often talked about it and told about the things she had experienced.

She was asked by the SSU youth organization to be the director for their political theater. She gained much recognition for this work and made many friends.

When her younger brother got old she cared for him until his death. Then she had to move because the apartment belonged to the estate and she was no longer able to work. That's when she moved in with us. She had all her stuff in a bureau. In it was everything she had accumulated during her lifetime. Father liked Emma and had great confidence in her and I was happy when he left me with her.

When Father was carrying me he noticed how distant I was, and the same at first when he left me with her. But if he went out and peeked at us through the window he could see that I was in contact with Emma in an entirely different way than he ever managed himself. This made him realize that I was able to be in a natural contact, albeit only with her. He wondered a lot about this but couldn't understand the difference. He tried to talk to Emma about it but she just said if he stopped scaring me he would surely be able to make contact with me also.

He couldn't understand that I might be scared of him because he didn't notice any of that. But he understood that there was something special about being in contact with Emma, since he loved to be in her atmosphere himself. He felt glad throughout his body and she always said something thought provoking. But when it concerned me he never could understand how it all functioned.

During the lunch pause Father lay with me on his bed or on

the lawn and tried to hold my eye. Sometimes he succeeded. That made him happy, but then I immediately disconnected. Then he cursed. He discovered that if he was the least bit expectant or anxious it was impossible to make contact with me, only when he was completely neutral and concentrated. He also discovered that the contact was always on my terms. He was unsure if it really was him that I saw or if something else had caught my interest. He couldn't determine which. But he noticed that I pulled back if he himself had the least little need of his own. He had to play and entice forever and until finally he succeeded in making momentary contact.

He also perceived that I saw right through him, that I had a different way of observing than what he had seen in other children. He thought a lot about what this could be.

My brother was not like that. He was always accessible, laughed for joy, trembled with fear, raged in anger, cried when he was sad, and grieved when he lost something. He was full of activity, curious, inquisitive, and he was very, very social. He played constantly, could play with anyone and at anytime, could adapt to most situations, was easy to have along, and never hurt himself or others.

Sometimes Father found contact with me uncomfortable. He got an awful feeling of being wrong, incompetent, bad or mean, and most of all inadequate. He told me he sometimes got so angry that he wanted to fling me into the wall, and sometimes he got very scared or sad. It was as if I exposed some awful secret that he had. It was as if I constantly tugged and tore at his feelings even though I was completely absent. It was like I placed some kind of demand on him that he didn't understand. He had the perception that I existed in another world than the one he was born in, and which he actually didn't want anything to do with because it was not good.

His struggle was about him wanting me to be in "the ordinary world", the world where a person is a regular person with faults and merits, good points and bad points, where we are in contact, become friend or lover or foe and enemy. He didn't want me to be in the strange world that he didn't understand and that he believed could not lead to any personal satisfaction.

I preferred to be in my inner world, in what I later called "the real world" or "Out". "The ordinary world" – the one you thought about if you were hungry, cold, longing, yearning – was very strange to me. Sometimes for short periods I ended up there and it was very unpleasant. It made my body feel like an unmoving piece of meat that often hurt. Then there were a lot of dangerous demons and horrible noises that scared the wits out of me. Then I would often scream, bang my head and scream until it quieted. The light was also so unpleasant in "the ordinary world". Everything changed constantly, and my head burned and ached.

In "the real world" there was always a different kind of light, and it was very pleasant. In that world I associated with my friends. There were two of them, a light and a dark being; their names were Slite and Skydde. They were boys, but they didn't look like people, they were beings, they were "sweeps". You could think of them as a scrap of silk fabric that floats in the air, that sweeps through it, that sweeps through "The real world". That's what I was also: a sweep_but I didn't see myself as light or dark.

Father did everything in his power to keep me in "the ordinary world". He realized that I didn't develop like other children while I was in my world. Among other things, I wet my pants until I was nine years old.

For a long time he worked with me every day on potty training. It didn't work, so he made a special stool that he placed above the manure gutter in the barn and placed me on it and let me sit there until I had pooped. He showed me how, and demonstrated and tried to get me to understand that I was supposed tell when I needed to go. He did not succeed with that, but he made it a habit to place me over the manure gutter every morning and leave me there until I had done what I was supposed to do. There was a problem only the few times we traveled somewhere.

The peeing business worked only now and then. When the feeling of pee-urge arose I could feel it in the body but I didn't understand it. It wasn't connected to peeing. Little by little, I was able to get the thought in my head that when I had this kind of feeling in my body it was time to pee. It took until I was eleven before I understood that the feeling in my body was pee urge. And gradually I learned that when I had the pee urge I should go pee. If there was a toilet available then I went there, if not I still wet my pants.

Father wondered much about how I actually functioned on the inside, why things that were so natural and automatic at a certain age, weren't for me. He saw me as an unsolved riddle and he really wanted to solve it.

He puzzled a lot about my tendency to expose myself to dangerous situations with such precision and cunning with no thought for the consequences, while at the same time I was in some ways like an unknowing infant. He was afraid that I might get killed, at the same time he didn't want to limit me too much, but wanted me to experience reality and become anchored in it, which I was not.

He could see that at some level everything was well developed in me, but as soon as some knowledge or skill I had was to lead to an action, a consequence, or a function it just turned into peculiar stereotypy and irrational behavior and long incomprehensible harangues of words. This didn't concern me for a minute, but it concerned my surroundings a great deal. Not least because I was so helpless in daily life. I was not able to dress myself or even think to wear clothes, no matter what the weather. I was unable to get food if I was hungry, and anyway hunger didn't signal for me that food was what I needed. I didn't know to protect myself from dangerous things. I burned my hands and got ugly wounds and blisters, I wore shoes that chafed and wore the skin down to red meat. My need for continual watching was both worrisome and burdensome.

Why wasn't I interested in my surroundings and other people? Why wasn't I open to being interested in and playing with other kids? Why didn't I learn to speak by conversation instead of just saying a bunch of words and phrases right out in the air? For me the words were a game: words had shape, color, light, and sound, that was like a multimedia show, and I loved saying them. The more complicated the word, the better. For me they had a special sensory meaning but no content meaning.

Why did it seem like nothing meant anything for me, not animals, not toys, not other children, and actually not other grownups either? Why wasn't I interested in eating or drinking unless somebody enticed me into it? Why didn't I want to have clothes on and why didn't I want to give up dirty clothes no matter how dirty they were? There were a thousand questions that were buzzing around me.

Many told Father that there must be something wrong with a child that screamed so much and that he ought to seek help. But he said nothing would come of me if I couldn't get real help to develop. He was not against seeking help. He often asked others: "What can you do with this kid? I can't come up with any good ideas."

He tried to talk with mother about it but she was not interested. She just thought I was troublesome and impossible to get straightened out. I drove her crazy because I didn't do as she said, because I didn't adapt so I could fit in, and she thought I was dumb because I couldn't learn the same way as other children. She felt he was spoiling me so that I would never turn out OK.

He tried to talk with the doctor at Mjolkdroppen many times but he said there was nothing wrong, it was just father that was overexcited and overprotective and spoiling me. The doctor said the girl was a little late in her development but she would most likely catch up later. He saw me only when I was secure with Father who could keep me from screaming for that short period, so he never got a real picture of the problem. In addition, the doctor was more interested in appendicitis and other sicknesses than in a child's mental condition, so he was quite uninformed in that area.

Then Father tried to talk with the teachers and other people at school but there he just got a bunch of criticism. Nobody was interested; most gave him the advice: "Send her to an institution so they can straighten her out. There she'll learn to behave."

He saw I had no instinct of self-preservation; that I would do dangerous things without the least concept that I could be hurt or killed. Therefore, he always arranged for somebody to be responsible for me, and he would have skinned alive anyone who failed to take the responsibility seriously.

Sven was the only one he could share his worries with, but unfortunately, Sven was even more worried than Father, so that increased the burden, instead of easing it. Sven was an alarmist; he expected the worst; that I would be bullied, sexually exploited, raped, or damaged by ignorant people who didn't have a good hand for dealing with me. His black-painting made Father even more depressed than he normally was. He stopped talking to people about my peculiarities and made up his mind to teach me all he could, and hoped it would be enough to make me sufficiently functional that I wouldn't become a target for other peoples' aggression. When he had made that decision he proceeded to address all the difficult situations that I got myself into.

He figured he would stay a step ahead of me and this meant that he was constantly conscious of me and my behavior, that he constantly was reflecting on what I was doing and how it looked, that he constantly engaged me in contact if possible, and kept doing something that held my involvement. He understood that it would be bad for my development for him to leave me alone and not think of me and what I was doing. The attention he gave me was of a different kind than he gave others. There was nothing like expectations or demands, no wishes or visions about how it should be, only a cool, concentrated attention.

What was it he was trying to teach me and what was it that I actually learned? That was the great question that father lived with.

He kept wondering what my problem was. He understood it was something like what people had said about morfar, the hobo, but this had not bothered him so he didn't understand why so many people thought there was something wrong with me. His older sister had a son before marriage who was twenty years older than me, and he had a bunch of peculiar behaviors without there being anything wrong with his intelligence. Maybe I was something like that?

Father compared me with other children and how they developed. He realized he needed to study how children functioned naturally to learn what he needed to practice with me on how to help me develop in the best way possible. He had realized that it didn't pay to start asking others, because they immediately started talking about how he was spoiling me, and that I was so different that I should be in an institution.

He had already noticed that I was not interested in the outer world, I didn't play with toys, I didn't babble; I stayed silent up until the time I started to say difficult words and repeat them many times, as if saying them was important in itself. But I seemed to understand what the words meant. When somebody said something I could see what they meant, but I didn't connect it with the words they said. I never pointed and never looked at things that were connected to the word I said. In another way, I seemed to understand what was meant by what they said, but it never led to me reacting to it. It was as if I didn't care what had happened, what situation I had been in, or about what was going to happen either. To refer to something that had been, or was going to come was totally foreign and worthless to me and consequently it was impossible to get me to do things through rewards or punishments.

Father had got his interest in making contact from his morfar. He was interested in taking care of the cows and just like morfar be able to milk them without manipulating them. To milk a cow Father massaged it, talked to it, coddled it and when he achieved real contact she let go of her milk. With certain cows it was enough that he came close and said "let go" and the milk ran out into the bucket. Then both the cow and Father were happy.

His dream was to be able to have contact with all twenty-three of his cows but he did not succeed. There were some new heifers which were not the least interested and which required a long time to make contact with, and then there were a few old grumpy cows that blankly refused.

When he was tired he put me down in a calf's pen. Sometimes there was a newborn calf there, sometimes it was empty. There I would sit by myself rocking and being in my own world. He knew this was not good for my development but he had no alternative. He often thought that the worst part was that I wasn't part of the togetherness, that I couldn't share my feelings with others, and he intended to do everything in his power to gain me my entrance there. He was not so interested in what would become of me. That's what many people asked: "What will become of her if you just keep her here? Wouldn't it be better put her in an institution so that she'll learn how to behave?" Father answered: "Become and become, she is the way she is and on a farm there is always something she can do, peel potatoes or something. There are so many of us here, there so many hands that we easily can take care of what needs to be taken care of and look after her, just like we look after other people who are not fully functional, so she can always stay here. Someone like her can teach us things that we can't learn except by real contact with somebody like her. The function she performs is that she forces others to solve her problems and that isn't so bad. Just think, if every soldier had somebody like Iris to care for and worry about, then there wouldn't be any war and the world would be a different place."

People in the neighborhood thought he was peculiar, but they knew this from before, so you might as well just shrug your shoulders.

I sat up as an infant, but was not inclined to crawl. Father devoted an hour per day for several months sitting with me on the floor moving my hands and knees. Mother thought it was useless, but he kept at it even though he didn't see any results.

So he finally gave up, and suddenly several months later I started crawling beautifully. This happened often: he practiced and practiced and practiced without me seeming to learn a single thing, but he continued far beyond the bounds of what could be considered sensible. He said it was the only thing he could do to avoid losing interest and giving up. And long thereafter it turned out I could do it. This was incomprehensible for him. He realized that I learned things easily, but he couldn't understand why I could not apply what I had learned. He never quite got the hang of how that worked.

What he didn't understand was that it was so pleasant and enjoyable when he was practicing with me that I had no impulse to do what he tried to teach me, because then the pleasantness would stop. Not until much later did I notice that it had stopped, and that emptiness had set in. Then first, came the impulse to do the thing myself.

Retrospectively I have come to realize that the deal with me was that I understood everything that was said and done, but had no impulse on the inside to do what was asked of me. I had no will of my own in the sense that curiosity about the world outside awakened impulses in me to search for something. It wasn't clear to me how one should use all the stuff that came out of other people. What came out of them were wishes, expectations, requirements, needs, and such. I saw all that and I understood it in my own way, but what was lacking in my world was that I could do something or take part in it. I often liked it when Father was practicing with me, when he put me on my knees and moved my arms and legs, when he stood me on my feet and poked my legs to make me walk. I understood very well what Iris was, it was a she, it was the one that father was working with; I observed Iris objectively, from the outside. Or else, I was in the real world, and there I had no concept of myself. Inside it was empty, or not empty but quietness. I knew there was a lot on the inside, but because it didn't move it wasn't alive. It was like a painting or a sculpture, and I didn't know you could do anything with it except observe the movements and changes in the surroundings. That's what I often did, observed everything and everyone, unreflectively.

As long as Father kept working with me there were no stereotypyc responses, but when he lost interest the outer world disappeared. And when the inner world stood still I tried to make the outer one move so that I could feel that I existed and was alive. I started to flap my hands around my face and bang my head, grimaced and developed tics and looked pained. If I was able to rock back and forth, the veil released and I went "Out".

Togetherness, to be in connection with other people is what lights up the inside and stimulates the impulse system, and since I was not in contact very much, very little was happening inside me that was visible on the outside. The universe was in my inner world, in what I called "Out" or "the real world" and I was part of it, but in the ordinary world I was a stranger; I did not understand it.

Father noticed one difference between me and my twenty year older cousin. I didn't seem to have any problem being outdoors, while he, in contrast, exhibited signs of anxiety, powerlessness, despair, terror, and panic. Much later – when as an adult I had been tested in Gothenburg and been told that I probably would have received the diagnosis autism if those testing methods had existed when I was a child – Father said: "If you were autistic, you were in any case a happy-autistic child. The only emotion you expressed was joy. Although you often looked pained, with a frown on your face, all hunched up with legs and hands in front of your face, and you often ran off and crawled behind a chair or under a bed, especially when visitors came."

Some people said if Father would leave me alone I would be much happier and not have any tantrums. He relented for a while but it led to me becoming anxious, and when somebody came and tried to contact me I reacted much more negatively than I had when he had been with me in all situations. It strengthened his opinion that the togetherness was good for me even if I didn't seem to like it. After that period he didn't doubt that the best thing was for him to have me with him as much as possible.

When I was just over three years old he succeeded in keeping me in contact so that I couldn't disappear but stayed connected. This opened something new in me and I started to cry. A quite ordinary cry, like children cry when it hurts. I didn't disappear into my own world but remained in contact and feeling. Before that I had never cried like that and Father perceived it as a great step forward in my development.

Earlier I had not reacted at all, or noticed other people; they had been like props in my world. Now I reacted in a different way.

Now the problem was that I screamed the minute somebody else came into the room, and if somebody came to greet me I had a tantrum. To the people around me it seemed that I screamed constantly, that now I was really intolerable to deal with; that I had taken a turn for the worse. But Father insisted that it was progress. Everyone was in deep disagreement with him about that. Somebody often had to take me out of the room so people could converse and socialize normally. Father said it was only when somebody new came in the vicinity that I screamed, and that when I was with him it didn't happen, and the contact was much better than before. Nobody believed this, but my brother and Sven affirmed that it was true. Most people considered him defensive because he didn't want to face the truth and change his opinion.

Father at least viewed it as progress. Not because he worried about how much I developed but because he liked that I was reachable, that this was life, that it was a quality that I hadn't had before.

Now a new language appeared. I could speak for hours, talk, talk, talk. I could say very difficult and complicated words, could talk about inner and outer events in a holy mess. But it was not communicative; if Father interrupted I just restarted with something new. I never went back and said the same thing; if I was to repeat something I did it each time in a new way. He called it my imagination. In my world it was contact. I had the company of my own voice and loved the motion that came outside me when I let out the words. It was a new game and it pleased me very much. It simply became a new reality within me and it never disappeared.

I understood what words meant, but in a very limited way. The word lamp meant just that lamp standing there. If somebody said lamp about another lamp in the room, then that one wasn't there. It didn't exist until somebody added something that distinguished it from the first one, for example table lamp or wall lamp.

Father discovered that I didn't say "I" about myself. Iris was known, but when Father said I or you or we I got confused and started talking about something else. I didn't grasp the concepts of I, you, or we. It was difficult. Father wondered how he could teach me that "I" was I. He understood that I saw everything as outside of me, as objects, and that nothing had anything to do with me, that I was untouched by all the phenomena and feelings that surrounded me.

One day the cat and the dog were fighting about a piece of food and were tugging it in opposite directions. I laughed heartily at their, for me, unexpected behavior. Father saw them and also laughed, but he noticed that I laughed first and was extremely happy that I could react normally in the ordinary world. I registered his joy at my laughing and learned from this that my laughing out loud was something valuable for others. After that event, to the irritation of people around me, I went around and laughed aloud in all manner of situations because I thought that was how you were supposed to act. My laugh was not normal in the ordinary world, but I was applying what I had learned from Father's joy.

When I reacted emotionally I was not really involved myself, it was only a stereotypyc reaction, an inexplicable behavior. He noticed that when I was unhappy, probably because of some need I had, these strange reactions came instead. And when somebody tried to make contact with me and expected that I would react naturally I had different kinds of crazy reactions like shaking my head and hands and withdrawing from all contact or throwing myself on the ground and having a tantrum.

As soon as someone came that might expect that I would greet himher (my word for both sexes) or that wanted to greet me I fled and hid. I could stay away very long, usually until Father pulled me out and held me. Then I would twist like a worm until the atmosphere was calm, and then I could become quite still and sit quietly for hours. If I didn't manage to escape and someone came towards me with the aim of making contact I ended up like in a white milk, a kind of fog, and then I often heard an awful sound – it was me screaming – and I flew backwards, others said I threw myself backwards, and hit so hard that it hurt. Then the situation changed and the person that had approached me disappeared from my world and I was again back in the real world. Father said that "I lost myself" and in my world that corresponded to that "I was home", was "in the atmosphere". There was a state that was midway between being in the atmosphere and being in the ordinary world, and in that state I could perceive something which could be called feelings. Not in the sense of feeling sadness, fear, or rage, and express it myself, but in the sense of recognizing it in the state of others. Then I could do the right thing, say something, touch, and fetch something, so that the other person realized that I understood himher. It occasioned great surprise since I wasn't really present, and still I could get a feel for something and express a compassion that was stronger than what people generally showed each other.

Once, a neighbor sat gossiping in our kitchen. The minister and a policeman came in and told her that her son had just been killed in an automobile accident. Mother was speechless and the neighbor turned white from shock. I crawled out from under the table and put my head in her lap and looked at her until she started crying. I knew. This was very contradictory and confusing for my environment. Mostly, because it was not possible to dismiss me as retarded.

Father observed this and had so many occasions to brood about it that he finally concluded that there was something else the matter with me than retardation, but he didn't know what.

What was toughest on my environment was that I always needed to be watched, that I couldn't be left alone, because then I disappeared and they had to go out and search for me. I was not reliable, and since I didn't have any instinct for self-preservation or normal aversion to pain I could readily place myself in deadly peril. It was impossible to rely on anything I said. I could sometimes answer sensibly, it seemed, but it was often taken out of thin air and concocted at random. They tried to teach me what was right and wrong, what was truth and what was lies, but these were notions that I could not form any relationship to, so that didn't work. It could happen that I sometimes answered correctly, but it happened so rarely that nobody paid any attention to it.

As long as Emma lived there was no problem with the supervision because she always wanted to take care of me, and with her I didn't run away, I wandered around like a little troll around her legs. She, who could hardly see or hear, always had time and she told me about herself and about her life.

Father had observed that my problems disappeared when I was with her. It was like I then could hear and understand, could do as she said, had almost no stereotypyc behavior, and my face looked different. As soon as he came in the door I changed and all the special reactions came back, but if he looked at me through the window I could function adequately. This was his hardest nut to crack. He realized that no diagnosis known to him fit me. He was certainly conscious of the fact that I was dysfunctional in many respects, but retarded I was not nor mentally ill. And what is one then? This was his concern all the time until I was an adult and could explain to him how my world had functioned. Sometimes he thought I was just stubborn and didn't want to be in contact, but at the same time he realized that it couldn't be that simple. He knew that being in contact was much more pleasant and natural, and I wasn't; that was something not right.

My dilemma was that the state I found myself in was so secure and pain-free that I always wanted to remain there. But at the same time it was completely lonely and this I could not stand. I filled the emptiness with all kinds of things: I scratched myself, bit myself, banged my head in the wall, and chewed my lips bloody. I would cause myself pain, and the emptiness eased and I could laugh.

Father had made up his mind that, in spite of my resistance, I would be in the general togetherness as much as possible. He understood that my development for social life depended on people around me being available to help entice me and draw out my interest in other people.

I was often under the kitchen table when everyone was eating, and sat there and rocked myself in to the real world. That world consisted of all the normal material things, but also of the immaterial, the information that is in the atmosphere around us. It was like the real world was universal, but that I experienced only the very nearest part of it. I might sit on a swing, or on the toilet, and find myself in the atmosphere, in the real world, released from the ordinary world. If nobody came and got me and activated me, I stayed in it, because I had no interest in the ordinary world. My bodily needs took me down to the ordinary world, but I had no impulse to actively make sure I got what I needed, that kind of self-preservation instinct was something I lacked. I didn't have any concept of real dangers either; therefore I exposed myself to deadly peril several times per day.

People didn't exist for me in any real sense. My life was populated with everything between heaven and earth – chairs, tables, plants, animals, and people – and everything was just circumstances that I was aware of. People were more troublesome than animals and other things, because they changed all the time and wanted things from me that were incomprehensible, and often painful and disturbing.

I loved to bite small children. They screamed bloody murder

and this sound pleased me and I couldn't understand why I wasn't allowed to bite them. The atmosphere got so beautiful from the child's screaming, and even more beautiful from the upset feelings that the grown-ups around me contributed in addition. I was very attracted by excited feelings in others, and I succeeded in producing these from time to time.

I was grumpy, hard to restrain, loud, and aggressive. I wasn't interested in things, but sometimes something caught my attention, and then I could often destroy it. I often bit people and animals so hard that they screamed bloody murder, and then laughed. I laughed even more when the people around me became enraged and the air became full of crackling light tongues in different colors. I scratched myself, bit myself, licked the wounds to make them sting, tore the skin inside my lips, chewed my nails until they bled, refused to move, or just kept walking in some fixed direction, and screamed, screamed, grabbed things, dropped fragile things, bit small children to make them cry, walked in front of cars and other machines, pulled animals by the tail or ears. When I wasn't making trouble I used to flap my hands around my face, bang my head, and hum monotonously or walked round and round and talked to myself.

I retained many of these behaviors all the way into my teens, but no new ones emerged, and one by one they disappeared as I made more and more contact with regular life.

My daily screaming had started when I was about three, when Father had succeeded in holding my gaze and kept me in the ordinary world. For years I screamed every day for anything and for nothing, and became an even greater pain for my surroundings. But when I was a little over six, one day a peddler came into the kitchen and addressed me, perhaps only said "hi". My pain started as usual and I started howling. But this time, something different happened. The peddler roared at me: "Goddam it kid, nobody is trying to kill you". This took. I shut suddenly up, the fog cleared and I stood completely still and saw a whole new world. It was like my eyes had changed in some way. That peddler had the same presence as Emma and later Fil.

After that event my daily screaming ceased and returned only for brief moments in pressure situations. This was a relief for everybody; also, after this I became easier to manage, both in terms of using the toilet and washing and combing. I now could tolerate being handled by other people, just standing still and letting happen what others wanted. I became instinctively accommodating and seldom caused difficulties. Occasionally I could give relevant answers when spoken to, but most of the time I was off in the blue and my answers were an unintelligible mishmash.

Despite everything, I became more and more functional as time went on. Even if I still lived in my own world I could be with the other kids for hours without getting into danger or running away to hide somewhere so they had to send a search party for me. I exhibited signs of unease when I got the pee urge and didn't wet my pants as frequently any more. The same, when I was cold and freezing, or when I was too warm. People could predict and guess more accurately about my needs even though

I still didn't express them adequately.

At about six, another new thing happened. I started to be all over my brother. I began to be concerned about where he was and to tag along behind him. I also showed signs of having understood a great deal that they thought earlier I was ignorant of, for example pictures in books and certain toys.

I grew and was early in my physical development. I looked quite functional but I had a lot of difficulty learning the elementary things in life. Many things Father had ritualized with me so they were automatic, even though I didn't have a feeling for what I did. It had no significance for me, but I did them on autopilot, as for example going to the toilet or putting on outer wear.

I had no ability to calculate and remember. I could not hold something in memory and think in several stages, so when there was an opportunity to act I always grabbed it quick as a weasel, almost like a conditioned reflex. There are innumerable stories about this crazy behavior, and today they are funny incidents that people use as their anecdotal showpieces. Once I came running to the barn and told Father that the neighbor who lived on the other side of the cemetery had got a maggot infestation in the root cellar with all the root vegetables, carrots, and potatoes and that the whole harvest was destroyed, and they were just crawling all over when they opened the door. Shocked by what I had told him, Father went to the neighbor to commiserate about the terrible thing that had happened. The neighbor had no idea what he was talking about and finally it dawned on Father that he had forgotten his usual question to me when I told him something dramatic: Is it for real or is it inside you? I was always able to answer that question. I knew that Father's "inside you" was what I called "out in the real world" in contrast to the ordinary world which he called "for real".

I knew quite well that we meant the same thing, Father and I, but I never adopted his definitions of reality but stuck stubbornly to my own words and descriptions. He sighed heavily and sometimes he became depressed because I could never accept the normal way to look at things.

If somebody else asked if something was for real I sometimes didn't answer at all or gave them some arbitrary answer that had nothing to do with what the person asked about.

Since I couldn't understand the dimension where I could say "I" about myself, but could only understand Iris as an object, he started wondering how he could train me in that area. He understood that I could never think independently if I couldn't be a subject, from the inside out; he thought this would be a real problem in life.

He mounted a big mirror in a clothes closet without windows. Then he took me there and held me in front of the mirror. In my world it was like a big black hole that sucked me in and I screamed, bit, and squirmed to get free and get away. He held me in front of the mirror until I discovered that it was harmless. He realized he was on the verge of abuse, and he was careful not to do it longer than I could stand. Then one day I showed signs that I could tolerate the situation, I went there of my own without protests, and then he could start to train me. He explained what a mirror was and that it reflected the picture. I didn't see any picture, I saw only a typhoon-like spiral that went into the dark, that was like a suction that sucked me in and I got lost in.

He repeated this practice many times until I could stand still and keep from fending him off. When he had got me to stand still and look I saw something fuzzy that moved sometimes and stood still sometimes. I saw two different shapes. Father was like he was, quite distinct, but the other was a peculiar little thing, I don't know what, and it was that he told me to look at.

He held my hair and said this is hair. He told me about hair and the color of hair. He showed his own hair and talked about it. Little by little I could see the hair on my head, see my eyes and their color, see my face, my body, my clothes. I was told to say "I have yellow hair, I have blue eyes, I have two hands". He practiced with me every day in front of the mirror for two to three hours depending on how much time he could take off.

He continued to teach me life, through mirror practices and by showing me all the phenomena he ran into and he let me paint and draw, especially on a slate with white chalk. The problem was that I sometimes ate up the chalk and was hoarse for a whole day.

He observed how I slowly changed during this training, and finally, a couple of years later I was able to say "I" about myself. Completely understand it I did not; since everyone said "I" about themselves it was very difficult. This every-person usage was so peculiar, that others could be the same as me.

To be able to say "I" about me opened new possibilities

since others seemed to become less concerned with focusing on me, my words, and my behaviors. I could also see that there was a difference between someone talking about somebody as a third person, as in a story, and somebody addressing "you", talking to the "you".

Little by little, "we" came into the picture and this I found easy. "We" was everyone who was in the room; hence there was no problem for me to say "we". But one day the Road Association had a meeting in our kitchen. A board member told my uncles: "We have decided to use oil-gravel as paving for the road and plan to start with it soon." My uncles looked at each other and one of them said: "But *we* don't agree with this. We heard on the radio that oil-gravel is toxic for the soil." Then I understood nothing again. Here there were some in the room that said "we" about themselves and some others who also said "we" about themselves and who were in disagreement with the first "we". I asked Father and he finally realized what it was I didn't understand and told me that "we" meant that a few of them were in agreement about something and that one spoke for them all, and that they all didn't need to be present in the room. This was very complicated for me, because I couldn't even imagine that a person existed that wasn't present in the room.

My mother's aunts and uncles were very poor and very gifted. The uncles joined the military, which was their only chance to get an education, and they eventually became high officers and policemen and joined the Conservative party. The aunts who were just as gifted were sent to work in a factory and eventually married shipyard workers who were socialists.

During the Christmas holidays when these rightists and socialists came to our home with its social democrats and farm-unionists, the question of which "we" was under discussion became very complicated for me.

My mother's uncle, the major, leaned over on the table and said: "Public health insurance is unacceptable. We all know how people goof off the minute you turn your back."

The husband of my mother's aunt, the shipyard worker, leaned towards him from the other side of the table and raised his fist to slug him.

I was quicker than him and had time to ask: "Who are "we" who know that people want to goof off instead of work?"

The shipyard worker got distracted by the interruption and not a word crossed his lips.

"Don't you understand you're not to interrupt like that" the major said angrily.

The argument that everyone had charged up for got derailed and everyone got mad at me instead.

The usual opinion about me was that I was impudent and disturbed people's peace of mind. I interrupted and shifted the topic of conversation to something else that people in general were not interested in. They got frustrated because they didn't get to finish talking, especially when it involved gossip. I asked: "What's her name? Who is she? Who is he? Why do you say he is dumb?" And I didn't wait for an answer. I wasn't interested in the answer per se; I was interested in people's reactions. For me it was what came out in the atmosphere, -- emotional charges, how they changed the light, sound, and moving shapes that preoccupied me-- that was the interesting and important. That this led to a bunch of other people feeling confused and irritated, and was something negative for them, this I had no inkling of. I had been told that emotions were the most important thing in life, that to have feelings enriched life and made it sweet. Not that I understood what it meant but I thought people wanted to have feelings, so I didn't grasp it was something negative when they got the kind of feelings that I engendered.

People found my presence disagreeable. At first they saw me as a nut-case that you didn't need to pay attention to. Later when my questions revealed that I had understood every detail of their conversation they became ice cold inside and wondered if I was reliable, or might divulge their gossiping and create embarrassing situations. It was a justified fear, because much later in another crowd I could very easily scandalize everybody without the least consideration or feeling for tact and tone. We were at a birthday party. Somebody told a story about bed straw. That reminded me of a story I had heard half a year earlier when Signe, one of the more elegant neighbor ladies had paid a visit.

Without any thought about the consequences I blurted out: "Signe said that Andersson went with Svea into the barn and did something shameful in the straw, and then they came out and Svea was all red in the face."

There was a dead silence around the table.

Svea became furious and said angrily to Signe: "That's the most ridiculous thing I ever heard."

Signe looked beseechingly at mother to get her to say that I had made the whole thing up but she didn't because she knew very well that I had heard correctly, and Father was there at the party so she couldn't lie about me.

Signe started crying and got up and left. Her husband apologized and left also.

Svea's husband said to Svea: "You know how women are; it is nothing to worry about." With that the whole party was over and everyone left. Mother bawled me out when we came home

Besides finding me impudent, people perceived that I saw right through them and touched something inside them that stirred their emotions. One warm summer evening when there was a barn dance at our place I sat, as I often did, in the lilac arbor and listened to my Uncle Sven. He was quite close to me talking with Monica, who had been a "summer child" with us, and now some years later had come for a visit. They talked about everyday things. Suddenly I saw a story appearing in the atmosphere like a film which was now for me to tell.

With a dramatic voice I declaimed aloud so they could hear me: "When a young poor girl came to the estate as a nanny there was a squire's son who was a bachelor. She looked at him and her heart almost seized up from love. But she was afraid that he would not notice it, because it was impossible that this rich man's son would care for a poor uneducated girl from the city. She began to weave secret dreams about life together with the squire's son, about how they got their own place and how she would take care of the household and make it pleasant and care for their mutual children which would be well-behaved.

She pined and longed for a close friendship with him and she would make sure that he had a good life. But she suffered in secret. Oh how hard it is in life when one must conceal all one's strong feelings, all this love she couldn't show. This was a feeling she would have to take to the grave, because it was impossible and would not be something the strict demanding squire's wife would take kindly to."

When I was finished, Sven said to me: "You always have to inject yourself with all your stories."

I didn't know where my story had come from, and Sven didn't understand it either. He and Monica continued to talk about everyday things, but there was a warmth between them that had not been there before.

Many years later Monica told me she got the chills when she listened to my story as I sat there on the ground in the lilac arbor. She admitted that I had seen through her great well-protected secret, that she was deeply in love with Sven, but never ever intended to show it since he was from a farm family and she was a poor uneducated girl from the city. What had scared her that time was that with a single word I could have destroyed her feelings by laughing at her or making fun of her, because she felt I didn't have an ounce of compassion for her or anyone else either.

I was flabbergasted myself. I hadn't had any idea that the story came from her. I didn't see *inside* people of course, I didn't grasp in those days that there was something *inside* other people; I only saw what came *out*, what ended up in the atmosphere.

Monica confided that she had talked about me with others and had found out that I had similarly seen through other people in my surroundings, and they had discussed whether I was a witch or possessed in some way.

I sometimes would pick the skin from under my upper lip so that it bled and the lip got swollen and then I would strike the swelling with my thumb to make it even worse. I sometimes would suck my upper lip into my nose or lick my nostril with my tongue. Also, I often sat rocking back and forth flapping my hands. It was all very uncouth and disturbing to others and made it unpleasant for them. Many wanted to try to civilize me, and I often got admonished about what not to do. In my world this led me to think they were satisfied by saying what they said, but that was not the idea. I was supposed to stop, but I never knew exactly what I was supposed to stop because I seldom knew what had caused their disapproval.

When people who came to visit caught sight of me, they quickly took care of their errand and left. But I liked the atmosphere that arose when they were unaware of my presence, and therefore I often sat in a closet or under the table, quiet as a mouse, and with the tablecloth hanging down it could take some time before they became aware of my presence. This way I got to hear a good many of their stories about others. They were in the ordinary world looking at events fragmented out of their greater context and didn't have an understanding of the real world. They didn't know that I was in the real world and thereby listening to them non-judgmentally, so many times they felt uncomfortable when they became aware of me and had no idea of how long I had been in the room.

A neighbor was sitting in our kitchen gossiping about the minister: "As if it isn't enough with the oldest son, a sinner who drinks and fights and carries on. Now the daughter has met a guy from the *reform school* and stays out late at night. And you can imagine what they do."

"You don't say! The reform school. That's awful" mother answered.

I said from my place under the table: "She is only doing what her daddy says!" It got completely quiet around the table.

What I had seen coming out in the atmosphere, in addition to what he said with words, was that he in some way also had understood that the minister's daughter had taken the Christian message seriously and wanted to help this delinquent straighten out his life, but that they preferred to wallow in the scandalous.

In my world, I was present in the ordinary world as an observer, not as an active participant. I wasn't in an "I", but inside an Iris who observed the world. It wasn't like I thought and reflected about others and about events and things. Not like I even had a desire or ambition to be more in contact. In reality, people were like objects for me, objects without an inner aspect. The idea that you could be in contact with them didn't exist in my world, so for me observation was the only alternative. But on the other hand, people often got upset or indignant with me, and the fact is I could with great precision and timing get people very agitated. When a child misbehaves it tends to be because of anger or rage, but that was not the case with me. I made people react to get the emptiness to disappear and to get something to happen in the atmosphere so that I could be calm on the inside. I started to walk across the room. Somebody stood in the way. I wouldn't consider going around, and I couldn't communicate directly with the person either. But I had figured out that if stood right next to himher and shook my head and hands and hummed aloud it would irritate the person and heshe would move out of the way. And then I could continue straight ahead.

People are so unpredictable. They could suddenly change in unpredictable ways, and then I was forced to rearrange so that it would be "right". I could spend all kinds of time on rearranging until everything was "right".

When somebody shattered my "observation world" and addressed me directly it got threatening and unpleasant and then I often had screwy reactions. One day when I came from the kitchen, a relative appeared unexpectedly in front of me outside the kitchen door. He looked straight at me and said testily: "It is awful how you look. Can't you wash yourself and put your clothes on?" In my world he became like a demon. He grew gigantic and his face got grotesque like a troll's. What came out of his mouth was like a slimy mass that would stick to me like syrup to a butterfly, and I tried to avoid it. I threw myself backward and screamed and then it got like a white wet-warm fog around me, like milk without being liquid. That was liberating since then the demons disappeared, didn't exist anymore.

Sometimes in such situations there would be a voice that broke through the fog and revealed itself as something horrible and then I would disappear into a haze that was like sleep. If somebody grabbed me roughly, so rough that it hurt, it would calm me. Then I could concentrate on the pain, and the pain was secure for me, it caused there to be something in my mind, and then it got totally calm on the outside, and I didn't notice anymore what was happening around me.

Later I have understood that people perceived me as disconnected, in my own world, and that all attempts to make contact with me failed. This triggered feelings of powerlessness and inadequacy in them, and that in turn gave rise to guilt feelings. Especially, since they sometimes got so rough it caused me obvious pain. Then they felt they had been abusive towards me, something they considered unacceptable. They couldn't understand why they got so desperate and aggressive and reacted so violently. My mother would throw dishes, or whatever, to the floor. My farmor would grab me and shake me, all hysterical. One of my uncles once banged his fist in the window sill so hard that one of the panes cracked.

Today I understand their anger was because the worst thing for a human being is to be refused, to feel unable to make contact because the other party fails to respond by making a connection that would lead to communication. That turns their autopilot on; feelings with roots in humanity's childhood arise and express themselves in the kind of reactions they learned in infancy. A deep knowledge and understanding both of the person who can't communicate and of those around her is required to master these automatic impulses and refuse to follow them. People often get the feeling that those of us who have these communication difficulties set ourselves above others, as if we were better than them, as if in some way we talk about them being dumber than us. This leads to aggressiveness in them that expresses itself in the impulse to dominate.

In my world I was present; I was together with the others. I had no concept of what connection was, but thought I was with others when I sat under the table or in the closet, or when I sat on the milk platform when the other kids played around me. In my world there was no reference to the idea that "being with" is something different than sitting and "seeing" what is happening in the atmosphere.

To "be there" in the ordinary world but to actually be in what I called the real world, this was my normal condition. I didn't know that there was any other way to be. I didn't know that you could be a subject that has feelings and meet another subject that has feelings. But this started to dawn on me when I was ten, and with that another picture of reality emerged for me. Then I got a glimpse, a first clue about what it was, and after that I have been looking for it my whole life. I know that when you are in an emotion-blocked state like I was in, you lose the point of being human. Just being in contact, togetherness, and communication, living with the ability to feel and react relevantly and having a connection between the outer and the inner, that is life, and the value in life, and that is what I have constantly been in search of.

I had a period around four when I lost the impulse to eat. I had never felt the feeling of being hungry or satiated, but it had been pleasant to get something inside of me. I gladly put stuff in my mouth, and in the potty they often found different items, among other things a safety pin and some thumbtacks. Apparently they had not got stuck on the way.

But then suddenly, the impulse to eat disappeared; I blankly refused. It was impossible to get any food into me and hardly any drink either. Everything that had to do with the mouth got unpleasant and I threw tantrums and kept away. For half a year they struggled desperately to get me to eat, and finally a neighbor who was a nurse wanted to have me admitted to a hospital for force feeding. This Father said no to. He felt that if it got so bad that I might starve to death, then so be it, but he understood what a terrible abuse it would be to force feed me, and he feared that it could never be repaired. He couldn't stand to see me as a thing: it was preferable to let me die a natural death.

Later he said that he probably wouldn't have let it get to that point, that he would probably have given in and let me be hospitalized if there was a real crisis.

In his desperation, when he had me with him in the barn among his beloved cows, he placed me under his favorite cow, the one he told all his troubles to, and whispered in her ear "let go" and she did: milk started pouring over me and after a while I started licking. He saw that and gathered the milk in a liter jug and let me drink it. For a long time after that I drank only cow-warm milk from that liter jug. I became constipated, but that had to be accepted. Eventually the diet was expanded to include pancakes, which it was also possible to get me to eat. For half a year this was my only food and I lived well on it.

However, it led to all my baby teeth rotting to little ragged stumps, but also to slowly get me started eating other food. I couldn't stand to touch food or look at it on a plate, but if I got to sit under the table when everyone sat around it and somebody took some food and held it under the table without looking at me, I could crawl over and take it with my mouth. This method of feeding me prevailed for about a year before I could eat in a normal way, and it returned from time to time until I was ten.

When I "ran away", as others saw it, in my world it was that I just went someplace. I had no thought of orienting myself. I walked right into the forest, and if I got tired I lay down under a tree and entered the state I called Out. There, I could lie for hours. When they noticed that I was gone, they sent a search party. People gathered and went through the forest with a fine tooth comb. Then they would find me and be relieved. Somebody said: "Wasn't it lucky that we found you so you didn't get lost completely." I didn't understand this at all because I knew exactly where I was, that I was in the forest, and that I was under just *that* tree. I didn't understand what they meant by saying I got lost because I hadn't had any thought of going back home. It never happened that I thought of going home of my own accord.

After a few of these escapes the neighbors got tired of the search parties and then Father got a sheepdog. He went around with it on the outer limit where I was allowed to go.

Then he taught to dog to bark furiously when I got close to the limit. The dog hated me. I was mean and kicked him when I wanted to go and he pulled my clothes. He growled and pulled till he got a piece of cloth in his mouth, which irritated mother, but I still made good my escape. Often, Father heard the dog and came running to look, and sure enough he found me on the way to the forest.

When this had happened many times and he had retrieved me many times he wondered what he should try next. The dog loved Father and obeyed him slavishly. When he was in the barn and I opened the door to go out he said to the dog: "Now go and watch Iris." At this command the dog laid down flat on the floor, ears drooping, and crept toward the door. He looked like a pleading child, but he did his job.

As time went on my behavior patterns got more predictable and most people felt confident that I wouldn't hurt myself, and hence there was no longer the same pressure to find me when I disappeared. Most of the places I escaped to were also known, so there were ten or so places to look, and I was often found in one of them. Father did not like for them to leave me alone for as much as several hours. He figured it was enough with a half hour or so, and the half hour wasn't for my benefit but for the others who needed a rest from me. Mother thought it was nice when I was gone, just so long as she knew I was somewhere where she didn't need to worry about me.

In spite of the dog, I still managed to escape sometimes but Father eventually discovered that I escaped to a certain place. I went through the pastures toward the woods. There lived a hermit who hated people and shot at them with a salt pellets in the shotgun if they got too close. I sat down in his ditch. After a while he came to me; he patted me on the head and so I followed him to his house. He knew where I belonged, so when it suited him he went back with me and placed me in the pasture and remained standing there so he could see that I got home.

His name was Fil and was the son of soldier. He lived in the little soldier's croft where he was born and raised. He went to sea when he was sixteen and didn't return until he was over fifty. By then his parents were dead and nobody knew if he had any other relatives. The croft stood abandoned so he took it over and moved in.

The cottage was small. It had a dirt floor and a fireplace in the middle of the room. There was a pot hanging there so he had warm water all day. He cooked his food over the fire and hung his laundry on the fireplace wall.

His bed was in one corner. It wasn't actually a bed, but a compact pile of spruce twigs on the floor packed with heather. It always smelled good around his bed for he changed the bottom often.

On top of the twig- and heather-bed he had a sheepskin. It was a skin stitched to felted wool cloth with strong tendons. He had one such skin rug under him and one on top of him. He also had a pillow which was filled with chicken down. I sometime got to lie next to him in the bed and it smelled strongly of wool, spruce, and heather.

Fil used a wooden box as his doorstep; in it lived a black snake. Once he caught some rats for the snake, and then it got so thick that it couldn't get out but had to lie there digesting the food for a long time.

Fil told me about his life. Actually he didn't tell it to me but talked to himself with me at his side. He talked about his childhood, that they had been short of food, especially when the father had been on maneuvers on *Axvalla Hed*. The father got paid for it, but he spent his money on booze so he came home empty handed. The mother did day work on the neighbor farms and this way earned some eggs, butter, turnips, and such. Fil received a lot of beatings from his alcoholic father. His siblings were much older than him and had moved away and never came back for visits, so he had no memory of them.

Fil hated his father, and his experience of childhood was very black, only misery. Somebody had taken pity on him and arranged for him to go to school every other day, and then he had learned to read and a little arithmetic. Otherwise, he worked as an errand boy on a farm nearby; the pay for that was one meal per day.

The family never associated with other people and he was not allowed to be with other young folks. The only ones he had met were his classmates, and since he was so odd he was bullied. He was tall, skinny and sinewy, but strong, so he was a fierce fighter. This caused the bullying to diminish, but he didn't make any contacts either. The girls thought he was ugly and giggled behind his back. He had pimples on his face, unkempt hair and homespun clothes and he smelled musty. When he was fifteen a man came and recruited him as a seaman. It was the brightest moment he could remember.

While he was talking to me, he kept busy at the same time with something practical, like gathering food for the animals.

He kept a goat, a pig, about a dozen hens, a flock of sheep and a few rabbits. As house pet he had a cat, a great big yellow tom cat that ran around in the community and came back with torn skin. The cat lay on the kitchen table below the window all winter long. There was a single window in the cottage and the kitchen table was an old desk with three drawers. In them he kept his knives and forks, plates and other kitchen tools. In front of the table was a patched and repaired kitchen chair, which was the only thing to sit on. He sat there often, talking with the cat, eating his food, fixing something or just philosophizing. Sometimes we went into the forest and collected wood and twigs for his bed. In the fall he collected a lot of heather so he had plenty to take from during the winter. He picked lots of mushrooms, blueberries, lingon berries, sloe berries, juniper berries, all kinds of berries and fruit and root vegetables that he raised. Then he preserved them and put them in the root cellar. He also repaired his outhouses and insulated them with straw so that the animals could keep warm in a little room.

He loved animals, both his domestic ones and the forest wild ones. He could imitate many different sounds and calls which often caused the animals to come forward, or stop and listen.

Once each year he went to the local store and bought salt, sugar and other stuff that he didn't produce himself. He also brought with him the Billy-goat which he exchanged for a new one to get a new brood without inbreeding. The other male animals and the ones he didn't want to keep he sold for slaughter or breeding. With the money he paid for his purchases in the store.

Everybody knew about him and nobody knew him. People thought he was crazy or psychotic, but he was saner than most people, just very, very bitter. He understood so much about the evil side of humans and how much suffering it caused others.

He talked about the evil in life. About how things had been in his childhood, how things had been at sea, what ships he had served on, and what hardships he had been through. He talked about people he had met, some that he had become friends with and liked, but that finally had betrayed him, cheated him out of money after getting him drunk. He often sat and looked at his tattoos and told me which ports they had been made in and what stories were connected with them.

One story that I loved, that he had to tell over and over, was about a port he came to when there was an auction for a girl who wasn't much older than me. The auctioneer held her by the hair so she wouldn't run away. She cried angrily when some dirty old men came and pinched her. She looked wild and bit anyone who came too close. Fil came forward and bought her and let her go. A few hours later, when he had been at the bar and was on his way back to the ship, he found her under his coat that he had laid in a corner. She followed him but he could not take her with him onboard. He gave her all his money and sent her away. They were sailing the following day and he figured he would never see her again, but in the morning she was on the quay pleading to be allowed to go with him. Then he took her to a woman who had a small store and negotiated with her and paid for the girl's keep for a year. Then he came back every year and continued to pay. She died at fifteen from a burst appendix. She was the only human being that he had grieved for in his entire life. He cried quietly every time he told the story about her.

The years passed. I escaped to Fil almost every day. He was a part of my life. He didn't expect anything, especially not that I would be in contact and togetherness. I was just a part of his day that was present there. When I was seven, I was not allowed to go there anymore. I was stopped from escaping there and they succeeded in keeping me away from there for I don't know how long. Much later when I managed to get there everything was changed. No Fil came to get me by the ditch. There were no animals. There was no fire in the fireplace, and there was a bar across the door.

When I returned from Fil's empty house I was confused and withdrawn, I had peed in my pants and was rolling around on the ground. Somebody said that Fil had died and was no more. Death didn't exist in my world, so I understood nothing.

I continued to go there, sitting in the ditch for hours. When I was there, Fil was close by and I could "hear" him talk and I could "see" him doing all the chores he used to do with me in tow.

I heard him say: "Today the weather is good for changing the bed. We will let sun and wind air out the skins." I saw him carry out the sheepskin fells and hang them on a rack outside the cabin. I saw him carry out all the old heather and put it in a pile that he was going to burn later. He said: "Thanks you old bed for having performed your service. Now you will be transformed into something else." He said: "I remember the fall when it rained so much that it was impossible to bring home any twigs. And then the snow came before things had dried out. So, that fall there was no new bed." He got a hoe to loosen up the dirt floor and raked up the spruce needles. "Now I'll get a little topsoil and mix in to make the floor smell properly." Then he tramped around with small steps to make the floor firm again. He got an axe. I asked: "Are we leaving now?" We went into the woods to get fresh spruce twigs. "Now we'll look carefully so we don't hurt the spruce trees." I asked: "Do spruces suffer?" "All living things can be hurt if you are not careful." Careful was a word he often used. He smelled the twigs because they had to smell right, and he was careful to take just one twig here and one twig there. He took the twigs home and got a basket and then we went to a place where there was lots of heather. "Here's lots of heather. But one shouldn't think that there is an infinite amount of heather whenever. Here's a knife, take this much here and this much there. But no more. Be careful so you don't hurt the roots." We filled the basket with heather. He said: "That's enough. Now we go home. One must never take more from the earth than one needs. People are altogether too greedy and that will eventually come to haunt them. People are so dumb that they don't understand that."

At the cottage he stuffed heather in among the spruce twigs and spread the rest on top. "A person has it pretty good when he can sleep on such a good bed. Once at sea on a ship to the other side of the globe I had to sleep on straw where there were both fleas and lice. It was a pain to try to sleep when they were itching and biting. This could go on for weeks." The he got the carpet whip that he had made from a thin tree sapling and beat the sheep skins.

When it was all finished he stood in the middle of the floor and just smelled. "Can you feel how good it smells?" I had no concept of what smelled good or bad, so I wondered a lot about how you could say that something smelled good. How could a smell be "good"?

In his old age my uncle told me that I used to walk round and round on the floor and talk with Fil, sometimes aloud so you could hear what I said and he used to eavesdrop. He told me how I behaved and how he could hear my part of what Fil and I talked about.

When the winter cold really set in I stopped going there, and then when spring came, he and the entire memory of our relationship was gone from my world. It was no longer there. It was like a photo where I know, but don't experience. My uncle worried about me because for a long time I stopped laughing, which otherwise was my normal mode of expression.

It was a strange time. According to my uncle I was four when I started escaping to Fil and seven when he died. In my world, Fil had disappeared and nothing else came instead.

The one-armed Emma traveled to Gothenburg to visit relatives and died there. When she came home she was lying in a coffin that was to be buried. I didn't understand why everyone was so sad, since she herself had come home together with the coffin and the dead body. The children were not included in the funeral so I snuck in and sat in the steps leading up to the church steeple, and there Emma sat with me during the whole funeral service. After that she continued to be there in the real world. If I got stuck in some stereotypyc behavior it got totally dark. And then there came a light that I knew was Emma. Sometimes I heard her say: "Come", or "Stand up", and then my behavior was broken.

That's how it was with all the dead people in our family. They were still there in the real world; it was just their body that was gone. Nothing to grieve or be sad about. But that's not how it was with Fil. When he was gone he disappeared from the real world also.

Emma called me her little sweetheart and she never tired of being in contact and listening to everything I talked about even if it didn't make any sense. There was always a stream of people, especially youths that came to visit her. She told them about the secrets of life and gave advice which she didn't require anyone to follow. The remarkable thing was that no matter how dumb the question or comment was she always managed to answer in a way that made the person feel good. This ability to relate to the world this way, this consideration and respect, this healthy humility without derogating herself came from the experience of a long life.

Father was one who often visited her. He often asked her to talk about what she had experienced in life and she did this happily. Sometimes he lay on the floor with me stirring her mustard and he often helped her with whatever she needed.

Mother used to visit her for an hour each day and read the newspaper aloud. Emma had poor vision and was no longer able to read and this was of great sorrow for her. She got a radio and this was her treasure. She also had difficulty hearing but she sat up close to the radio and listened to all the programs. She followed all the debates, especially the political ones, and then she discussed and commented on them. I was often at her feet and took part in what she said, although it would be many years before I could put it into any context.

Emma learned everyone's secrets. I told her about my two playmates, Slire and Skydde, the beings I was with when I was "Out", and who were mine only, and that nobody else could see. I used to meet them when I sat on my swing by myself. They came and got me and took me with them Out. We flew away and played "whirl round tree-tops" and came back all exhilarated and giggly. I told Emma about everything I saw and everything I learned, and Emma listened with interest. She commented: "You don't say, that's really something" and then smiled secretively and her love beamed all around her. I am sure today that she knew, that she also was in the real world sometimes. She understood things about life and people that others hadn't grasped, and this she got from her deepest inside.

Emma is the only person who still continuously is present within me and can show up as a relation without me consciously trying to remember. Normally there is stillness and emptiness inside me unless somebody comes and says something or asks something. Then I surf backwards in my memory, like a film running backwards. I stop the film and pick out the sequence that is relevant for the situation... Otherwise, it's like a vacuum or dormancy within me and no impulses pop up spontaneously on the inside. If I stay in that state too long, obsessive thoughts crop up, thoughts that continually repeat and have no meaning and lead to no result.

One such thought is from a film I saw early in life: "Impossible, You Don't Get Money." When I have been without contact for too long it comes and keeps on and keeps on and keeps on until I get crazy and start screaming.

These days I seldom let it go that far. I know that this, and other, obsessive thoughts come after about four hours. I make sure that I get into contact before that, call somebody, turn on the radio or TV, go visit somebody or talk to myself in the mirror. I have become quite good at breaking this before I reach collapse and my autistic stereotypy shows up, and I have also learned to get out of it as soon as I hear a human voice.

I sleep today no more than three hours at a time just to make sure I don't wake in that state, because then it is often like a nightmare. The body is immobilized and the mind is in this nothingness that suddenly is filled with demons and terror.

As a child I rocked myself out of this nothingness and ended up in the state I called Out. Then I didn't get stuck in the kind of lock-up I now sometimes get. Then I wound up in the immaterial and met my companions Slire and Skydde. I could sit on a swing, or go round and round on the floor, or sit on the toilet and hum monotonously, or lie and bang-twist my head rhythmically back and forth. I could put myself in this state anytime I wanted, so long as it wasn't a time when my body had some need, because then I was drawn into my body whether I wanted to or not.

Summertime the family went to the lake to go swimming.

I went straight out in the water. It made no difference how warm or cold it was, if it was windy or calm. Water equaled bath, which I loved. I never left the water of my own accord so someone had come and get me when it was time to go home. Mother found it very simple and pleasant by the lake because then she knew the whole time where I was. She was afraid of the water so she was never the one to come and get me out.

The others took turns watching me because I might suddenly walk out in the water or into the reeds where it was almost impossible to find me. Also, dogs were not allowed on the beach so Father did not have access to that extra help.

There were many incidents of near drowning so he decided that I would learn to swim. This was quick and easy. A summer student got the assignment to teach me. He wrapped my hair around his hand, dragged me along and said: "Swim, swim." That's how I learned to swim.

Then came the next problem. I swam straight out in the open water without thought of turning back. Somebody spotted my blond head way out so Father had to take a skiff and row after me.

To float in the water was like a dream. The water clucked and flowed in and out through nose and mouth. I could be above or below the surface, but to breathe I had to be above, otherwise the coughing came. I loved to lie on my back in the water, either on a sand bank or just floating in the water. I could lie there for hours looking at the clouds in the sky. I could fly up among them, and play. Then I was in my world with my playmates.

Once there was a party at the swimming place. There was

a funfair and a bunch of booths, there were performances, and horse and dog shows. It was decided that we all would stay, since the weather was nice and warm. Normally Father was the one taking care of me. It was like he had facet eyes that could look in many directions, and like he was an octopus with many arms that caught me. But, for some reason it was my mother who was watching me that day.

Not many minutes had elapsed before I disappeared. Panic, I was gone. I was paged on the PA system but Father knew I would never answer, so he organized a search party in the reeds. It was August and nights were getting darker so he figured that I would probably sit down someplace and rock myself into my state. His worst fear was that I would find the railroad and start to follow it. He knew that I would never notice it if a train was coming so this was deadly dangerous.

Two men went opposite ways on the railroad but no girl was found there. The partying broke up when the police came and started looking for me.

I was on the pier. I went up on the ladder and jumped in the water and stood there and pushed down my boucle dress, went up and did the same thing again. It looked so funny when the air bubbles kept the skirt above the water, and so funny when the water pulled down the fabric. I heard a splash from somewhere and went under the pier and sat down. From there I could see the man who had just jumped in. After a while I forgot him and went back to the ladder and continued jumping. When the man came back from his swim he spotted me on the pier and recognized me.

He got dressed and took me with him to the funfair and lifted me up on the stage.

There was a huge commotion. Everybody talked all at once. The atmosphere became beautiful and I laughed. The stage light was pointed at me and I stood there and looked at the wooden floor where small rivulets flowed from my legs down on the floor and down between the floor boards. I saw a pair of hairy arms, and I was down on the ground and somebody took off my clothes.

In addition to Sven, I had two uncles who lived in the bunk house. One was tall, blond and handsome. He loved to dance. He started dressing for the dance many hours before it was time and the others made fun of him for his vanity. In his youth he had had many women, but he was too egotistical for any woman to want to marry him. One of them he named Prissy because she wouldn't take a drink and that was the end of that relationship.

He played the base violin, preferably jazz, and there were often visitors with instruments in the bunk house so there was a lot of music going on there. He also had a great interest in nature. He often took long walks and then he brought me and the dog along. We went over fields and in the forest; we went on a small trail and on untouched ground. He talked to himself about what he saw and experienced without wondering about whether I was listening or not. To me he was a person who resembled Fil, but not exactly.

Nobody could humanize animals like he could. He argued with them, talked with them, and saw them as having human characteristics. Once when he was plowing with a horse in the yard he constantly scolded the horse for tromping in the row or going askew. Finally the horse stopped, turned his head and glared at him until he was finished with his noise making, and then first did he start walking again.

It was a fun performance for me. I often sat crouched on the side and watched the atmosphere and just laughed. He didn't care, so for me it was a learning place.

He also had a special relationship with the hens. He had a name for every one of them, and was the one who fed them every day. For a while we had some turkeys sharing the pen with the hens. He was mad at them because they stepped on the hens' toes when they tried to drink. He thought the turkeys were so big and his hens so small that they ought to leave space for the hens. He waged a constant struggle against the turkeys and never tired of scolding them. They didn't care, but this dynamic was very interesting to me.

The bachelors had the attitude that it was enough that one of them got married and produced children for the sake of reproduction. That way the others could be carefree bachelors who lived their life and died within the extended family kinship.

The other uncle had black hair and dark, tanned skin all year round. He looked southern, as if he came from another country. Farmor had the same coloring and we assumed that there was Walloon blood in them, probably from his morfar's side. He loved sports and circus tricks and was in very good shape. Ten-twelve year old girls admired him greatly and he loved to show off his tricks for them. He also helped them ride on our work horses, so he was often surrounded by girls of that age. He was good at arranging games that could go on for weeks – today we would call it life play – and this caused a bunch of half-grown youths to always come to us as if there were a youth center at my uncles' bunk house.

In the winter they spent time in their room, listened to Radio Luxembourg with modern music from all over the world, played jazz and improvised, or played cards long into the nights. The other uncle played the clarinet and saxophone, and he taught it to some of young people staying with us instead of being in reform school. This type of social life was condemned by the pious, but it continued for many years anyway. Here, all the gossip was exchanged and all the vagabond stories told, one worse than the next.

Between Emma's room and the uncles' was an old kitchen. It wasn't winterized and wasn't used for cooking. In there was a loom that different people used and a ping-pong table that was also used. Tournaments were held regardless how cold it was; you sometimes had to play with mittens to avoid frostbite.

I liked to sit curled up in one of the beds furthest in the corner, often unnoticed. The room was almost completely dark. There was a stove that gave warmth. It was standing in front of the tile fireplace and they often fired it so hot that it glowed red to keep the room warm. The fuse blew if both the ceiling light and the radio were on, so either the light was on and they played cards, or the light was off and we listened to Radio Luxembourg.

There were a lot of conversations about all kinds of things. Especially about all the mystical and magical that somebody had heard of. Most of them were afraid of everything occult, but at the same time interested. Sometimes hobos from the nearby brick factory came by, and they told the strangest stories you could imagine.

In the real world all this was present and visible. I noticed also if somebody just wanted to show off, or if there was something in what he was telling. I loved to sit there and look at the fears that took form in the atmosphere. It was like fireworks of light that lit up the gloom in the room. There were also a lot of odors from everything musty, often damp clothes that gave off various smells: straw, manure, clay, bricks.

Often my beings Slire and Skydde came and played with me. We flew around among all the words and phrases, went in and out of peoples' clothes, played with gestures and dove under the table and buzzed around their legs. We were careful to not disturb anyone, to not go inside somebody's skin for then they got very scared. I loved to be unnoticed and left alone, but still be present where everything was going on.

Then I was discovered. "Iris, are you still sitting there dreaming, go to bed right away", somebody said.

Thus the fun was over for that time; I was brutally brought back to the ordinary world and taken into the house and the normal routines.

The two brothers had their own traditions on Sundays. Either somebody came to visit, and they played darts or had some other contest depending on season, and weather and wind, or they took their bikes and rode off to visit with somebody for a few hours. Sometimes I was nearby and when I had good periods and didn't disturb people too much, or when Father demanded it from his brothers, I got to go along. I got to sit on the package rack and hang on the best I could.

One destination was to a man who had the artist name Ariman. He was a hypnotist and entertained at fairs and amusement parks, when he wasn't in jail because of what he did. He got people up from the audience, hypnotized them and made do some of simulated actions, for example go fishing, or be a lion in the jungle, or be a clown in the circus. They didn't remember anything afterwards, and when they were told what they had done they got very upset and felt injured and reported him. It wasn't only that, some of them experienced severe anxiety and insomnia, and in some cases it triggered mental illness, so it was not a harmless thing he did.

When we got there, they sat around the kitchen table in winter time, around the garden table in the summer, and asked him to tell about his experiences. I sat under the table and was with him in his stories and learned to hypnotize. I had no judgment and did not understand what it could do to people's mind so I used it blithely whenever there was somebody to do it on.

At one occasion I hypnotized all the hens so the whole yard was full of apparently dead hens, and when Father came home he was horrified and wondered what had happened. Then one of them shook herself and got up and started running around cackling and laid a wind egg. One after the other did the same thing and soon they were all awake. The worst part was this thing with the wind eggs. They are eggs that haven't yet formed a shell, but only a membrane so they often break or are eaten by the other hens, so there was egg loss the next few days.

Sometimes I put the dog in a trance so he stopped watching me and then I could escape to wherever I wanted. Other times it was some ewe or pig that was bothersome that I wanted to put to sleep. When mother forced me to go along on something I didn't want, I could sit and fixate on her until she got so tired that she forgot that she was taking me and she went without me. Then I was very satisfied.

The other kids who played at our house sometimes would bother me and then I could fixate on them in a way that made them feel terror and very unpleasant feelings inside, and then they stopped immediately. When some other kid approached me when I wanted to be left alone I sent out a wordless: "Beware", or "Watch out" that got himher to become frightened, without understanding why, and then they lost the urge to do something with me and I was left alone.

There was no strategy in this, or conscious wish or curiosity, I just practiced what Ariman told us and then it happened.

The older I got and heard more about Ariman's imprisonments and what my uncles told me about what had happened to people who had been hypnotized the more I understood that this wasn't really OK. I had no morals that prevented me but felt anyway that this wasn't something you should play with.

In our teens many of the kids found it exciting that I knew how to hypnotize. Not that I had talked about it much but the rumor had spread and the subject came up in different contexts. The mystical, the occult, the unusual attracted.

Once I let myself be persuaded to hypnotize a boy about sixteen. I didn't have the judgment to understand that it might be harmful, especially since he had been drinking, and didn't realize it could go so wrong. He became totally psychotic, landed in a world of terror and fear that was totally devastating. He screamed, struck out, threw himself down and carried on. I had to spend ten hours to try to get him grounded again. It was a tough job, and then I understood how seriously you could harm someone with hypnosis. It taught me something for life and about other peoples' constitution.

On the side of the yard, on the way to the outhouse, was a big sycamore. It had a huge branch about five meters above the ground, where somebody had put up a rope swing. I often went there and sat in the swing. It was possible to swing very high and I loved to swing, especially so I could be in my real world and play with my being friends. From time to time somebody passed me on the way to the john and talked to me. I never answered but everybody knew that I heard what they said even though it didn't result in any contact.

When I swung the highest I could see our house in one direction, the church in the other; the outhouse I couldn't see since it was behind me, and between me and the main house was the bunk house. Under my feet when I swung high was a snowball bush big as an arbor. In front of it, towards the main house was a lilac hedge that formed a half circle, and in front of that were ten bee hives on a small lawn. It ended with farfar's peonies and after that came the gravel yard. In the middle of it was a flowerbed. It was mother's pride and joy. She redid it every year, and gradually it became a rock garden with boulders that the uncles had dragged home. It was filled with plants that flowered from early spring to late fall. Even in winter time there was a bunch of pretty frozen plants.

In the main house there was a large kitchen on the ground floor. It was the gathering place for everyone... When I was very little, farmor was in control there. She was always nervous that food would not be ready in time so she prepared it several hours ahead of time and then it stood in a water bath until meal time, and then there was basically no flavor left.

The door from the kitchen led to a hallway. There was the stairway to the second floor where our family lived until I was about one. Then we swapped so that farmor and farfar moved upstairs and we moved down. The door on the other side was the kitchen entrance that everyone used.

Farmor had raven black hair that had now become more pepper and salt. When she let it down to brush it, before she tied it up in the tight knot she always wore, it reached to her knees. She had never cut a millimeter because that was sinful according to the bible and it had to be followed to the last jot and tittle. She had small pepper brown eyes that could stare in a way that made folks uncomfortable and she had a shrill voice that cut through bone and marrow, and that was instantly obeyed. Somebody likened her to the witch in Hansel and Gretel.

When farmor and farfar had moved upstairs one could often hear her voice in the open window when she hollered: "Farfar, come in immediately with ..." and then everybody knew there was no alternative or answer, there was only to do as he was told.

She was pious, or rather scared to death of winding up in hell after her death. Most of it seemed sham religious, because the most important thing for her is what people said. She went to church and participated in all the church activities so that people wouldn't realize how bad we actually were behind the scenes. She was ashamed for everyone and felt the rest of us also ought to understand that we should be ashamed. She was most ashamed of Father because he was so bold and did everything his own way, just like her father had done. She often said: "Him, I got for my sins." Father used to joke with her and say: "Mother must not have sinned very much if I am all she got for her sins."

The best thing about her was that she was naive and easy to fool. The children and youths that were home did that some times and it led to many funny moments even for her. She was very worried about me and she often said: "What will become of this unfortunate child?" She thought that the great misfortune was that I could not accommodate myself, couldn't be polite and say "Good Day" and "Thank You". This made her think I would come to a bad end. Now, in retrospect, I understand that she was scared to death because I had no self-preservation instinct, so that if somebody communicated with me the right way they could get me to do any craziness they wanted, and that I could be sexually exploited if there wasn't somebody watching over me constantly.

She used to mash potatoes with butter and feed me and

that worked much better than anything else they wanted me to eat. Food was "a chapter all by itself" as mother expressed herself. Farmor saved all the leftovers, and we had to eat it all before we got new food. This meant that all food got old before it was eaten and father detested this when he was a child so he lived on home fries.

Mother was allowed to use whatever products she wanted to prepare all the good food she could think of. Father made sure first that the family should have good food, after that came all the new innovations and conveniences. He also made sure she got all the latest kitchen aids before he used money for improvements in the barn. She got refrigerators and freezers, food processor and dish-washer, new washing machine and drying room. All the neighbor husbands were unhappy and complained to him because their wives wanted them to be as nice as father.

When I had done something that farmor thought was very sinful and wrong she would call me up to her. Then I had to stand before her as she scolded and admonished me. This I liked. I stood totally still and stared out in space. Her words were flying around and formed shapes, it was different lights that sparkled. It was beautiful, and you could never predict how it would look. I stood there and was entranced. I flowed into the colors, shapes, patterns, let myself be carried back and forth, up and down. Everything changed shape continuously and I flowed in with it. Suddenly I felt my arm being pinched. Farmor screamed with a shrill voice: "You hopeless child, you don't even hear what I am saying to you. What will become of you when you grow up? Nobody can train you and you don't behave like a Christian human being." Then she sent me away with the admonishment to be careful going down the stairs, and when I came Out I was back in all the beautiful I had just been in. I could stay in that for hours. Sometimes I went to the swing and could continue to float around until somebody came and took me back to the togetherness again.

Farfar was the nicest person on earth. He loved to walk by himself humming some tune. Everyone knew he was completely irresponsible and if it hadn't been for farmor he would have been a penniless hobo. Farmor was the one who kept track of everything, and most of all of farfar. Once, the story goes, he had gone to the market to sell a cow, but he was no good at doing a business deal so he got cheated. When he discovered this he got drunk and didn't come home until the next day, without the money and without the cow. After that, farmor took care of the finances.

He loved to putter in the garden. He was mother's helper on things like tending flower beds, raking the yard, and taking care of the roses. He also picked all the fruit and berries as they ripened so mother got to take care of the rest. When he was raking the yard to pretty it up for the holidays I got to walk in front of him and make a bunch of figures in the sand. He showed me and I played, and then he came with the rake got it nice and straight again.

Inside the kitchen was the guest room. There was the radio, which we listened to often. The news and the weather forecast were the most important and then everybody had to be silent.

They were the source for all the discussions around the kitchen table. All the different happenings had to be discussed, and you had to have opinions about them. If opinions differed it caused the conversational volume to swell. It was an opportunity to ventilate political profiles, religious ideas, and the myths and strategies that were there as undercurrents. One such was that most people were egotistical human beings who were concerned for their own advantage, and then the whole thing concluded with the agreement that "after all we have it pretty good here in *Svedala*".

Saturday evenings there were entertainment programs on the radio. Everybody took their places in the guest room and all lamps were turned off so the fuse wouldn't blow. I sat under the table or hidden in a corner behind somebody's chair. One program that ran a long time was *Speldosan* (The music box). It was a program with many hit artists and quiz contests. There were many funny episodes and everyone laughed and enjoyed the quiet, each other's company, and the entertainment from the radio. I liked the atmosphere that arose in the room. It was like Bengal fire with colored smoke that filled the whole room with coils that curled around each other and that I could float around in. That was fun. Everything that streamed out of the radio, and everything that was said by the listeners continually changed the atmosphere and I got new ways I could float around.

Then it was over, everybody went back to the kitchen and had coffee, and then it was good night.

On Tuesday nights there was radio-theater, fairly late. Then we gathered to listen to that and then that special mood also arose. Even those who went dancing on Saturday nights were there so there were more people than usual that sat there listening in the dark.

One serial was called "The Man in Black". It was a scary mystery with many murders. Olof Thunberg was the man who read it and his voice was special, all agreed. Chills went up and down the spine listening to him and everyone sat in great suspense waiting for the resolution.

Actually, children weren't supposed to listen to this, but since I was like I was, and since the grownups didn't think I understood any of it, nobody worried about it. It was true in the sense that I was not interested in the murder mystery, which did not awaken any thoughts or feelings in me. In contrast, I was interested in that part of the story that led to the murder: envy, rage, greed, revenge. I was also very interested in the atmosphere that arose in the room.

But sometimes the difference grew too great between the black awful feelings that Olof Thunberg described and the listeners' feeling of being engaged and entertained.

The murderer knocks on the door of a house. The mood is tense and everyone sits mouse-quiet and listens intently. A woman comes to the door and opens it. The murderer composes himself and asks with strained voice: "Is there room for a stranger here?" A quiet rush passes through the room. The woman does not know that he is the killer. But then a drunken voice is heard from inside the house: "Ask if he has any whiskey, then we'll let him in." Everyone guffaws, except me, and then there is chaos in me for in the same way that I can't understand humor, I can't understand how revenge and murder could be described in a way that could amuse and entertain people.

Then I put myself in the state where I could leave the body and go Out in the real world, which was known to me. There I could observe everything that was happening, hear everything that was said, and understand a bunch of things without having a tantrum or other crazy behavior and stimming. Then I could see how it was in reality: the voice streaming out of the radio, and everyone being in the ordinary world and therefore unable to grasp the reality in the story, which is how they could be amused and entertained by it. There was nobody who was interested in what the story really was about, they were quite satisfied to be entertained by it. This I never understood. I couldn't for the life of me understand what it was that entertained them.

On the other side of the guest room was the parlor. It was a big room with tapestry and a fire place. There was a huge dining table with lots of chairs, where we ate on holidays, or when we had guests. Normally it was used as a large bedroom at night. There were two bed cabinets with three beds in each, sort of like Murphy beds, only bigger. The beds were collapsible so that they looked like a bureau. There was also one bed cabinet with two beds. The bed cabinet was vertical and looked like a linen cabinet. This conversion happened every night and it created a very special atmosphere there. I fell asleep last and awakened first, because I couldn't sleep when anyone else was awake, so I focused on the atmosphere while I waited for them to fall asleep.

Often there was somebody who read aloud or somebody who told something: fairy tales, jokes, stories, something experienced, dreams. In all these words I could be in my own world. I understood the things I heard in my special way, and that resulted in a lot of interesting experiences. It filled my otherwise empty inner for a while, and I appreciated it very much. Suddenly I could start laughing for a long time and everyone in there wondered what had happened.

When I listened to their stories I didn't hear just the story itself, but also relations and situations that lay behind it. My uncle told the story about Hansel and Gretel. While he was telling it I perceived that he saw his mother as the witch, himself as Hansel and his sister as Gretel. I noticed both his fear and his defiance of his mother, my farmor, and I noticed how satisfied he felt when the witch/mother got kicked into the oven and died. I laughed because the happenings in the story coincided so comically with what I saw in the atmosphere and said to my uncle: "You are Hansel and farmor is the witch and you think it's fun that you and Gretel can fool the witch and push her into the oven so she dies." Everybody fell silent and felt uncomfortable, except the young ones who giggled knowingly. My uncle screamed: "That much meanness isn't allowed, even if your name is Iris." And he rushed out of the room.

That's how it was in our house: farmor was sanctimonious, and was afraid that we were ungodly and wouldn't get to heaven, and had a bad reputation among the neighbors. This caused her to be constantly dissatisfied, continually correcting and controlling everyone. Everyone except Father and I were controlled by her; my uncle, who constantly had a guilty conscience and feared her, sucked up to her and accompanied her to church even though he was not religious.

I felt the others had not seen what I saw when we listened to the story, and I couldn't figure out how to get them see what lay behind it so we could talk about that, because that's what I could have talked about. Then I could have been in communication with them. What I didn't realize was that they were guided by values; they considered it ugly or mean to talk about certain things. Their reactions got very confusing and sometimes it ended with me having a tantrum.

This is what distinguished Emma and Fil from all the others. They saw things the same way that I did, we were in the real world, and therefore I could communicate with them and be secure with them. And together with them my cramp released. But as soon as there were other people along, who lived in the ordinary world, the values world, the cramp returned.

Father was in the ordinary world, but in contrast to most others in the ordinary world, he wasn't trying to force me into it, but gave me the possibility to live in it just as I was. I think he knew that there was something beyond the ordinary world since he had grown up with morfar who lived in the real world, but he wasn't interested in it and lived as a wise man in the ordinary world, without either accommodation or defiance.

Periodically there were various other people living with us. One period there was a brain-damaged man that Father helped to become a shoemaker. Once there was a homeless couple. From time to time youths that couldn't fit in to society or had other problems. It was a constant jumble. Some lived with us and worked somewhere else; others lived away but spent weekends with us. Some were summer children, weekend children and stayed with us when school was out, and the mindset was always: if the heart is big enough the house is big enough.

For me these elements were a never ending series of new fields to observe. It also led to the family talking about how to act and behave to get everyone involved, and there was a lot of engagement and togetherness the whole time. Father used to say how great it was to have so many hands to do the work because then it went so quickly and easily that there was a lot of time left to socialize and have fun together.

Other people lived in the ordinary reality that was full of values: the right and proper thing was to obey the Lord's rules and commandments; they must not sin, and in their world there was so much that was sinful. I saw how they lived piously by those values on the surface, but under the surface they were still wicked and sinned on the sly, and their real aim was not to refrain from sinning but to avoid being found out. If they had lived in the real world, they wouldn't have had a need to sin. Sin in the real world —without values—is, for example, to avoid somebody that you love in order to avoid being criticized or judged in the values world. When people evaluated, it looked to me like they isolated themselves from the real world and lost contact with it.

I know a girl who had a wonderful singing voice. She sang like a nightingale and she loved to perform. She was sweet and friendly and knew the art of performing. Her great dream in life was to develop her voice, to be able to study and get to express herself in song. Whenever she talked about singing and her hopes she was in the real world. But those around her had no appreciation for this and called it "dreamy fantasies" and thought it was something she could do on the side. The important thing was to get married and get an "honest job". Eventually she adopted these values and then she disappeared from the real world. She withdrew herself from song and accepted the idea that the singing was only a dream and then she ended up in the ordinary world and stayed there.

Most people existed in the this isolated state all the time, but there were also some that were in the real world, but who still were only interested in the ordinary values world and wanted to belong in it. They wanted to be there, because that had status and that counted, and one received praise there, and authority, and approval. For me it was impossible to abandon the real world and be choked with values and isolation from the real world.

The real reality is a phenomenon. All life, all movement is a phenomenon. It means that one doesn't focus on being required to do something but on the possibilities one can chose among. Then, of course, it was possible that what others said "have to" about possibly was the best one, but not because they said "have to". And the real reality was so much greater than the values reality.

Furthest back in the house, beyond a hallway from the parlor was the outer room. That was the Parson's room. In there was an altar with a stool in front of it. On the wall was a telephone.

It sometimes rang with a shrill sound that cut through the room and made me fly out of my skin. There was oak furniture, big and heavy, a desk, a book case, a big glass lamp, a couch, a table, and stuffed chairs. A solemn silence prevailed there. The wall paper was pale yellowish with an almost invisible pattern. There were brown velvet curtains and white lace curtains underneath. There were tapestries with Christian motifs, and velvet drapes in the same brown color as the curtains. On the floor was a brown linoleum mat and on it a big oriental rug in subdued colors and beautiful patterns, which I loved. I often sat under the desk on a sheepskin and followed the patterns in the rug with my gaze.

Every third week Parson Karlsson came there and spent the whole day composing his sermons. He came and sat down early in the morning. I was awake and up so I stood in the doorway and then he said please come in. He knew that I would quickly sneak by him and crawl in under the desk. When I snuck past he stroked my hair lightly with his one hand even though I tried to avoid it. Then I sat quietly there until he took a pause to go out and relieve himself. Then I snuck out and did the same.

My place was under the desk. I rocked quietly with my body and everything else disappeared. The Parson was sometimes quiet only to burst forth in a cascade of words. He read from the bible and then made unction-filled declamations with lots of words that formed the most fantastic colorful scenes in the air. I seriously doubt if the pictures I saw were the same as the bible intended, but for me they were like fairy tale. He often addressed me and asked afterwards if it was good enough, what

I thought, but he never waited for my answer, but answered himself: "That way is much better Iris." He concluded by reading the epistle and the sermon.

I dove into the world of the bible and I loved it. There was drama and excitement, there was sorrow and grief, there was bliss and ecstasy and ... everything imaginable.

It was a different world with people who were dressed completely different from those around me. The outside was also different. Completely different trees and sand, lots of sand, which came in many different colors. The only sand I had seen was the one at our swimming place but this sand looked entirely different. Lots of stories played out. It was about sudden death, about baby birthing in the stable, about good and evil, about crazy and wise, about a bunch of people who were brave and honest and did a lots of things that fit in my world. I saw many people who walked about in a bunch of sand and among houses which were like white boxes without real roofs. They had beautiful flowing clothes and carried urns with water. Sometimes they were hunted, sometimes there were crowds walking together, sometimes they were following somebody, and sometimes they fought. I saw the ladder to heaven when the Parson spoke about it; it went straight up among the stars and hung free in the air. It looked funny and I laughed. The Parson looked at me under the table and asked what I laughed about, but he knew he would never get an answer.

I was afraid of the Parson. He was big and he had only one arm. He had had cancer in the other arm and had it removed. He looked like a huge bat with his black cape, his solemn face which looked extra strict because of the hooked nose. His voice sounded like a doomsday sermon every time he said something. I never heard him engaged in a conversation. He gave his commands and got everything exactly as wanted. In a way he acted as if he was above the people. But he was just reverential, not the least judgmental. Every third Sunday when he preached in our little church he put on his cape and walked across the yard. He was big as a monster and when he walked out the door he bent his head so that it looked like a bow. Maybe he bowed for the lord, because he could have made it through the door all straight up if he had wanted to.

I often snuck into the sacristy and sat in a corner under the desk there. The caretaker tried to chase me away but the Parson always said: "Let her be, she doesn't hurt a fly, and she probably needs to hear the word of God also."

Sometimes I snuck into the forbidden outer room in our house when the Parson wasn't there. It was strictly prohibited and I knew it but I couldn't resist. The bible often lay closed on the small altar by the side of the desk. I opened the bible and crawled under the desk. I rocked and went Out in the room's atmosphere. I dove down into the bible and images appeared the same as when the Parson was talking.

"What does it say, tell me what it says" I was thinking over and over and ... I dove right into the book and out the other side. There was another world with people with funny clothes and different houses. It was like in a foreign country where the ground was full of sand all over. People walked past me without seeing me, it was only I who saw them. Farmor's stories about

God came back to me. I saw the ladder to the heavens; it looked like a string of pearls glittering in the light and so long that I couldn't see the end. I saw a great crowd of people and especially a man who walked in front. They walked toward a city that was already filled with people. I guessed that it was Jesus who went into Jerusalem. When I looked up I saw a great form sitting on a throne. It looked like everything was made of ice, faintly translucent, even the old guy, though he was moving. There were wonderful colors in the ice, and it was like a fairy tale. God looked like king Bore in a children's book we had, but the whole thing was much more beautiful this way in real life.

Riiiiing…. The telephone rang. It hung on the wall, inside the door. It could be used by the family only when there was something important and when they needed to contact the Parson. I was terrified of it. When I tried to answer, it was as if the Parson was a giant eagle that attacked me and grabbed my neck with his talons and flew away with me. I was in the room without permission and knew that somebody would come running to answer. It got very unpleasant. I crawled into my corner under the desk and sat there until the person had finished talking, hung up and left. Then I sneaked out and disappeared into one of my other hiding places.

Father was not religious but he could respect that others were. He wanted, however, that they should respect him too, but this was not always the case.

One day some Jehovah's Witnesses came to see him in the barn in order to save him. They stood in the doorway and preached. Father declined and asked them to leave. He said there was no point in trying to save him because: "I have nothing against God, but his representatives on earth I don't have much use for." He felt that the church and its men had sucked the poor people dry and failed the needy, judged and condemned as if they were gods, and this he could not stand. Nor that they threatened people with hell. In his world, there was no hell except the one we might have here in life on earth, so he thought they used unfair methods to scare people and that was not his way. He also said that he had the church so close by that he could go there every day if he wanted. Then the Jehovah's men commented: "But you don't really do that, do you?"

"Yes I do" said Father, "because I am the one who rings the bells."

Thus that conversation was over and they wandered off a little disappointed.

The county paid for some of the people who came and lived with us. Father made sure that this money wouldn't be squandered and make us dependent on it for income, so instead it was used for bicycles, skis, and such that we wouldn't have been able to afford otherwise. We basically lived a good life. We always had food, clothes, and a roof over our heads, but we were always short of cash. The farm provided us with the necessities, but there was nothing left over for luxuries, and it was a luxury to have a bicycle, a moped, a car, skates or skis. Father often said that it would never happen that somebody would have to leave our house because we didn't get paid for taking care of himher, so the farm had to feed all the mouths.

He also was concerned that everyone should carry hisher share of the load. That meant that everyone took part in the work according to hisher ability and interest. One person took care of some animals, somebody else other animals, a third person felled fire-wood in the forest, a fourth drove the tractor, a fifth helped mother in the kitchen. All the young people and children also had their tasks. They got to chose between indoor work and outdoor work, between animals and field work. Everything was produced and utilized at our place, the sheep were sheared, the wool was carded and spun into yarn, dyed and knitted or woven on the loom. The bees gave honey for sweetener all winter. The chicken down was plucked and used as stuffing in pillows. There was a smithy where all the required tools were fabricated and repaired, as well as a carpentry shop where handles and such were made. In the winter, the men worked on fixing harnesses and other leather things.

Thus life was lived around me. Work was always being done but there was no stress or hurry except at harvest time or in case of bad weather; then it was all hands on deck, things had to happen in the shortest possible time. I was an observer. I was there and was taken care of by whomever had the possibility. Mostly I was with Father in the barn, since he was the one taking care of the cows. It was a motley life, a mobile life with lots of jollity. The grownups sang a lot and told each stories. Sometimes there were conflicts, but Father took charge and made sure everything was out on the table and ventilated, and gradually peace was reestablished.

One morning when Father had just placed me on the

stool above the poop gutter, one of the uncles, Nils, came into the barn.

"I heard on the radio how they talked about that one shouldn't be satisfied with charity, but that one should actually get a wage for one's work. It isn't fair that we who do the real work on the farm don't get to keep the money for the work we do in the forest and on the fields and with the animals and instead it goes to the common." The common, that was farmor, farfar, mother and all the children and youths that lived with us but whose work did not directly lead to any income.

"That's the stupidest thing I ever heard" father said, "Of course, everybody should have it equally good."

Nils muttered that it was unfair that they had to wear themselves out while others went there and had it easy.

Then Father said: "I'll take this up at the eleven coffee." "No, that isn't necessary" Nils said embarrassed and walked away.

Father walked around in the barn and talked agitatedly to himself and I saw in the atmosphere how his idea that everyone in the house should share alike in what the farm produced had gotten undermined by what Nils had said. It wasn't completely broken, but it was like a dark cloud had come and darkened the sun.

At the eleven coffee I sat in my place under the table.

"I have something important to bring up", said Father. "Nils apparently thinks that he doesn't get enough of the money that we make here on the farm. And I am wondering if there are others who think there is a problem with the way we have been sharing the money that comes in?"

"I have also heard on the radio that those who work on farms also should get a wage" somebody said. "Just like factory workers and everybody else."

At our place nobody got a salary. When somebody needed something he brought it up at the eleven coffee, and if there was money available he got it. All requests were considered and the money was divided fairly, not based on performance but on need and requests.

Discussion started around the table. Somebody said: "Those that haven't done anything useful in their lives might as well starve." He was referring to the youths who lived with us, and who would otherwise have been in reform school, and who did not do much useful work.

When everyone had had their say, Father said to Nils: "If you got money and you didn't need it what would you do with it?" Nils said: "I would save it."

Father asked: "What's the point in saving money when you know that you can get everything you need from the farm?"

"Then I could use it any way I liked."

"But you can already request anything you like and generally you get it."

"Yes but I want to have my *own* money."

Father said: "You must understand that everyone contributes, and that everyone should get what they need. Not all the work here on the farm generates money, like cooking, cleaning, taking care of the children. But have you thought about how much it would cost if we had to pay for it. It's so expensive that then all our money would go to that and there wouldn't be anything left over for the rest of you."

But everyone did not agree with this. These are different times. Now, one wants money in the wallet. There is another freedom out in the community. But not at our place.

"How much money are we talking about? Who wants to have their own money?"

It was only the two uncles that wanted their own money, so it was finally decided they would get their own bank accounts and that a small amount would be deposited in them each month as spending money.

The others were relieved that the unpleasantness was over. And then we went back to the old familiar way. The new age had to wait.

I was often in the barn with Father, and from time to time a calf was born. Father noticed that contact with calves was good for me, so he put me in the pen with the newborn calf, and there I could sit for hours and just pet the calf until he got up on shaky legs and started walking.

Once when a calf was born I said: "It will die." Nobody paid attention since the calf was completely healthy, but after a few hours it died. Nobody understood why, and nobody understood what made me say that it would die. After this, many calves were born and I didn't say anything about them, but later I said the same thing about yet another calf, and it died also. Some years later I said the same thing for the third time about a newborn calf and then Father laid the calf in a pen with its head in my lap and put a bucket with raw milk next to me. So then I sat there with the calf and dipped my hand in the milk and let the calf suck on my hand, and this calf survived.

Father didn't say anything about this, but he came to realize that I had a gift that he hadn't known about and that I didn't know about either. When he said that to me, something lit up inside me and just then we were both in the real reality. The important thing for me was not that the calf survived, but that Father and I for a short while were together in the real reality. This one moment caused my life to suddenly have a value that I had not been in contact with earlier.

There were calves born on other farms as well and since father had told them about the surviving calf he went there with me and sometimes I said "It will die." Then Father arranged it the same way as at our barn and those calves survived. Many were skeptical and maintained that they would have survived anyway, and maybe so, but on those occasions when I uttered my laconic "It will die", the calf died if nothing was done.

The thing for me was that when the calf didn't have any atmosphere around it, when it was empty around it, it meant that it didn't have contact with its own life force. The calf could be as healthy as anything, but if nobody made contact with it, the natural function in the calf ceased. When the calves were born out in the field and could suckle their mother and the mother could lick them and keep them close they never died in this way. But in the barns it wasn't like that. There the cow stood in a special stall and right after the birth the calf was put in its own pen, and the raw milk was collected. The calf certainly got some of it but it was taught to drink it out of a bucket and therefore didn't get the relationship contact that some calves needed to make contact with their own life force.

I think it is the same thing that happens with many children that die in early infancy, crib death. When they are laid down by themselves and don't feel the mother's heart sounds and body heat they lose contact with the impulse system that causes the life force to take over, and then life ceases without there being anything wrong with the child. If the child gets a little colder, a little less comfortable, a little more motion around it, then the life impulse system gets going; otherwise there is the risk that it gives up.

Mother had told Father early on that she didn't want any children because she wouldn't be able to care for them when they were babies. She knew about herself that she would find it so unbearably painful that she would just throw them away, or anything, just to get rid of the pain. She could not imagine herself taking care of them.

When my brother was a toddler, mother could take care of him. Then it wasn't painful anymore. It was only if he defied her that she got crazy, but he did this rarely, plus there was always someone who could take over. In this way, mother was effectively prevented from solving her problems, but her difficulties did not have serious consequences for us kids since we had so many others who protected us.

Father spent a lot of time trying to understand me. It was hard for him to understand that sometimes I was able to do something perfectly and at other times be totally dumb and just stand there and stare and not follow a single instruction. He didn't understand why it sometimes was possible for me to be in contact in some activity and on other occasions impossible, only dead stop and resistance. He would keep on practicing a behavior or habit for the longest time without the least type of result. Then half a year might pass and he would discover that I was doing exactly as he had taught, and as it was supposed to be done, without anyone saying anything to me. He understood that there was something tricky in me, in the learning system itself, and that I didn't have any judgment or realistic picture of the future.

If father carefully reminded me of something that had happened in the ordinary world I could describe the event reasonably realistically, but when he let me speak freely then the real reality crept into the ordinary one. Sven took me with him on the tractor to get some hay from a neighbor. When we came back Father asked me: "Was Agnes at home?"

I knew that he meant the wife of the farmer. I answered: "I got strawberries, and they were in my hands and I could put them in my mouth and they were super good and nobody ate except me. It was red and flowed and poured in a bottle. I also got juice and it turned into a pink cloud that bubbled and foamed in the glass."

Since I had got strawberries and juice, Father knew that Agnes had been at home.

I almost never obeyed instructions, but my brother always knew how to get me where he wanted me. He might walk past me and say: "*Vinninga*."

I turned mean and hostile..

Ten minutes later he walked past and said: "We are going to Vinninga."

I didn't react at all.

The third time he had my coat with him and said: "Come, now we are going to Vinninga."

Then I took the jacket and ambled behind him.

When he wanted me to do something, washing dishes for example, he sat on the bench with a crime mystery in his lap reading, and simultaneously was giving me orders: "Put up the plate, change plate, get another plate." He kept it up until the dishes were all done and he had finished his book. I enjoyed this situation very much, because then I could be in my own world and at the same time in somebody else's. He liked it also because it took some time and he could keep reading without anyone complaining. Otherwise, he often hid his detective books inside his school books and looked like a diligent student instead of a reader of escapist junk.

All the regular routines that people follow were totally meaningless for me, and I didn't have any inner conscience or impulses that told me what it was time to do, for example change my clothes, wash, brush my teeth, eat, go to bed. These were just bothersome interruptions and I tried to avoid them. But I couldn't. There was always somebody who made sure I was included in the normal rituals. The thing that didn't happen was brushing my teeth. Nobody came close to my mouth. Then I bit, scratched, kicked so that the person gave up. My bad diet and brushing habits caused my teeth to be practically destroyed. I had 28 cavities in the 24 teeth I had left when I went to the dentist at fourteen. Earlier they had pulled some teeth and that had to be done by force because there was no other way.

Mother had a constant battle with me when it came to changing my clothes. She grabbed me and held me fast and it was a tough job, since I bit, scratched, kicked, and hit, and when she finally had done it she had to hold me until I got used to the new clothes, otherwise I just ripped them off. Father did it the easy way. He filled a tub with water–I loved to bathe– and put me in it. Then I undressed myself voluntarily, and he could take my clothes to the laundry without me reacting. Then he put out clean clothes, and when he took me up I was already weaned off the old ones. Mother thought that this method was dishonest; she felt that I should learn to change my clothes like everybody else.

I also had a bad habit that sometimes cost me terribly. I felt that I just *had to* smell things, and also taste most things. Father had a carton in the milk closet with a white powder that appealed to me. Once when it was open and reachable I stuck my face in it and got a mouthful of the stuff. It was a cleaning powder for the milking machines, called *Skurit*, and consisted primarily of soda. I got burned all over the inside my throat and couldn't eat or drink for two weeks. They tried to give me liquids through a straw and I managed to survive. When my throat had healed and I could start to eat again I went back there and did the same thing with the same result. Father was desperate because I couldn't learn from my experiences, and because I liked things that were harmful for me.

One winter day when it was 20 below zero, I licked on a

metal railing by the kitchen entrance and got stuck with my tongue and lips. Mother had to warm up water and pour over the railing to get me free but the skin came off the top of my tongue and the lip was red meat. I did the same thing two more times, and they had to watch me so I wouldn't get that impulse when I went outside. I loved the blood flavor I got in my mouth, and when the wounds scabbed over I picked on them constantly which caused them to take very long to heal.

Every time we butchered animals at home on the farm I was allowed to be there. They collected all the blood, and it needed to be stirred so it wouldn't coagulate, and then I could stick my finger in it and taste it. I loved the flavor of blood, both my own and others, so that was a high point for me.

Father was often puzzled by my paradoxical way of functioning. In one way I was like an infant that couldn't fend for herself and wouldn't hurt a fly, and on the other hand I could come up with all kinds of dangerous things through far reaching strategies to achieve something I had fixated on. He didn't recognize this from anything he had experienced before. There was no predictability in my reactions. I could react a certain way several times in a row and then suddenly react completely differently, and the old way of reacting didn't return.

Sometimes he was struck by amazement over my stubbornness and creativity, only to find that there wasn't a single conscious thought or impulse that steered me. He didn't know if he should laugh or cry, and sometimes he worried that I might actually expose myself to something that could cost me my life. At the same time he wanted me to have my own experiences, because he noticed that this started a good process that I could devote myself to for quite long.

He often asked others: "What do you do with a kid like her?" Unfortunately there was nobody who took his question seriously and discussed the Iris phenomenon with him, instead most people gave him the advice to send me to an institution, then maybe I could turn out OK also. Eventually he stopped trying to involve others. He realized it was futile because there was no interest in learning about these difficulties, only a desire to be rid them as quickly and painlessly as possible for the sake of others...

Father pondered much on how he should think around me. I was odd and had a lot of different behaviors. I liked things that others had been brought up to be disgusted by. I was able to do different things, for example go and fetch something they asked me for, because I knew what everything was called and where everything was, but I didn't do it except in very special circumstances. Unless he was wholly present in what he said to me and simultaneously was thinking of the exact thing he wanted me to fetch I got no impulse to act.

It was not possible to control me with rewards or sanctions because I often got fixated on the reward and was then driven to obtain it independently of what I was supposed to do to get it. I didn't learn any of what I was supposed to learn and most often I never did what the reward was intended to strengthen. Same thing with sanctions and punishments. I often liked them, like being locked in a room, get thrown out, not be allowed to go with somebody, not eat certain things that others liked.

Moreover, I had no constancy, so if they promised me something or threatened me with something, I didn't remember it after a minute so then it was ineffective. I just could not get into the state of conformity that everyone seemed to expect. I didn't know what it was, or even that it existed, and this worried Father for he wondered what would happen in school.

He was sure I wasn't retarded even if I in many areas was undeveloped, and he knew that I wasn't psychotic, even if I prattled about strange things when I was relating something, and he knew that I had my own special world that I lived in. He knew I could distinguish between the inner and the outer reality, and that I didn't have a split personality like psychotics have, but he didn't know what this should be called. He also understood that there were several among our kin that had different variations of the same problem and that it probably was something in the family genes, but there was nobody who could do anything about it, so he figured the only thing was to give me the best possible care so I could grow up with as little damage as possible. He saw my older cousin who had managed quite well until he was seven and ready to start school. Then he became people-shy and developed anxiety demons and got tics and stereotypy. He wasn't completely normal before either, but before school he just had the same peculiarities as me.

Father also had to struggle to keep me present here so I didn't spend my time in the state I called Out. It was a continual tug of war. I sought out places where I could be alone and rock myself into that state, and he tried to keep me with him to minimize my opportunities for disappearing Out. He realized that even if I only marginally developed it was still better than if I got to remain in my state. He knew that I avoided all contact and therefore did not develop constructively unless he engaged himself consciously. I had the tendency to back slide and got more hang-ups and peculiarities.

He understood that my state Out was pleasant and problem-free for me. That it filled me a substance that I otherwise lacked, and that it was tranquil compared to the ordinary life which constantly involved conflicts, not least with other people. In the ordinary there were lots of expectations, requirements, and wishes that washed over me in the atmosphere and which I couldn't escape unless I rocked myself into my state. What was expected was that I should want something, but it was just empty, blank, nothing inside. It was also expected that there would be some type of model that I would live by, which I never understood. Nobody grasped that I had no contact with the emotion field that would give me the information that other people seemed to have access to. It was not like this field was missing, but a bridge was missing, some kind of transfer, some kind of feeling for others and for situations that could be connected to memories of experiences that could give guidance for how to behave and what the consequences would be.

The peculiar thing about my condition is that there is so often such emptiness, a standing still, no impulse whatever, and even though I can see everything and understand everything around me it doesn't give me any impulses for action. It's like being in an invisible glass box. You see and hear everything, exist and function, but it is like a nightmare state, the body can't move, only the psyche is active.

When I was together with other people there were always a lot of things required of me. I couldn't say what I wanted, because then I was impolite. I had to greet people in a certain way; otherwise they got angry and called me impolite. Sometimes farmor said I was sinful when I said something, and sometimes she made me say forgive me though I didn't know what "forgive" meant, or why you should say that word. I saw that people calmed down and lost interest in me and then I acted up again, and the same story was repeated. Some could laugh at it all, but most thought that I should be sent to an institution. Life was so complicated sometimes. It was like you absolutely can't be yourself when you are with other people, that they are disturbed by it and you mustn't disturb their peace of mind.

Unfortunately for others, I loved disturbing their peace of mind. I loved it when they got emotional and reacted. I didn't realize that it was only certain feelings that are pleasant. In my world I had heard that feelings are the most important thing, and for me there was no difference between bad and good feelings. Mother's feelings were the easiest to activate. She started up on almost anything, and I had a whole battery of alternatives, and she reacted every time, so she was a slam dunk. Often it was enough for me come into the room. She got angry just by seeing my look, or the "smirk on my face", as she said. She said that I could "provoke gall fever on a dead horse." When she started up, the emptiness and nothingness disappeared for me. She thought that I provoked her deliberately. This, I actually did too, but I didn't know it was mean. I heard her say it but it didn't mean anything for me and I had no conscience that could guide me and no self- preservation instinct either, so when she screamed that she would kill me if I didn't stop, this didn't mean anything for me either. It was only beautiful words that formed beautiful patterns in the atmosphere. She often said that she could have had ten kids like my brother, but not a one like me, and that she had got me for her sins. I waited often to learn what these sins looked like. It was such a fun word, it had such a special form and I loved it, but she never explained how her sins came about or how they looked.

I did a lot of dumb things and I was considered clumsy and unintelligent. But the fact is that I did these crazy things with great precision. When my brother was testing to see if the plank across the silo was strong enough by sending me out on it I would never have done it if I hadn't known that it in fact was strong enough. When I ran out in front of the neighbor's car so I could listen to his squealing brakes, which I did many times, I did it at exactly the right second. A few seconds sooner and he wouldn't have to brake at all, a second later and he would have run me over. When I ate Skurit the second time and licked the cold railing the second and third time it wasn't because of stupidity, but because I liked the pain. When the horse bolted, I knew the exact moment to jump off so as to not get hurt. My brother on the other hand would jump into the nettles and thistles.

Father brooded much about my incomprehensible behavior: that I seemed so calculating and cunning and could create the most complicated situations and get past most obstacles without the least fear or self-preservation or thought of the consequences. That I could so easily put observing grown-ups out of action and expose myself to the most hazardous situations, while at the same time I appeared so ignorant and intellectually undeveloped. That I in one way was like an oblivious infant, and at the same time a full-fledged swindler that developed the most complicated strategies to achieve her devious goals. It just didn't compute, he didn't know if he should laugh or cry, let alone how he should deal with my behaviors.

This mixture of stupidity and clumsiness on the one hand, and my skill in manipulating people for my own hidden aims and getting them agitated on the other is a paradox I still don't understand.

The only one who didn't keep telling me to behave was Father; Emma hadn't done it either, but she wasn't here anymore as a body. Instead Father told me how he believed people wanted me to be, and asked me if I couldn't do that because it would be nicest that way. Then I did like he said as far as I could, but it depended on what clicked in my head at the time.

He tried to teach me that you don't need to take it personal when you think other people are stupid, you can just think they are batty and let it pass. This I couldn't, I had a tantrum instead, but occasionally I succeeded in just staring at the person and "let it pass", and that was fun, because then it was the other person that had a tantrum. That was not exactly what Father meant by "not minding". But when a person was irritated I somehow got caught in it and couldn't stop "carrying on" so the other person somehow lost it, got really angry or got a head ache. Often heshe started scolding Father or mother because I was spoiled and that it wouldn't hurt if I got a good spanking.

Father answered that hurt was exactly what a spanking would do. He knew that it wouldn't help, that it would further reduce my ability to be polite and well mannered, and he felt that grownups ought to be mature enough to not let themselves be rattled by an innocent child.

The word "innocent" used to be the source for new arguments among the grown-ups, and the air was filled with the most wonderful colors and forms. I used to sit under chair or a table and follow the play in the minutest detail.

At some occasions it ended with the person going home in a huff promising to never come back again. They thought that Father was completely screwy and ought to be locked up, that he was worse than me. He smiled kindly, said so long, and asked the person to think it over and come back again, since he didn't carry a grudge and he hoped this applied to the other one also.

Mother heard such arguments and "crept to the cross". She prayed and pleaded with the agitated visitor, apologized and humbled herself, and sometimes the visitor remained as a favor and sometimes heshe left anyway, and the mother wrote apologetic letters and abased herself even more. Most of them came back, and these events eventually turned into funny stories.

Nowadays I have learned to surf on other people's wishes and now I am able, often better than others, to read others and see what is expected of me. I have learned to understand the content of the atmosphere in a whole new way, and thus I can behave normally even when I don't have any feeling for what is normal behavior. I have no autopilot that reflexively steers me from unacceptable to acceptable behaviors; instead I have consciously trained myself in the art of making internal lists and follow them so that others are disturbed as little as possible.

During my entire childhood I maintained an autonomy where I didn't run the risk of becoming docile or defiant. Every time someone has placed demands on me to obey I have reacted with tantrums and stereotypy. This has been the cause of a lot of trouble, and at the same time it has protected me from blocking out the real reality. Most children give up their consciousness of the real reality very soon and allow themselves to be compliant- or else they turn defiant. By not blocking out the real reality I caused myself and my loved ones a lot of complications. But when I eventually acquired an understanding of the ordinary reality I was old enough that I could maintain my consciousness of the real reality and of how humans could function if we functioned the same way as animals do. And I understood by and by that humans have decided to live in conflict, and destroy much of what would work fine if we lived according to our nature, like the animals do. There are groupings, religious, political, and others, which are interested in separating a human from her nature, because so long as she lives by her nature they have no power over her. When she lives according to her nature, she can imagine doing as others wish when she perceives it as sensible, but nobody can make her do something that is harmful.

This way, what was a burden when I was a child has become an asset. Others can't provoke me and draw me into mental games and intrigues, and get me to say something about somebody absent. One Sunday I sat outside the church after the service. A churchgoer said to me: "I know your mother, and she is so nice, but she cusses so terribly. She should stop swearing, because it isn't godly. Otherwise, she is a good person." He stopped and waited for concurrence – or perhaps disagreement – from me so that he could continue to complain about her cussing.

But I had no opinion whatsoever about whether my mother should stop swearing or not, so I answered: "Yes, some people cuss, and others talk with God."

"Ah hem?" he said surprised and hesitated. Then he smiled and said: "That's one way to look at it." Then he went inside and let mother treat him to coffee.

It isn't possible to threaten me with rejection or scandal either. I still retain my consciousness about the natural and how it is defeated, and therefore I am able to show people how to avoid extinguishing the natural within them.

Father had made up his mind that I had to choose this world. He wasn't going to give up until he had made me understand there was something good, something exciting and fun in living in contact with other people. And, being the person he was, he first decided this and then tried to figure out how in the world he could to get me to discover it. He couldn't bear the thought of forcibly training me to see it, but slowly nudge me towards it until my interest awakened. That's how he got me to use the toilet, and that's how he got me to eat, so he thought that it had to be possible to get me into the ordinary world also.

He pondered much on different periods in my life. First, how I avoided all contact and gave no signals of my needs and how he, when I was three, nevertheless got contact with me. Then about how this contact caused me to be so badly perturbed by other people that I screamed whenever a new person appeared. That habit disappeared three years later when the peddler came into the kitchen and roared that I wouldn't die.

Later he pondered how I could sit in school beside my brother and be entirely satisfied. How tediously I still developed and learned things that eventually functioned, even if it was in a different way than for other kids and often only after they had abandoned hope that I would learn it. How I could appear completely normal and capable one day, or together with some special person, only to be just as incompetent as before the following day. All this and more were questions that remained unanswered, and which I myself have wrestled with trying to describe in order to help others understand what communication is.

He wondered later with a shudder what would have happened if he actually had put me in an institution, or if he had followed the advice to leave me alone instead of struggling with me about everything. He understood that if he had stopped caring I would have sunk down in my state where no reasonable development took place, where my talents would have remained useless in reality.

He was grateful that I was such a difficult enigma to solve, that I was so hard to figure out, because he learned what it was like to give up old concepts and think anew. He felt that he had developed greatly himself. Once in my teens, in an attack of normalcy and curiosity about what other people thought about me, I said to him that I had been so much trouble and worry for him. Then he answered that he couldn't think of anything more important in life than to care for someone like me. He said I didn't understand how interesting and valuable it had been for him. And that is true. I still don't know quite what he meant by it but I have begun to get a hint of it.

I am beginning to understand if you take care of dysfunctional human beings, you get to have a tough life and at the same time a development of your personality and character that you couldn't get any other way. This is what we handicapped persons give back to others so that from the beginning we have already discharged our debt, therefore there is nothing we need to thank somebody for, we do not owe a debt of gratitude to anyone. There is much we can be thankful for in that others focus on us and thereby undertake their own development, but we have paid back by not giving up and by forcing others out of their comfort zone and learning new things about themselves, deep down. It can take long time to discover that the only reason to take care of broken humans is to actualize oneself.

One advantage with growing up in the fluid environment I did, with so many permanent people and so many transients has been that I finally became used to the atmosphere of the new people, that the new and strange didn't scare me anymore. In the beginning it was hard for me to handle, but I finally managed by having Father as the security and constancy in a world where everything else was changeable. This mix of having enough that is known and familiar while there is also always something new; this is the difficult balance for everyone who takes care of persons with different types of handicaps. This applies to the person herself and the person she is caring for. Both need the stimulation of the new and the security of the old. The ability to balance between secure and new is a great art.

The tug of war between me and Father continued until I was ten. Then Father asked me to choose the ordinary life. He explained to me if I stayed in what I called the real reality I would be so strange to those around me and therefore so uninteresting that I wouldn't get much contact with others. Personally I was then in a questioning mode: "Why are people enemies when they know that they sooner or later will die? What's the point of being enemies when it solves itself through death?" I posed this question to Father and he answered that most people didn't understand that they were mortal, and that's why they got caught up in feelings and thought patterns that caused them to be enemies and remained so. He also said that since I knew a little more, maybe it was my task in life to explain this to them so they could stop being enemies.

I had by then discovered that humans were humans and not just a species of animal among all the others, so when Father asked me to choose the ordinary I already had so deep an interest in the human that I really didn't have a choice even if I thought so myself.

After this, a new phase commenced, a phase of cooperation

between me and Father which made the world, as I experienced it in my daily life, completely different. It wasn't that I got much of a will of my own, but I learned to surf on that of others and thereby the world expanded and grew much bigger.

Later in life, this is how I see the universe: That the universe can be the smallest thing, and then expand to be the biggest thing, only to collapse and be small again. It seems to me this happens in our physical development as humans, in our mental development, how we are born unaware of ourselves, how we develop consciousness, and how it is slowly quenched by the rigid patterns of our upbringing and later by senility. This is a principle that is present in large and small, and which man tries to eliminate, but which always wins in the end. There is a wisdom in this which can be used to solve hang-ups in conflicts, and I hope to one day be able to communicate it so that people can let go of their misunderstandings and live life like an explorer with constantly curious eyes that see the novel in the everyday. Our worth consists in that we are humans and that this cannot be changed, can't be added to so that we become more valuable or taken away so that we become worthless; it involves our thought patterns and our view of life.

CHAPTER 2

School Days
(Iris in the eyes of others)

When my brother had to start school, a year before my formal start, he was super scared, his face turned white, he had a stomach ache, got sick and threw up. Father went with him and took me along. Every day for a couple of weeks we were in the school with my brother. His phobia didn't get better, but it was August and Father was needed at home for the harvest. He hated leaving him in the school in this condition, and he couldn't let the grain go to waste either, so he put me on a chair next to him and said: "Now you have Iris here, so I am sure it will be ok. She will go with you and sit next to you so you won't have any problems with your stomach." He accepted this and I ended up sitting in the amazing world of school.

It was the best school semester of my life. Nobody focused on me. I sat and looked at all the letters, all the pictures that the children drew, heard the hymn they sang in the morning and other songs, was with them outside during recess, and sat among all the other kids. The one called ma'am, I heard her voice the most, and sometimes there came fantastic stories I could play with in my own world. Strange new words that formed light, colors and shapes that I could play with inside. I got to participate in all the nice things there, the reading aloud together, all the stories that ma'am told, I could watch all the games and the calisthenics between the desks; I got to eat milk and sandwiches in the cloak room. I got to be in my world and at the same time be present in the ordinary world in my way, and nobody expected anything or demanded anything of me. The other children used to play at our house, so I and my behaviors were not unknown, and children don't judge, unless grown-ups teach them to.

My brother probably didn't need me for very long, but I got to sit there the entire semester anyway. But after the Christmas break I was not allowed to continue. Father tried to arrange it so I could stay there, but with my peculiarities and my strange development I was seen as anything but ready for school. Father said I wouldn't be much better a year later, but it didn't help. After one semester school was irreversibly over for me and then I regressed and got depression.

I started to wet myself again, stopped responding to attention from others, and resumed some stereotypy: I flapped my hands, spun my head, drooled, resisted undressing, and ran away every day. Father was worried, but decided to give me all possible care and kept at it with a lot of effort until summer came. He often asked: "Iris, what is it with you? What should we do with you? Now you are just as difficult as when you were little, and we can't have that." But I couldn't answer, in my world there was no answer, there was only empty and nothing and I didn't know what was missing, only that it was empty.

The summer after this spring semester turned out to be a nice time. It was like I knew I would start school in the fall and I became lighter and lighter in my mood and easier to handle. Father was glad that it was easier to make contact with me, and I didn't go into my state as often, or as soon after contact. I wet myself less often and ate better.

I started school, but it wasn't the same as before. Now I had to sit at a desk, sit like ma'am wanted, and I was supposed to perform, which was completely incomprehensible to me. At the first opportunity I ran over and sat down where I sat during the first semester and ma'am came and brought me back to the desk. Ma'am got irritated and upset, thought me defiant and careless and punished me often by sending me out to the cloak room. I liked that a lot. I could sit there with my ear to the wall and hear everything happening in the class room. I often went Out and floated into the class room and was there in their atmosphere. It was lovely. Then I could float about among the word pictures; to A as in ape, B as in banana.

It took a while before I could stop humming, and since I always used to make some sound to keep me company, it was strange to not hear them. Father had taught me if I wanted to stay in school I had to hum on the inside instead of the outside, and this I had learned to do. I sat there and sounded inside and then others didn't mind, and I got to stay.

Then there was the bell that ma'am rang. As soon as it happened the kids went into motion and ran away. In the beginning I didn't understand it, but after a few months it dawned on me that the sound meant that if you were inside you were supposed to go out, and if you were outside you were supposed to go in. Not so that I thought it, or that it would have worked if I was alone, but passively I knew it. That's how it often was, somewhere inside I knew what different things meant, but I couldn't translate it into any appropriate action or show that I understood.

And then there were the questions. Somebody asked me something and I often knew the answer when it was about some everyday concrete thing. But I never knew what I should do with it, and this led me to start dancing, spinning, rambling, or screaming instead. This inner state where things connect indiscriminately instead of naturally has been the hardest thing for me to get straightened out. It took many years into adulthood before I succeeded in organizing things so they hung together sensibly.

I was also wont to provoke ma'am like when she had just thought of something she was going to sausage-stuff the students with. When I saw what she was about to say, before she formulated it in words, I could pick any word at all, that had nothing to do with her thoughts, and then this word came out of her mouth, "dress", or "blue paint", which made her really confused. If I was really mean I could get her to say a cuss word, and then she was crushed for the rest of the day. But it was risky to try to stick in a word that was too much in conflict with her own morals and values, because then she might come to a dead stop, and say nothing at all. Then she would start over, frustrated and irritated, and eventually some unfortunate child who wasn't paying attention received the brunt of her irritation.

She never connected any of this to me.

I had learned this trick of influencing people to keep my mother from killing me. When I made her crazy and got her impulses going she was unable to control them. She was frustrated because I wasn't a normal child and sometimes got the urge to attack me or kill me. For that reason she never wanted to be alone with me and just said: "take her away" instead of doing something to me. That way I was protected from being hurt by my mother. But when I was around seven or eight I figured out that I could divert her anger away from me. When her impulse came, there was a kind of space between her and me where I could stick in something, for example a thought about the "stove", or "the water faucet is running", or "somebody is coming". Then she got distracted and turned her attention to it instead of against me. She didn't feel manipulated, but was happy that her impulse had been diverted.

In my world there was only one thing of each kind. One person had one name, another had another. If somebody's name was Erik and there was another named Erik, only the first one existed. The other one fell away. Then you had to say Erik Eriksson and Erik Andersson. It was so difficult to generalize, because if there already was one, you couldn't in the same sentence mean something else by it.

This also became my problem in school. First we learned A for apes, B for banana. No problem, I knew the alphabet before I started school. But when the apes and bananas and the citrus were put together to form completely different words; when you had to think completely differently, it became chaotic for me and I developed a bunch of strange reactions. Then ma'am sent me out in the hall so I would calm down, and I sat there and became calm. The problem was that I missed learning to read. I didn't grasp that the letters were abstract symbols that could be combined to form different words, and it took until I was fourteen before I figured that out. Ma'am didn't understand how to help me, she just got frustrated. She was sixty-four years old and she had never had a student she couldn't teach to read and write. I was an abomination that destroyed her peace of mind because I was so strange and incomprehensible.

Ma'am was concerned and called for a meeting. Father was there and said he was sure I learned stuff even if I couldn't produce results. Ma'am said she had been a teacher all her life and she would indeed make sure that even I would learn to read and write. If not, I was retarded and then I should be in a special and not a normal class. It offended her greatly that I was such a spoiled child who wouldn't submit to the rules like everybody else.

She said she indeed remembered Father as a pupil, and his willfulness, and she certainly remembered what he had done when mother came to the school, how he had chased the other kids with his wooden clog and how he had let mother sit beside him though they were in different grades. She understood that a headstrong person like him couldn't have anything except a headstrong child, and it was a wonder that my brother was as capable and normal as he was.

She tried to get me classified as retarded with the help of various experts, but that didn't succeed because Father did not go along with it. He agreed that there was something the matter with me, that I was underdeveloped, but not that I was retarded. He had dealt with retarded persons so he knew they were unintelligent all the time. But with me it was different; I was especially talented in some areas and completely impossible and undeveloped in others. He couldn't say what, but something was different about me.

The experts got together to do some tests on me. Father asked to sit in a corner of the room since then they would find out what I actually knew, but this was not allowed. He had to sit in the waiting room. I was in with the experts and they gave me tasks which I didn't bother to do. According to the tests, I was completely incapable and undeveloped, but they could see that I really wasn't, so they understood that it involved some kind of immaturity. They tried to get Father to sign off that I was retarded and he refused. In my papers it says that I am "underdeveloped", with quotation marks.

Father's view that I wasn't retarded was based on his realization that I did understand, and also that I was able to do most practical chores, although most often it didn't occur to me to do them. Sometimes when he had the time and inspiration, he tested me. He got out all the clothes I was to wear and laid them out in the hall. Then he stood in the doorway talking with someone. Simultaneously he concentrated on me and thought intensively "Undershirt, undershirt, undershirt....", and after a bunch of rituals, climbing in the stairs, waving of hands, uttering of sounds, I got the undershirt on. He continued with panties, socks, long pants, sweater, shoes, and overcoat.

After about 45 minutes of sending these directions out in the atmosphere he got me dressed. Then he knew that I was able, but there was something wrong that caused me to not do it automatically or understand that I should do it because it was too cold to be naked.

Another of the many times I was to be tested Father again asked if he could sit in a corner of the room. He explained that I didn't see the point of answering all these questions, but if he could be in the room, even if I couldn't see him, it would become apparent how much I actually knew. They viewed this as manipulation, and hence he was not allowed. They only got one answer out of me, and from that they could tell that I understood more than a retarded person.

And since I could answer one question correctly they thought I was trying to provoke them by not answering the others also. They tried to entice me with rewards, but this caused me to be so intolerable that they gave me the reward without me performing anything. They tried with punishment, i.e. just sitting there quietly and looking annoyed, and then I just started laughing since I enjoyed myself in that situation.

On this occasion Father got a lot of criticism. They considered it his fault that I was the way I was, that I was spoiled and was just faking. They were agitated and frustrated because it seemed like a cat and mouse game to them. Father said again if he could sit in the room without looking at me and without saying a word they would get the result they were after, but this they absolutely could not accept. Moreover, their prestige was now involved so the struggle with me was one they intended to win.

The test was supposed to take two hours, but they kept at it all day, not stopping until their quitting time. On one occasion when they were relaxing and talking amongst themselves I was sitting in front of a game with asymmetric triangles, and in no time at all I had laid them correctly. When they noticed it and started looking at me I lost my concentration, but they could see it was correct. This was a riddle for them. They understood nothing.

The way it was in my world, when the charge in the atmosphere became orderly and familiar to me, which could take five hours, I became grounded within myself and then I thought it was fun with all the triangles, and it came naturally to place them in order to make a big triangle.

This puzzled them and created even more question-marks around my development difficulties. One of the experts understood why Father didn't want to sign a paper and have me declared stupid. She realized that he understood that I wasn't normally developed, nor well functioning, so underdeveloped was probably a better word than retarded. She said something to him to the effect that I did have intelligence but that I had a peculiar way of using it. This satisfied him, because that's how he saw it also.

This was characteristic for me. One moment I didn't seem to understand anything at all, and the next I displayed brilliant insight. Father had experienced this many times. I could motor-talk, fantasize, and recount and create all kinds of absurd conjunctions, all the way from the universe to the most everyday trivia. If you listened carefully you noticed that not much escaped me, but my way of using what I had picked up was nonsensical. In the middle of all the rambling I might pop out with the solution to a problem that they had wrestled with for a long time. That single sensible sentence I could address to Father and say it in such a way that he, in that moment, could not imagine that there was anything wrong with me. And a few minutes later I was into my word jumble again, and then it was clear that something was off.

Father refused to put me in a special class. Not because he was against a special class, but because then I would have to be transported to the city and be with a lot of strange new people, and he knew this I could not handle. He finished the meeting by saying: "There is a law that says that children have to attend school for seven years, but this law doesn't say what they have to learn, so then she'll have to stay in the first grade for seven years if she doesn't learn what you require for her to be promoted. In any case she will not go someplace where she can't orient herself, because that would harm her and this I will not subject her to. I don't care if she amounts to anything, but she will at least have a good life and not become shy and anxious like her cousin." With that the discussion was over and that's how it became.

Nobody knew what my problem was, and in those days in the countryside there were no acronym diagnoses, so therefore Father's "underdeveloped" was allowed to stand.

I got promoted. Not because I learned anything or could provide any kind of evidence for it, but because ma'am didn't want me in her next first grade class but instead wanted to be rid of me as soon as possible. And so she accepted that I was like I was.

We went to a B-school (a school with several classes in one room), so the first year my brother and I were in the same class room, and this was good for me. Partly because I got to go with him to and from school, partly because he was responsible for me putting on clothes when I went outside and ate my lunch in the cloak room during recess. It was like it had been the previous year and that was secure and pleasant for me. I often sat and observed when my brother and his buddies played and I felt like I was with them the same way I was with them when I sat on the milk platform at home. I never understood when recess was over and I didn't connect the teacher's ringing a bell with the idea that we were supposed to go inside. Those kinds of connections were unintelligible for me. Not until my brother said explicitly to me that bell ringing was *equal to* inside did I get it programmed into my skull. When that had been done I had no problem following that procedure.

That's how it was for most things. If somebody said how it was supposed to be in a way that I could program in I was able to do exactly what was expected of me. But when I tried to learn it on my own because "she ought to be able to do this at her age", and when on top of that, different rules applied in different contexts, then it didn't work. My learning system was very awkward and my memory system even more messed up. As a result, although I knew everything that the others knew, I couldn't use the knowledge in any sensible way, and it was the using of it that counted. It was about using it, but also about using it in a "normal" way. It didn't click for me because I could never grasp what was normal, how it needed to be for all unspoken expectations to be fulfilled.

We had a Christmas party. All of us children stood in two files in the cloak room with the parents somewhat behind. Ma'am stood beside me and just before we were to go in she couldn't resist saying to me: "Try to show now that you can go directly to your desk" and wagged her finger. If she hadn't said that I would have gone directly to my desk, but her turning towards me and talking to me without warning made me completely rigid. It got cramped in my body, and the whole room pressed in on me and I entered another reality that made it impossible for me to go directly to the desk. I was forced to find some way to make my body happy again so that I would be able to go to my desk. When the other kids began going inside, first the one file, and then the other, I started to whirl around and round and whirled myself to the other end of the cloak room and back again and I whirled into the class room behind the last child in the file. Ma'am couldn't say anything because with the parents there she had to smile the whole time. The whirling was finished and when the other kids went directly to their desks, I made a right turn and walked behind the teacher's pulpit and the organ, which was forbidden territory. Then I squeezed myself in behind the long bench with instructional materials that stood in front of the windows. In each window I drummed a couple of times on the window sill. When I had got furthest back in the classroom and drummed on the last window sill my body felt glad again and then I could squeeze behind the materials bench again and go to my desk. I sat down without waiting for the order from ma'am and then all the other kids also did it, and ma'am became all red in the face. If the parents hadn't been there she would have told us all to stand up and wait for her to tell us to sit down, but she knew I wouldn't comply so she was forced to bite the sour apple and accept that for a brief moment she had lost power in the classroom.

I had waged this kind of battle with my mother thousands of times. When she ordered me to do something it made it completely impossible for me to do as she said, because then I would get annihilated by climbing into a dark empty space, or catch fire or blow up. During that time there were two states for me. Either I was in the emptiness, which for me was the same as dead. It wasn't something I was actually afraid of, but it wasn't life. Or else I was in a state where I heard and saw and was aware of my surroundings, which I liked better. Actually I wanted nothing more than to do as mother said, but when she ordered me I lost my grip on that consciousness and went into the emptiness again. And it was like being forced to go to sleep while I was having fun. To avoid this and remain in the consciousness I had to wave my hands, or whirl, or hum, or motor-talk and to keep doing it until mother had stopped thinking about what I was supposed to do. Then first, was it possible for me to approach it. I felt that I *had to* do it, just not in a "normal" way and not as long as mother was expecting it. What mother usually didn't notice was that I eventually did as she said. And the times she noticed it she still wasn't satisfied because I hadn't done her way.

As an adult I still have this behavior pattern but in place of whirling or doing other things that scare or provoke people I have learned for example to ask a question that causes the other person to lose focus on what she just said, and I have learned to do so naturally and pleasantly that she usually doesn't realize what happened. And when she has lost her focus on what she said I can do what she asked me to do.

The second year when my brother and his class had moved to another school, Father practiced walking to the school with me. He took the dog along, and it learned the way and to follow me. So that year the dog went with me and turned around at the road crossing. He sat on his side and waited for me to get inside the school yard, and when it was time to go home he was sitting in the same place waiting for me to come out from the school yard. This arrangement only worked if I came across the road. If I went in another direction, the dog sat there and barked all he could but he didn't follow me. It was too far from home for Father to hear the dog barking, so then it might take a while before I got home.

I often went to a small dam where there was a tree with a big branch growing out over the water. There, I sat in hiding and rocked myself Out into the real world. Other times I went into the woods and sat under a spruce tree that I loved. Eventually I went home. Father had followed me a few times and knew where I went so he waited strategically the hours I normally was away. I always went the same way home, and the dog sat faithfully and waited until I came.

A few weeks into the new school year a new boy started in

my class. He was short and skinny. As a child he had dumped a pot of hot water on himself so his chest and arms were scarred. He had an under-bite and poor vision. He had an atmosphere that I liked. There was something about him that awoke me out of my state of floating in somebody's presence without making contact.

I could sit and watch him during the periods and follow what he learned. I saw when he understood things and could enter it in my lists. In this way I became more cooperative and pleasant for ma'am, even though it in no way was sufficient.

Then there was a doctor's examination and they found that he needed glasses. His dad had arthritis and couldn't work, and his mother had to take care of him and everything else so they couldn't afford to buy glasses for the son. Then the county stepped in. He got a pair of "county-round" glasses, which he got teased and bullied for.

There was a boy in the first grade, big and tall, red haired and freckled, who took the lead in bullying. He got a few others with him and tormented my classmate every day, especially after school when it was time to go home, since then the risk of detection was less.

One day when I passed the school after a few dream hours in the woods, my classmate sat in the ditch and cried. His glasses were stomped to pieces and he didn't dare to go home with them. He told me that the big first grader, together with some other boys, had laid in wait for him behind the school yard hedge and beat him up, and that didn't matter, but they had stomped on and broken his glasses that he got from the county, and this he was in despair over.

From the place where he sat you could see the road going in a wide half circle through the open fields. I saw the red haired boy leisurely making his way home. I took a shortcut across the field so that I caught up with him before he made it to the houses and rushed right at him. I beat and beat him till he lay on the ground and begged and pleaded. I stopped but by then he had a black eye and a bloody lip, and he was all dirty from his red hair to his shoes. He was half a head taller than me and lots stronger, but he was stunned by the rage that hit him.

Then I went back to the classmate and told him to go home and said that I would tell Father about it and he was sure to fix it. He did so and I ran home to the barn and related the story. To start with he didn't understand anything and thought it was my usual fantasies, but he sensed that there was something else in what I was telling him, something unusually real, so he asked me to tell it to him again, several times. I told the same story several different ways, but with the same gist. The boy's broken glasses, the one who did it, that he got beat up by me, and also a bunch of other details that had no proportions.

A short while later, the father of the beaten boy called and berated him about his daughter that was so wild and violent that she attacked his son. Father asked him if he thought that there was a reason for it but he maintained that I had just been mean and wanted to do harm. He had indeed heard about me through ma'am so everybody knew very well that I was peculiar and liable to do anything: throw tantrums and scream, bite and kick.

Father asked the man to come with him to my classmate so they could straighten things out. No, that was not possible, that had nothing to do with this matter. Father told him they were poor people, that they had gotten their son's glasses from the county, that they couldn't afford to buy new ones, and Father wanted absolutely that the boy be able to tell his story in a safe environment, namely his home.

Father took me along and we went home to my classmate. We waited there some hours but the father and the other boy never showed up so my class mate told his story to his parents, Father, and me. Then it came out that the boys, with the big one in the lead, had harassed him ever since he got to the school, and that they made sport of getting him to cry, and this time he had managed to not cry and then they took his glasses instead and stomped on them.

A few days later Father was called to the principal's office. He went there and told the whole story. The principal had received a report from the boy's father and now I was to be punished. Father straightened everything out and got the principal to write a report so that my classmate got new glasses and that was the end of the matter. Any punishment for me didn't happen either.

After this event the bully-boys had respect for me and stopped bullying my classmate, despite the fact that I long since lost my focus on the issue and would not have reconnected to it if they had continued. The spirit in the school had changed and I was present in another way, even if I didn't behave any differently than before.

I got up earlier in the morning than anyone else. If mother

had taken away my Iris-smelling clothes and put out new clean ones, the normal spectacle ensued. If she had put out a flannel shirt I turned it inside out because it was softest on the outside and I wanted to have that next to my body. This was not acceptable and we would have a struggle that could last half an hour. I also wanted the buttons in the back so that the collar came above the knitted sweater at the throat; there was also a fight about that every time.

Mother didn't understand how much trouble I had with my sense of touch. If it wasn't nice and soft it would be intolerable, unpleasant, and anxious for me. Because of this super sensitivity, if somebody caressed me with a light touch it was like fire in my body and I got totally freaked out, threw myself backwards and screamed. I always avoided that kind of contact and therefore I always had an urge or need to lean against something.

When the clothes were "broken in" they were soft and they smelled of someone known, that I called Iris, and then it was easy and pleasant for me to put them on and be in them. When I came home from school I was able to change to different Iris-clothes and that also worked for me. But every time mother changed them and I got new clean clothes it was the same hell for me. But she thought I was just defiant and stubborn, that I just wanted to make trouble for her and create a scene to get attention. Such was not the case. That's not what motivated me; it was the discomfort with my skin that caused my reactions.

The same difficulty arose when I had to start to wear shoes in the fall. I couldn't stand shoes, so I put on boots. Mother wanted me to wear shoes when the weather was nice; she was ashamed of me when I walked in boots in warm sunny weather. Then I would normally go barefoot, but that wouldn't do at school. Ma'am complained about it and mother hassled me. Father tried to get me to wear shoes but that didn't work any better. He didn't understand either that my feet hurt so much it was unbearable to wear shoes, that I got all preoccupied inside and it became a kind of anguish that caused everything else to disappear from my world. This struggle continued until I was eleven. Then I inherited a pair of leather shoes that were just right, that were made of real leather and fit like a glove.

The same story took place when winter came and I was supposed to wear snow boots. They were just as uncomfortable as shoes and I put on my rubber boots instead. Mother considered it too cold and she didn't intend to be embarrassed by not getting me to wear snow boots. She put heavy wool socks on my feet so I couldn't fit in the rubber boots, but then I took my brother's which were bigger, and to her chagrin I was wearing rubber boots anyway. After a week she finally won the battle and I accepted the snow boots. The thing was, I didn't have a lot of perseverance, so sooner or later the function that had created the resistance got turned off. It had to do with my inner focus and nobody knew, including me, when it would shift, but it did shift all of a sudden.

Different periods came with different hang-ups, some simple that my surroundings could ignore as eccentricities, and others that were more difficult to deal with which they were forced to confront me with, and this was hard for whomever had to do it. It only lasted for a time because after a while it got integrated into my patterns and then it didn't bother me anymore. It could come back, but then only for short periods.

I was very dependent on ma'am having a structure: that she did things the same way every day. The important thing was not that she told us her plan for the day and stuck to it. The important thing was that she had a structure within herself. When she did have that, it came out in the atmosphere where I could see it, and then I could be present in my own way in the class. But when she didn't have a structure, like when she had a cold or was preoccupied with her own problems, no structure came out in the atmosphere and I wound up in the emptiness.

The content wasn't too important, it could vary, I liked that, but the pattern needed to be the same. When we got to school we put our outer garments in the cloak room, and were in our stocking feet or slippers. Then everyone lined up in a file and went inside when ma'am opened the door and rang the bell. Everybody said: "Good morning ma'am" and she answered: "Good morning" and said the name of the pupil. I didn't answer but I waited anyway for this event every day. Then we sat down on command and ma'am told us if there was somebody who was ill. Then she read a verse and we sang a hymn. The hymn was written on the board so everyone could read the text. It was changed every week, so it was about forty hymns per year that were used.

I didn't sing but I learned the words and played with them in my mind, let them pass in review as long patterns forming the strangest shapes. At my confirmation I could recite all the hymns that had been used during my school years, but without understanding the religious meaning. Connecting to something as abstract as an invisible god that somehow constrained people's thinking, acting, and doing, that fell outside my range.

There was nearly always somebody who misbehaved during the first hour of the morning and it often ended with himher getting some form of punishment, dunce cap on in the corner, or sitting in the cloak room until recess, later to be allowed inside and receive the admonishment from Ma'am. I loved these kinds of interruptions. It got like fireworks in the atmosphere and I could be floating around in it while it lasted. Then Ma'am took over command, and if nothing else happened to enrich the atmosphere, my stereotypy soon started. I waved my hands, pulled the skin off my lip, and jerked my head sideways. Then Ma'am usually got irritated, or some classmate complained to her. Then she dealt with me, and after a while there was movement in the atmosphere and I could stop.

Thus the second school year elapsed with many small incidents. Like my mother, Ma'am was disturbed by my mere presence and wished the whole time that I wasn't there, or rather that my disposition was like the other children's. But it wasn't and Father tried to tell her the only thing was to ignore the disposition I had. But this they couldn't, they got frustrated and irritated and felt I was the one that caused their discomfort.

In a way I needed to have somebody in an emotional state, whatever the emotions were, so that I could be present and participate in the ordinary life. Otherwise I ended up in my own world and was far away from contact with the human sphere, and that was even more irritating for Ma'am, because then she knew that I didn't learn anything useful. I never knew that people distinguished between positive and negative feelings. Since I didn't experience them myself, I thought one kind was just as good as the other.

School was good for me and I learned a lot, even if it wasn't what the intended, i.e. reading, writing, and arithmetic. I learned to copy words, almost like drawing a picture of an object in the room; the word I drew was just a picture and I knew what the picture meant, but I was not receptive to learning. I observed what was around me but did not participate in the sense that impulses and initiatives arose in my mind that would cause me to respond, learn, and have new insights. The little that I memorized was mostly parrot knowledge. Then it was over when it was over, and I had no reconnection to it later so as to be able to repeat it in a test or in practices. Then I would do something completely different, because I didn't understand what I was supposed to do; what was expected of me. It was a great source of irritation for Ma'am because she mainly thought that I was sassing and provoking her. She felt hurt and offended and thought me rude and inconsiderate since I had no regard for her feelings. This was true. This I didn't know how to do. I didn't understand a whit about that you could get such feelings, or that they were negative.

At graduation Ma'am cried and said this was the worst school year of her life and moreover it was her last before retirement. She said she had not been able to manage me and that I was a blot on her professional pride as a teacher. I didn't grasp that this was something negative so I was quite pleased that she talked about me and mentioned my name several times. It got very light and beautiful in the atmosphere. People commented later on how I could look so pleased about having been such an affliction for the teacher.

The third school year we attended another school and there we rode the bus. My brother had already been going there for a year and ridden the bus so that was no problem; he was responsible for me getting on and off the bus, going and coming.

There were pupils from several communities, so we went from being a small class to one of about 30 students. It was hard for me because there was so much new all at the same time. A new teacher, new students, a new school all in combination often caused me to escape to a bath house in the park and sit on a boulder behind it. There I could sit and be in my own world. When the lesson had been under way for a while some of the others came to get me and I followed them inside. The new teacher had heard about how strange I was, and Father had met her and gone through most of my behaviors and how best to deal with them. She had no prestige vested in having it done her way and this made it easier for me to be in her atmosphere. She was a joyful person and quite boisterous and this made the atmosphere around her animated.

We sat two by two which suited me very nicely; I could copy my seat mate's exercise book. She was left handed so it was easy to see her word pictures or figure pictures since her hand was not in the way. Consequently it was not clear what I knew and didn't know, because what I turned in was often ok even if it suffered from the same errors that the other girl had.

Fortunately she was very good and made few errors so it wasn't too obvious that I copied her.

As for reading, I didn't know how to put letters together but I was good at listening and remembering. If I had reading homework, my brother read it to me a couple of times while I was looking at the book memorizing the word pictures I looked at, and eventually I learned the whole thing by heart. The problem was when I had to read aloud and had missed some little word like "and" or "it". If the teacher stopped me then I couldn't continue on, but had to start over from the beginning. What saved me was that the teacher didn't have the patience to listen to it again, but let the reading be continued by someone else, and this way I got along ok.

I had this teacher in the third and fourth grade, and was considered an anomaly but was allowed to participate anyway. The teacher had heard Father's way of thinking about remedial class and she understood him, so it was no problem for her to let me continue.

Then it was time for yet a new school and a new teacher, a man who had a masters degree. We were the same students as before so that was a known, but there was a whole new atmosphere around this teacher. He thought I was interesting and he said already one of the first days: "I have no idea what's the matter with you but I will really try to make sure that you can learn what you are supposed to so I can give a report on you also." Then he placed me in the first row, just below where he usually stood and he always had his focus on me when he was talking to the class. It was a brand new experience that I had not had before. A person who was interested in me without being frustrated or irritated or wanting to train me to be something other than what I was, that was like a new world. Sure, Father had the same attitude but it was still something special, I had never met anyone else with interest in me, a real interest in trying to understand me.

He told the class that since I had some difficulty understanding the material by reading it myself he would go through it all during class and that this would make it easier for all the others as well, since they would need to only brush up on it at home. It got me some brownie points with the class that they got a new method of teaching that made it easier for everyone. It also turned out that the weaker students could absorb the knowledge more easily and thereby got better grades.

Now I know that wasn't the whole truth. I have since realized, after many years of study and mentoring in schools, that he was an extremely capable pedagogue, who was able to use himself in the teaching process in a remarkable way that is still just as unique. He had the ability to sense what the individual students needed to best be able to learn and to incorporate this in his teaching method, giving all the students the best chance of learning. For him there were no difficult students, only challenges to be mastered and turned into strengths.

He could see exactly what he needed to say and do to make the stuff he was talking about comprehensible for me. And he knew how to do it with the whole class involved. The class understood in the "small field" while I understood in the "bigger field". And this was something entirely new to me. He knew he was a good teacher, but unlike Emma and Fil, he wasn't aware of being present in the real world at the same time he was talking in the ordinary world.

He didn't care about my tics and my stereotypy. He didn't allow himself to be influenced or distracted by them, he was in tune with me the whole time even though he didn't get any answers from me.

He could see when I hadn't understood and then he repeated it again in a different way. During tests, he took me with him to the supply room while the others were writing in the classroom. There he read the questions to me and let me talk. When I said something that could be used as the answer he wrote it down, and continued like that throughout the test. When this was done he gave me a blank paper and I copied what he had written down, and he accepted that as my response to the test. He did the same thing in all the subjects; in this way I got a functional work book. He couldn't figure me out, on the one hand I had memory like an elephant and could describe details that most of the other kids promptly forgot, and on the other hand I seemed completely lost and couldn't answer the simplest question.

In Swedish class he gave different composition topics for us to write about. I made a bunch of incomprehensible word pictures that neither he nor I could read. Then he had me stand by the lectern and tell a story and he wrote it down as fast as he could. He knew if he asked me to pause, I would start on a whole new story, which he did not want. Then I had to copy what he had written on my paper and he accepted that as my composition. "It was told by you, composed by you, written by you, so I can use it as the basis for your grade."

In math it was more difficult but he gave me a template to fill in and then he read out the numbers over and over in different ways, and let me do it over until it was somewhat correct, then he accepted it as the answer. The whole time he was trying to find the entry point for me to get the concept, and he accepted what I managed to accomplish with his help as good enough. He succeeded in making me believe that I wasn't completely stupid, just had an awkward way of learning.

When I started fifth grade with him I had turned eleven during the spring. My year from ten to eleven had been revolutionary. It was during this time that I discovered that people were people, that something existed that was specifically human, that humans could have a different connection with each other than with animals. This was so transformative for me that I ended up in a different world than the ordinary world I had been a part of before. I started to see people as individuals and tried to understand them and what they said, thought, and felt; what they meant by what they said and how to understand the point of talking with others.

I discovered that boys were something other than girls and that there was something special between boys and girls that created light and movement in the atmosphere. I didn't understand what it was but it attracted me because it was so alive. I discovered that girls behaved differently when there were boys with them than when there were just girls or grownups, and that boys also became different when there were girls nearby and no adults watching. There was something about the contents of what was said also. Boys said a bunch of things for no reason and sense of where it came from, and the girls did the same, both to each other and to the boys. I realized it was something I didn't understand and I didn't have a clue how to find out what it was. It was something that other people had that I lacked, an ability that I didn't comprehend, or how I could get it. That's the mystery that I have been dealing with the rest of my life.

I had learned that if I could think of nothing to say I could listen to the talk around me and seize on a word I recognized and start talking about it as a topic. I could tell what I knew, I could listen to what others knew, I could ask questions. I figured out that you could ask in different ways. One way so you got a yes or a no answer, which was uninteresting, therefore I was always pondering how to ask so the other person would have to explain what heshe knew. This caused me to end up in some strange conversations with people, and I thought it was great fun. Some thought I was batty and others that I was interesting, in any case it allowed me to be included.

There were four girls around me paired two by two, and I was the fifth wheel. For me, in my world, I was included just by being in the same place. I didn't understand that friendship was a different kind of relationship than the one I was part of. The others were strong willed and sometimes their wills collided and one or the other of the pairs broke up. Then I was always there for the one that was left out. I didn't have a will of my own, I always wanted what the other one wanted, so with me there was never any conflict about what we would do.

The girl that most often came in conflict with some of the others became especially important to me. She knew everything about how to be and act, how to dress to be in, and how one should be as a girl. She was thin, cute, happy and cheerful, and a lot of kids collected around her, especially boys.

Father knew I didn't have a good self-preservation instinct, and he realized that I could easily be exploited sexually by boys. But every time I met a guy that made a pass at me and I seemed to be attracted to him I did like my mother had taught me: Can I see him across the kitchen table for the rest of my life? Most of time the answer was no and then I knew I shouldn't be alone with that boy. If it was somebody I could imagine across the kitchen table then the next step was to invite him home to talk with Father, and then a lot of them disappeared voluntarily, and there were very few left.

Father had confidence in that girl so she got the assignment to never leave me alone, but always go with me home. And that's how it was; we were never apart from each other if there were boys. What she did when she was with others or by herself I don't know, but she and I never separated and we always rode home together.

We had sports and different types of exercises and games in school. With individual exercises I might succeed sometimes but often I did something completely wrong and this caused the teacher to demonstrate with me as the guinea pig. First he did it himself, then he demonstrated with me, holding me and getting me to do it as he intended. This was fun and I liked gym very much. I thought I knew how to do it but if I tried it by myself, without his atmosphere and spirit, there were no impulses that steered me the right way.

When we were playing handball I did not understand the rules. I kept throwing the ball in all kinds of directions, which interrupted the game so nobody wanted me on their team. Then the teacher told me to "Shoot at the goal keeper", so I did. Wherever I was on the field I aimed at and shot with all my might at the goalie; they were hard balls so the goalies did not like to stand in the way of them. I didn't realize that the goal was where the ball was supposed to end up so wherever the goalie was heshe got the ball thrown at himher. This made me popular and all the teams wanted me and I was placed strategically and became the goal shooter.

During the two years under the kindly guidance of my teacher I found out what the reference for life was, and I discovered the value of life, that human values were connected to life. During this period my interest for everything having to do with life and everything one could learn about it grew. I developed a conception of our globe, how big it was, that it was round, where it was located in the universe, that there were people that lived in different places and that life on Greenland, for example, was different from life in Sweden, about America and the emigration, about Africa and imperialism, about the Soviet Union and the Cold War, about Sweden as a great power. I absorbed it all like a sponge and I loved collecting all the data I could get access to. Then I could use them when I wanted to talk and in this way I could communicate.

The teacher told us about the peanuts in Africa. The authorities accepted only peanuts as payment for taxes and this forced the farmers to raise peanuts instead of something they could eat themselves, and this led to malnutrition. I was fascinated by how it was possible for it to be like that. In the real reality I could see how they could farm in a better way. Why didn't people fix things when they noticed how bad they were? I talked for weeks about this but noticed in my classmates that they didn't give a damn. They often said: "So what? That's just how it is. Why should we worry about that, there are much more fun things to do."

I didn't get this at all. I couldn't imagine anything more enjoyable in all the world than collecting all this data, organize it into lists in my head and use them to communicate with. The friends around me thought I was impossible, they often asked me to talk about something else, or be quiet. They said what I talked about was boring and preferred gossiping about others.

Father was the only one who liked this and relished it with me. He listened patiently to everything I told him about what I had learned and how I thought about it. He asked questions and didn't seem to be the least bit bored. When I came home from school I went with him in the barn for a couple of hours and told him everything I had heard in school. He smiled and smiled and couldn't hide his joy at these –in his eyes- strides. He thought that I had grasped something essential in life. He said if I wanted to know about life I could ask old people to talk about their lives. Farmor and farfar had died that year so it was too late to talk with them, but I thought if somebody else shows up I will do that.

Now I started to think through all that Fil had told me, all that Emma had told and much that Father had told about his grandfather. Now I could think in a different way. I started to understand contexts and put different things together and discover that this led to new thoughts. It seemed like the world changed with each new discovery and I relished all the stuff there was to know and understand.

Not far from our place was an estate that had a brick factory. In the wintertime there were some hobos living on top of the ovens and they were responsible for keeping the ovens fired and at the correct temperature for making bricks. If they did a good job, the squire gave them a meal each day. My brother went there and hung out with them and sometimes I got to go along. He said that they drank and could be violent and you had to watch out for the DTs, and that they might paw on small girls. I didn't know what pawing was but I understood that it was a no-no. Later I have realized that the risk was minimal with a kid that threw a tantrum if you just touched her so I didn't really have anything to watch out for.

I went there, stood and waited by the doorstep until somebody came and asked what I wanted, and then I said I wanted them to tell about their life. This they were happy to do, they were loquacious and talked much about their lives and their history. They knew who I was because they had been at our place for a meal now and then. They had worked there a few days and got some beer, so they knew I was the parsonage girl.

For them I could tell about everything I had learned in school. They had all the time in the world to listen, and if I brought a basket of food, "goodies" they said, I could partake of all their stories.

My older cousin, who had the same problem as I, only worse, was often with these men. He had tics and flapped his hands in front of his face and looked in porno magazines, since they had plenty of those. Compared to today they were like Ladies Home Journal, but in those days they were very daring and forbidden.

The winter before I turned twelve in the spring, I got to hear on those evenings about a side of life that I didn't know existed. One of the men had lost his parents when he was six. He had been sold to a farmer who was very mean and beat him. He had escaped with a hobo that came there and since then he had been on the road. The first few years he kept away so he wouldn't get caught and sent back, and he got better and better at getting food. As a ten-year old he had arrived here and lived on top of the ovens. Looking back, I guess he was about thirty years old, but he was so dirty and ragged that he looked much older.

The remarkable thing was that these men were willing to talk about all the misery they had experienced in life, how many beatings they'd gotten, about all the drinking and fighting they'd done, about how they had starved and suffered, how nobody wanted anything to do with them, how they couldn't get work every day. Many of them had nightmares and couldn't sleep, others saw ghosts in the middle of the day, and could unexpectedly be struck by panic and terror. And still they had a will to live, a joy in life, a light cheerfulness. They were quick to joke and laugh, quick to play and goof around, even about the most serious.

They cared for each other and took good care of those who were incapacitated, those who were too psychotic to know what they were doing and the trouble they created. There was a different spirit of caring than was found in normal homes, that I could discern.

One of them was a *"tattare"*. This meant he had gypsy background, but he had broken with his "baggage", as he called it, and had wanted to be a normal decent Swede. Unfortunately, he had not succeeded. He couldn't get a job because he was so dark skinned and looked so foreign. That was something very suspicious in Sweden. He didn't know how to read and write and didn't know how to behave since he was brought up with different manners and customs. He used to sneak into the church on Sundays, go up in the balcony and sit on the steps going up to the bell tower so that nobody would see him. He had talked to Father and liked him very much because Father wasn't judgmental and condemning like other Swedes he had met.

The reason he broke off from his family was that his mother had fallen in love with a Swede when he was little and abandoned her husband and him. He was seven then and his father was a violent drunk who at any time would tear him out of bed and beat him black and blue without reason. It was so humiliating that he couldn't stand it. He asked for help but everyone looked the other way, and a few years later he left. He went from house to house and did day labor, but he was not allowed to stay. Everyone thought he was a thief but he had not stolen a thing in his life. The years from fourteen to sixteen were tough, but then he met an old hobo and got to accompany him here the first time. The old man was dead now but he remembered him and his stories, and he liked to tell them.

Two things most of them had in common. They had all lost their home and their mother early in life, and they all drank liquor, home-brew that they got hold of on different farms where they did day labor. Those who had the capacity to work did, and came back with the liquor ration that they all shared. They said it was the only fun they had when I asked why they drank.

Few of them had attended school and knew how to read and write, but two were very well read. They had attended the university, and become crazy, as they said, and therefore hit the road as hobos. They told about a life of drinking and carousing with the other students, how they never slept and partied all night, how they had had women, the kind that "lived off their body", and they had gone to lectures.

One of them was an aristocrat. He came from a fine family but had been very unhappy as a child. When he talked about it I understood that he had had similar problems to mine. But he hadn't had a father that protected him from being punished for his strange behavior. He was raised by a nanny who for practically speaking became his mother. When he started school she disappeared from his life, and after that his life became nothing but a great agony. Without her he was lost and didn't know how to behave and he was punished every time he made a mistake. When he was fifteen he ran away together with some hobos who had been there doing day work. He stayed in hiding for several days, and then he swapped clothes with one of them so as to not be recognized. He never looked his family up again.

Another was the child of a businessman and had a mother who went insane when he was little. He loved her, for she loved him and they played and joked, but when he was five she was sent to an asylum and the father remarried a very mean woman who tormented him terribly. He never saw his real mother again and he still grieved for her. When he was ten and ready to start real-school he was sent to a boarding school where he stayed until he had done his matriculation exam. After that he got a room in Lund and started at the university, but then his insanity emerged and he was expelled. That's when the two men met and became hobos together.

The summer after this winter of enlightenment was completely different for me from the previous. I think it had to do with the different hormone flow in my body, and that something had happened with my consciousness which made it possible for me to understand reality in a different way. I also discovered how little I understood which made me realize that I needed to learn a lot of things.

For the first time I met an older boy who could touch me in a way that wasn't unpleasant. We sat in a ditch and talked for many hours and he held me and it was pleasant. Hour after hour passed by and it was morning when I went home. When I got home they had locked my entrance door and I had to come in through mother's and Father's bedroom and got chastised thoroughly by mother. Father turned in the bed to look at me and happened to bump into my knee so I fell backwards into the closet with a crash. He burst into laughter which he tried to hide by putting the pillow over his face, but the whole bed was shaking; then I got to go to my room to sleep.

I devoted that summer to discovering closeness, to touch and be touched and not throw a reflex tantrum as soon as somebody wanted to have contact. My difficulty was that I had no clue how you should be or do. I asked all the others what they thought and how they got information, but they just said that they *knew,* or that it was self-evident, but it wasn't for me. At least I got to know a bunch of boys and we, the strong willed girl and I, had an enormously good time.

Then the last school year started. It was the same school building I had gone to my first years, but then I had been in elementary school. Now I was going to be in high school.

The teacher was an old man who was also the principal. Both my Father and mother had had him as their teacher and he was just as stupid then as he was now.

He showed from the beginning that he didn't like me. He had of course had a lot of contacts with my elementary school teachers, and he considered me the dumbest student you could imagine. He told me he would teach me to behave, and he certainly didn't intend to tolerate any peculiarities and privileges that I had had with my other teacher. He said he had indeed received reports that he was very dissatisfied with. He thought I was spoiled, and it was time that I learned to know my place.

He also considered me stupid, unintelligent, uneducated, and it was only because of stupidity that I hadn't learned to read, write and do arithmetic like the others. Later I understood that he was scared of me, but I couldn't understand that then.

Every time I asked something or answered something his face got all purple and he spit nasty words at me. I didn't understand the nasty words so I asked him what they meant and then he got even angrier and thought I was making fun of him, but actually I did not understand. This caused my classmates to laugh at him, and the he got even more enraged. In the beginning of the semester I sat furthest back, but he brought my desk to the front and let me sit there as punishment. He stood there hanging over me when he was talking to the class and this was very unpleasant. He got altogether too close and I had an outburst. Then he took both the desk and me and threw us out into the cloak room. I sat closest to the door, so it was easily done. I put the desk back up, put in everything that had fallen out and went home.

I went straight to the barn and told Father what had happened so he would be prepared if the teacher called. This he did, but the version he gave was very different from mine. But Father, who had had him as a teacher himself and disliked him, believed me more than him so he had no success in trying to make common cause with Father against me. This drove him crazy.

Unfortunately for him and fortunately for me he developed a hernia a couple of months into the semester. He ended up in the hospital and had an operation. Then he developed peritonitis and took sick leave for the rest of the semester. We got a young new graduate as a substitute.

The class had now been reduced to half since the remainder had transferred to the prep school after sixth grade, so we were a small group of sixteen students, and all of us were poor at reading, writing, and arithmetic. This meant the motivation was very low, and with the old teacher, who was a gratifying object of provocation and troublemaking, the class had developed accordingly.

This meant zero respect for the teachers, chaos in the classroom, few who were not tardy. Nobody did their homework and nobody did the assignments during class. We mostly ran around buzzing with each other.

The substitute grabbed me by my clothes and held me against the wall and said: "I respectfully don't care if you can read and write, but you need to be clear about one thing: you will not disrupt a single one of my classes again." Then he let me go and added: "I understand that you have difficulties, and if you want help with learning to read and write, I'll be glad to help you. We won't have time for it while I am the substitute here, but the elementary school near here will be changed into a special school, and I am a newly trained special teacher and I can help you after you have finished this school. That school starts this fall."

I couldn't answer then but as time passed it became more and more clear for me that he was a good human being and that he understood something that others didn't understand,

and in the fall I started with him to learn what I didn't know.

The teacher had me say the letters in all the words in a text. Then he had me sound all the words. Then I had to read through the whole thing straight and finally I could read and understand parts of it. To practice he gave me an assignment to read two hundred words every day. It didn't matter what I read so long as I understood the contents. My brother counted out two hundred words in the daily paper and put brackets around them and then I had to struggle through it. First say all the letters, then read the letters as words, then read the words as sentences.

When I returned to the teacher, I didn't have to read through what I had practiced, instead he read it and had me tell him the contents in my own words. It was difficult, it hurt terribly, the anxiety made me climb the walls, but he just sat there and waited, and corrected some home work while he waited. He never said anything about whether it was right or wrong, good or bad, only that it was good that I kept at it.

In the beginning I mostly rambled, and got very little of the contents, but he was not satisfied with that. I had to go home and reread and think through what I was going to tell. It couldn't be word for word, it had to be my own words. It took me half a year to learn to stick to the contents, to not make things up, add to or take away, to not guess as soon as I got stuck.

Then he said I was to write two hundred words each day. I had no idea from where I was going to get the things to write. He said I couldn't copy from something, that I had to write it from my own head. I got totally confused. There was nothing in my head to write. Then he said I could address somebody, write it like a letter to somebody if that was easier. Then I went home and looked in the children's magazine *Kamratposten*. There were fifty personal ads. I picked thirty-one of them and then I wrote a letter each day to them. For two years each of them got a letter per month from me. Some answered, a few I still have contact with, but most of them never answered. That didn't matter, so long as I had somebody to write to. How they could interpret my hieroglyphics with all the misspellings, and butchered sentences, I don't know but most of them thought it was ok, they have told me later.

The teacher didn't care if I spelled correctly or not, he thought the important thing was that I wrote and that I could keep it up a long time. The same with the reading, but after about a year he said it was time for me to try reading some books. That seemed like an insurmountable challenge but I asked where I could get the books from. He said I could go home and pick any book and start with it. At home there were no books, since there was no one who was into reading, but one of the uncles read wild-west mysteries so I borrowed one from him. It was a series of books about two buddies named Bill and Ben who took the law into their own hands when they thought the sheriff was too mild with the crooks.

I spent one year struggling through many of the wild-west books, and eventually I found it to be quite enjoyable. Each time I had finished a book I had to give it to the teacher to read and then he had me tell him what I had grasped of the contents.

As for arithmetic, it mostly amounted to practical application of counting money, and measures for baking a cake, or following a recipe when cooking a meal. To learn to do a reasonableness check if it was dollars or cents for a product, tens or hundreds. To understand the reasonableness of whether it was liter or milliliter that was intended in a recipe. He helped me understand the difference in length between a meter, a kilometer, and a mile as well as the smaller measures. We paced, walked, biked, measured and played store. He taught me to read fact books and think in terms of scale when looking at a map. That mathematics was a description of reality with a special language made me understand the point of knowing mathematics and I have had a lot of benefit from this. He also taught me chronology as applied to the sequence of events in history. We started with kings and then he switched over to all kinds of other subjects, modes of dress, lifestyles, means of livelihood. He got me to understand the difference between here and now and what had been before and what is coming later, that they were completely different ways to think. This I had not realized before.

After two years he said I had learned enough that I could continue on my own. I still read with difficulty and had to reread three times before I grasped the contents, but on the bright side I then retained the contents for the rest of my life, as he said, so it worked out. I could write freely from my head although I spelled like a rake, and after all, there are many who never write at all, and he thought it was better to write even it wasn't flawless. He gave me a dictionary and he wanted me to read each word many times and write it two hundred times on paper. If I did this with every word in the dictionary, I would eventually be able to spell correctly. This I did. I practiced for many years exactly as he had said and I actually learned how to spell those words most of the time. On the other hand the word order wasn't especially good and grammatically it was a catastrophe, but slowly, slowly, my self confidence grew in these areas.

CHAPTER 3

About the incomprehensible world Iris lived In

I studied pedagogy at the University and was supposed to do a group project. I have never understood the point with group projects. You get an assignment and then for some unfathomable reason you are supposed to do it together with someone else. Everyone chose their partners and there was one left for me. He wasn't really in our class, but he had missed this class before which is why he was with us now.

We started. He said: "Let's first read through this, then we make up a structure, and then fill in the contents." I answered: "Unfortunately, I can't read through something just like that, I need to take it home and have some time with it, but if you read through it we'll do as you suggest." He groaned. We argued about this, about my dyslexia, about group projects, and finally he bawled me out and called me a fucking autistic that was impossible to work with.

Since I was used to such explosions, and was never especially upset by them, I asked him what an autistic was. He calmed down and looked at me skeptically and asked if I was stupid since I didn't even know what autism was. "No" I said, "I heard about the diagnosis once, I think we touched on it briefly in the course on leisure-pedagogy but I never really got what it involved." Now I really wanted to understand why this student thought I was an autistic.

He took me seriously and started to talk about it. He was studying special-ed pedagogy, and was in our class only because he missed it in his regular schedule, and he had just finished a one-semester in-depth course on autism. He talked and talked and finally I said it was like he was talking about me when I was growing up. He became very interested and after a couple of hours he asked me to come to Göteborg where he could do some tests on me, because he wanted to know what it was like to be in another mind state than the concrete world of relations.

So I started to roll out the whole story about the incomprehensible world I lived in as a child. Many of the memory fragments I retain myself, a lot has been told to me, all the crazy things I did and got into. Much of it I have gotten from interviewing older people who knew me during my childhood. In addition I have had the opportunity to work with incredibly skilled therapists, who by their guidance enabled me to put together the picture of me as Iris. The fragments fall into place and take on a deeper significance.

I go back again, and from my new perspective retell the story of Iris.

I have a clear memory of Iris. I knew what kind of thing Iris was, but not what "I" was. "I" everyone said of themselves so that didn't mean anything to me, but Iris, that was she, that was the girl. In Iris' world there were no humans as humans, there were only things, one thing at a time, which sometimes stood still, and which you could smell, bite into, hold, or throw away. Sometimes it moved and made a sound, and then it was more pleasant, because when it made a lot of sound it created such a beautiful light all around, and ribbons of light formed such beautiful patterns which moved continuously in swirling shapes. It was like fireworks and like colors, although it wasn't colors, it was like a light although it wasn't light and it looked totally different every time, although it was the same for the same person, and it filled Iris' whole mind. Somebody jerked Iris away, she was not to do this, but Iris liked to do this, it got so nice and she could not desist. Saying that she wasn't allowed meant nothing; it disappeared from her head immediately.

The girl liked to ride on the father's back. There she bounced up and down. The father talked continuously, but not to her. He talked aloud about his musings, answered the radio, and talked with the cows, with the cat, with everything it was possible to talk with.

"Now, let's see if *Majros* got an extra goodie, she eats kind of slow, and she will soon have a calf, so we need to make sure she gets something even if she does eat slow."

"My, there comes the old cat, I haven't seen her for days, she's been out running around, we'd better give her some extra milk and a little cream; we can afford that. How ragged she looks … poor thing."

Then he knelt down by her dish and petted her while she was lapping up the milk and purred as only cats can.

The girl sat there and her cheek became warm from the

father's warmth and she heard his booming voice. She was with him in a rhythm, in a dance, when he was moving and walking and talking, and it got light inside. The atmosphere all around took on a special light and it moved like the ocean swells. It was like intoxication. She drifted in it and floated around in something very pleasant. It was like hovering in a dream even though she was awake. All that is normally present in the waking state was there but it didn't mean anything to her. The state she floated in was the only thing that existed. Sometimes she felt the warmth of his skin, sometimes a smell, and odor that tickled her nose, sometimes she bit into her hand and got a lovely sensation of pain.

Occasionally the father went to the granary and ground some flour. Then the air turned white and there was a bunch of funny shapes. There was an entirely different smell and it was cold in a different way. The father had a different voice and the girl laughed.

The girl heard sounds, usual sounds, sounds that disrupted the familiar, sounds she recognized and came to her and went in through the ear and became something inside. She loved this. She did not understand that the sound came from her, that it was she who was screaming, or that it was she who was banging her head against the cabinet door so it rattled. Everything else disappeared and she became light and glad inside.

Something had changed in the girl's world, had taken on a different meaning. The father had a form that the girl could recognize and be delighted by when it came back. She could distinguish his form as separate from all other forms, which also were distinguishable but without significance.

Usually the girl had a kind of thick fog around her which caused her to be alone; she saw, heard, or felt nothing except the ghosts that emerged in the fog. Sometimes the fog was transformed into the most beautiful projector-images you could imagine. But on another level she saw, heard, and understood much more than children in general. But there was no one on the outside who could sense it and the girl herself had no consciousness of it.

It was so calm and secure and nice inside this fog that it was painfully uncomfortable when somebody tried to enter. It was also paradoxical, because on the other hand she experienced a special calm when somebody had penetrated the fog. This is so hard to understand for those around her that it must be explained again and again.

When the father was unable to keep the girl with him he left her with Emma, the one-armed old lady that lived in a room in the bunk house instead of in a nursing home, where Emma did not want to be. Emma came into her fog and enclosed them both. The light in the fog went from grayish to shimmering silvery-gold. Emma talked about herself and about life, and her words formed long strings that twisted around them and were so beautiful. The girl laughed a lot. When Emma told her to sit on the pot and tinkle and poop she could do it. She knew exactly what Emma wanted her to do and she did it without question. Emma was also able to wash her hair. She laid her down on her back with her head over the edge of the tub and she lay there completely still. Emma washed, rinsed, and combed her hair until it was nice and clean. When the mother or somebody else tried to wash her hair there was always a terrible commotion, she screamed and squirmed the whole time and it was necessary to hold her fast, and afterwards it took several hours before she stopped banging her head against a cupboard door, scratching herself, or chewing her lips bloody.

It was completely different in the girl's world when she was with Emma. It was as if everything became clear and visible and she saw Emma's face. She saw eyes. It got completely different on the inside, there were sounds and reactions that didn't exist otherwise. Many years later this is still there. Emma is the only person who populates Iris' inner being.

The father also entered the girl's fog often and changed the color of the light. With him it was different because he always went straight at her and sometimes that felt right, but sometimes

there were a bunch of strange shapes around him that made it unpleasant, and which she was forced to suppress, and this she did in every way she knew how, flapping her hands, rolling her head, spinning around, letting her mouth utter a long stream of words.

She was liable to take off and go anywhere, at any time, without warm clothes and without eating. She didn't know to come back of her own, but lay down under some tree and disappeared into her own world. She could remain there for hours without the least concern for herself.

The girl was afraid of the dark; when darkness fell she hunkered down and whimpered and rocked till she entered her own world. She could be like this for hours until some need drew her back, she peed in her pants, or grew tired and fell asleep.

The father had to form a search party with people from the village. They shouted her name and she could hear them but in her world there was no concept of answering. She did not move, so they often missed her.

The girl never thought that she'd gotten lost. In her world she knew exactly under which tree she was sitting and what it looked like around her. She liked the atmosphere that arose when everybody came and were relieved that they had found her. She had no notion of them being worried and scared for her, and she did not understand that she had run away or that anyone could be worried about her.

The girl's favorite place was the swing. There she would sit and swing back and forth, hour after hour, if no one came and interrupted her. There she went Out and there she met the real reality. She sat there transfixed and didn't care about the other kids who were playing around her.

She also liked the outhouse. The father had made a special seat for her so she wouldn't freeze stuck in winter time. That was also nice place to sit. It smelled and she could use the smell to float away into the real world.

There was a bunch of farm equipment in the barn, hay turners, horse rakes, row seeder, ring roller, and all had seats mounted on springy steel bars. She could sit on them and bounce up and down for hours.

Another place was the church. The girl went in and sat

quiet, quiet; disappeared into some image or icon that she made contact with. She often went up in the steeple and sat on the window sill and opened the shutter. She disappeared into the real world and played with her spirit friends.

The morgue was another favorite place. The girl climbed in through the window and when there was a coffin there with a dead person in it she got up on the bench and clung to the open lid. Then she could talk. It was different from everything else. The one lying there was so still and it was so nice in the atmosphere. There were a lot of pictures. Some were of people and some were of events. It was like an album that scrolled down one picture after the other. The girl looked and looked and talked about everything she saw for the one lying there, unable to see. Then the pictures ended and she climbed out again.

The girl did not know how to play. She didn't understand rules and that they were to be followed. When she joined a game of hide-and-seek, where you were supposed to hide and then get back without getting tagged, she never got the idea, so she went and hid so well that the other kids had to stop the game and go looking for her. Or if she was to stand still and count to ten, she didn't understand that she was supposed to try to find the others but stood there and counted to ten over and over until the others got tired of it. Whenever possible they put her on the milk platform and played around her. This way they could keep track of her while playing happily, pleased that the girl wasn't included and messed everything up.

The girl was involved in the game anyway, in her own way.

She saw everything that was happening around her. She could go Out and be quite close, and in her own world be involved in the game. She loved it when everyone was running around her. It created a beautiful light in different nuances which swept in the most beautiful patterns and shapes, and she laughed often, apparently at nothing. When the father saw that the kids had put Iris on the milk platform he didn't realize that she was still involved in the game so he intervened and made sure that they included Iris in the game in the regular way.

Iris loved water but hated to take off her clothes. She would roll around in any puddle she found no matter how muddy it was, and she ran out and stood under the down spout when it was raining. She would sometimes tear off her clothes and run around naked even when it was so cold that the others didn't even want to go outside.

The mother had a fight with the girl every night to get her to take off her clothes, and when she got tired of fighting she would put the girl in the bath tub with her clothes on so that she took them off herself, or she poured a pitcher of water over her. To the mother, this was a failure; her aim was that Iris should undress herself without protests like other kids that age. Also, the mother knew that Iris loathed clean new clothes and that it was a struggle to get her to put them on.

That's not how it was for the girl. The clothes were like a part of her. They were Iris, and that you could not remove. If they got wet and sticky, then you could remove them, but then you couldn't put on something else instead. In that case the girl had to remain naked. That was nice, and free, and cold, and then she felt something. It was awful for the girl when somebody wanted to remove her clothes while they were dry. It was like she was in a boiling kettle and she saw hands everywhere. Long skinny fingers with hard nails and hands that grabbed her. It was unbearable and she tore herself loose. She tried to escape but there were hands all over. All of a sudden there was water and then the hands disappeared and it was pleasant again.

Then came something foreign. There was something she was to be stuffed into. Something that smelled strange and was hard and unpleasant. Again the hands came and were all over. They burned like fire on her skin, and they were attached to arms that moved quickly and were hard to get away from. The girl slid under the table but the hands followed and dragged her back. The girl tried to run out but the door was closed and often some other person was blocking the path. It also had hands that moved and hindered and grabbed her and held her.

Sometimes there was something pleasant, that the girl wanted to put on. That was flannel shirts, but she wanted to have the soft outside in against her skin. So that became a struggle also. The girl did not understand why these hands were so mean, why they weren't soft and warm, why you couldn't play with them like with your own hands or with the father's. They were like strange twisted sticks that burned and chafed and grabbed her.

The father knew that it was possible to get her to dress herself, but it was a long and tedious process, where he gave directions in the atmosphere, one at a time and waited until she had found the right item and put it on. During this process he must not have his focus on her for then she became completely stiff and distant; instead he had to be talking with somebody else, or singing.

The girl was in the entrance hall. There were a lot of shadows. She was naked and there was a lot of stuff there. A bunch of fabrics were hanging behind the door that you could crawl under and hide, and on the floor there was a lot of shoes and boots She was stomping around in there and laughing. Then she saw something in the air, something for the feet, something that would go on her feet, and they got there with the help of her hands. She climbed up the stairs a bit and sat there a while with the sock in her hand. Then it came on and something else came flying. She found it, swung it around, bit into it, smelled it, and then it came on. This way it kept going a long, long time; she thought it was fun, but suddenly it was over and then it was empty again.

Food was a problem. The girl never came in to eat of her own accord, even when the food was something everyone knew she liked, and it did not help to call her. Somebody had to go and fetch her, stand there and wait while she performed her rituals and then came trailing behind. She dropped to the floor and crawled under the table. She loved to sit there and look at all the legs that surrounded her. Then a hand would come down with something in it. This she took with her mouth and could chew and swallow. It did not taste of anything. It was like something that just was there in the mouth and that was supposed to go down the throat. Somebody poured a little milk into a glass and handed it down. She always drank the whole glass no matter how much or how little there was. Water she never drank, only soft drinks and juice, and the mother thought it was better with milk for everyday.

The father said, "If a Hindu can make it on a couple of deciliter rice per day for many years, then she can make it on what she gets in the stomach; just have faith mother, and see how it goes."

The girl loved to listen to all the sounds above the table. She knew exactly who was speaking and she saw the images that came from the talk. The radio also talked and sometimes the other voices would talk about what the radio had said. Once it was about a terrible war in Algeria and this horrified everyone. From this arose a strange atmosphere that caused the girl to be numb and unable to hear and eat for a long time.

The other kids could use Iris as a doll. You could dress her, undress her, put her to bed, sit her down, and control her however you wanted. She tolerated it all and allowed herself to be handled roughly. She would sometimes fall asleep without warning and wake up after a while and the game could continue. She peed wherever if no adult was there to tell her to go tinkle, and this was a problem for the kids that played with her.

The girl entered a special state of consciousness. She saw what they wanted to do with her and it looked like fun. Her whole body was like a brightly lit field that radiated and illuminated the atmosphere around the kids. She observed all the patterns and amused herself by floating around in them. Then it ceased and she was left alone. It got empty and she started rocking. Then she entered her regular consciousness again. Then father found her and took care of her.

To be Iris is to observe the world. Iris sees the world, sees the father who is there, the mother who is also there, and sometimes others as well, but they don't mean anything to her. When somebody makes contact with her it is like the fog breaks momentarily and something becomes understandable for a little while. Iris is piece of wood, a stone, a dog, or whatever. It is difficult to explain what it is to see, and to see, and to see, and still not be part of it.

While she seems to be sitting there idle she is also a sweep and participates in the games the others are playing. She is in her own world, she is Out, and there the others don't exist. No, they do exist, but only like any other objects whatever. Occasionally it happens that a child enters the real world and then she can see it even though she can't contact it. Sometimes something comes from somewhere else and then she loses interest in the other kid's games.

Mostly, Iris sees her hand or her leg or her dress or some other little detail. She concentrates on observing the detail; what catches her eye is the movement. Whatever is still doesn't exist, isn't seen, doesn't catch her interest, is gone.

Inside her head it's empty, like air that is just there, and sometimes there is a wind that you can feel and notice and then she is captured by that. Somebody's eye is looking at her. Then she wants to touch, feel, smell and go in, inside, but you can't; people find that uncomfortable and pull away or shove her aside. Then all she has left is the image inside her head and so she ends up in emptiness, with an image that hangs around and then gradually fades.

She can be cruel to animals; grabbing, squeezing, pulling and poking on them without the least feeling for them as living things. The most peculiar thing about Iris is that she has no feeling for aliveness. For her it is only motion, rather than feeling that causes thoughts and understanding.

The father manages to stop her and keep her from the urge to generate feelings in others by hurting them, and as time passes, this interest fades away completely. She has very little aggressiveness. She seldom gets irritated or frustrated, except when somebody is trying to get her to fit in and do things that she can't repeat in her world.

Suddenly, the grandmother feeds her mashed potatoes with butter. It melts so oddly in the mouth and becomes like water and runs down her throat, it comes again and again, for a long time and the girl just sits there and opens her mouth.

Sometimes, Iris sits behind the grandfather's chair and there is a nice cigar smell that envelops her. She draws it in and gets intoxicated by it and enjoys it.

Iris has two states where hearing is concerned.

One is that she hears the words as funny sounds that she is captivated by and that she can shape with her mouth and say and hear again and again. Sometimes the mouth starts and words and sound come automatically. Then she hears words coming out in the air and getting caught by the ears again, and that is pleasant. Inside the head it becomes like a whole concert and that is beautiful and fun. Sometimes there are words all over, people that words are coming out of, gadgets that words are coming out of, her own mouth that words are coming out of, and she listens and listens and listens.

In the other the hearing is something that can be seen. Sound becomes colors and shapes and all kinds of patterns in the atmosphere that the whole space is filled with.

Iris loves sound. Sometimes, screeching terrible sounds. Such a sound comes from the brakes on the neighbor's car. Iris can hear the car starting from far away and runs to the hedge and stands there hiding, and rushes out in front of the car at just the right moment. Then it screeches to a stop and the girl feels happy inside. It is like a whole serenade, like the world appears and becomes clear, only to quickly change again by someone grabbing her and then a lot lightning bolts come out of the mouth, shaking the body, and word-flashes that come out like balls and burst like balloons and fade away. It all blends and becomes like fireworks around her and she is in the middle of it.

When Iris has her focus on feeling, she is hypersensitive. Then she reacts by jumping high the minute somebody touches her. It burns like fire when something touches her skin. The gentler and more careful the touch the more it burns. It is terribly unpleasant. If the focus is not on feeling she doesn't feel anything, or if the touch is sufficiently rough it hurts and then she laughs. She loves pain for it feels like life. If she herself touches something and feels it she gets like color sensations inside, it becomes like warm, cold, shivery, painful in many different ways and generates a lot of images and associations. The girl often plays like that. Focus on the fingertips, touch something that the eye is fixated on, get different pain-sensations by squeezing, clamping, pinching, tearing, hitting to enter into a cascade of image-sound-smell-taste-sensations.

Sometimes she can't take the focus off feeling and then she gets scared, because then other people can come much too close. Then the eyes of the others become like black sucking holes, the voice-sounds strike straight in and overturn her inner world. Then she gets hysterical, throws tantrums. If she can shake her head and bang her head against the wall or scream loud enough she can overpower what invaded her and then it lets go after a while. Then it becomes like a lovely mishmash in the head, almost like euphoria, it "hurts good", a liberating pain that wipes away all the horrible impressions that had invaded her.

Odor is important for Iris. She smells everything. She is driven to pick up everything that can be picked up and stick it under her nose, or stick her nose into everything that comes her way. This bothers people around her. Somebody is always ashamed of her and says "stop that", "don't do that", "you can't do like that", "you can't come along the next time if you can't stop sniffing on everything". But she can't stop. It is like something invisible is drawing her to do it. Even when she hears what they are saying, it is impossible to comply. It's like the world begins then, like she makes contact with life, and the things that are around her become bright and visible. Not just the thing she is sniffing at, it is like the smelling becomes a bridge to the reality that the others are in. She perceives herself as being with them. She can hear quite well what the others are saying, that she shouldn't poke at things, shouldn't touch them, shouldn't smell and lick them, but she can't desist from it because that would mean being outside instead of included.

For her this is self-evident and she doesn't understand that others don't understand this. It never occurs to her that they might be different; that thought doesn't exist in her world.

Every odor triggers the inside-feelings. It's like an amusement park where she is riding the merry-go-round. It becomes a brief intoxication that causes everything to spin around, and then is gone. Then a new odor comes along and the same thing happens again and again. Sometimes there is no reaction to an odor and then she just picks another one, because the reaction will come sooner or later. Sometimes there are icky feelings that gag her, and that is pleasant also. She vomits easily and likes to vomit, to the dismay of the people around her.

Sometimes the focus is on hearing. Then she can hear things. It may be anything that grabs her interest, and she listens and listens. When classical music is coming out of the radio it fills the whole atmosphere with the most beautiful color movements. It's like being in a living work of art where you are drawn in every direction and become exhilarated. Somebody shuts it off. Then she can stand there a long time, staring at the gadget and not understand where it all went. Other times it is someone's voice that is flowing from the radio and becomes a pretty play of colors, or something else: like a motor noise from some vehicle.

Voices are funny. They can be like strange images in the air; they can assume different light-colors and patterns that are ever changing. If there are many voices at once it becomes uninteresting, but if there is just one at a time, the girl can sit for hours looking at it. When she is sitting under the table she can see the shape of the one speaking. Each person in the household has her own specific shape that is recognizable even though it's constantly changing. It's like a painting with wet paint that runs in different directions and forms new patterns depending on the way you tilt it.

Iris' concept of the world is like isolated chunks that she is in, and then disappear. Sometimes the focus is on sight and then she sees everything. Small things that interest her and that she can focus on forever. It is so beautiful to look at something; it changes as soon as you touch it. It is like you are in some special air, where only what you are looking at is clear. Then it's gone. Looking fills almost her whole existence and she can't keep from looking. Sometimes it is too much and she covers her eyes and just rocks back and forth, sometimes she stomps and spins to stop the seeing. But she can't. Almost none of what she sees is connected to realities and the everyday world. What she sees is feelings that are floating around, she sees thoughts, she sees phenomena and happenings. She registers everything where she is, not so that she can say what it is, but she knows through her registration-recognition. She sees how things are placed on the table, in the room, how different persons, whom she sees not as people but as other things, are sitting around a table, what comes out of each one, how it moves from one to the other, and everything that happens she sees. In the same way that Iris is "Iris" – an object – so everything she sees is also objects that are there in rows and piles around her.

When the nothingness comes and Iris doesn't get the innerness started, the focus ends up on the seeing. Something comes into the field of view and with that the urge to bite into it. The urge to let something come into her mouth becomes strong, so strong that she can't control it but rushes forward, grabs hold and digs in. Sometimes she knows intuitively that it is not allowed, and that results in her instinctively making sure that no one can intervene; she waits, or sneaks by, or finds a strategy for reaching the target. This instinctive behavior originates in a super mind that controls her actions; it does not have anything to do with conscious thought through intent, which those around her often assume. The girl gets punished if what she sinks her teeth into is something unsuitable, like a smaller child or an adult that was too slow to guard herself, but the punishment is meaningless because she doesn't know why she receives it. She makes no connection to what just happened; it is only a way to achieve life and movement inside and has no concrete meaning for her.

It is mostly bright in Iris' world and she is present in the moment and often she is satisfied with that. There is so much to look at, the atmosphere is never the same but constantly changing. She sees word-pictures, sound-pictures regular pictures, sparkling northern lights, fireworks and other color-light phenomena that captivate her. All is play and all is fun and she laughs often. Sometime the mother is working with her hair. It pulls and tugs and is felt. The girl is glad and can sit still a long time. Then it ends.

Episodes and deadheading, that's what it's like to be Iris. The father devotes time to finding a way to get inside Iris. He succeeds at times and then it gets completely different. Then the world becomes visible and coherent, then there is a room and things in a different way, with threads tying the different things together, and it is possible to understand things that don't exist for Iris at other times. The father describes, as much for himself as for Iris: this cow has delivered that calf, she has carried it in her stomach, and Hero is the father. Iris has seen the cow deliver that calf, but it is the father's description that connects the calf with the cow; then first, is there a thread for Iris between the cow and the calf. But the room remains only as long as the father keeps engaged with her. After that, the episodes and dead heading resume.

Somebody notices that Iris is sitting under the table and pulls her up. "You should be with the rest of us at the table." But Iris doesn't want to, she becomes a steel spring and twists like a spiral, she hisses and makes unarticulated sounds. If she gets the chance she bites and scratches the hands and arms that are holding her. She just wants to escape. Her heart is pounding and her head is throbbing. The colors become like tongues of fire that consume her and everything becomes unbearable. Then blackness comes, the darkness that separates her from everything. Then all the unpleasantness disappears and one can do whatever one wishes with her. Then she is placed in somebody's lap and she sits there totally apathetic and without volition.

When she is placed on the floor, the legs start mechanically to walk. She walks until there is an empty floor she can walk around on and she starts walking round, round, round until something grabs her attention again.

Iris doesn't do anything on her own other than walking around aimlessly in a figure eight, or sitting under the kitchen bench, or on the swing or in some other hidden place or crawling into a closet. Her body and her feelings are not connected with each other. It's like contacts between the different systems are missing. There is nothing to hang experiences on, and thus they can't be used as guides on subsequent occasions. The action itself has no meaning. There is no goal orientation or plan, only impulses that come from whatever catches her eye for the moment. It may be an odor, a taste, a sound or a movement that gets her to bestir herself as if on autopilot, wholly disconnected from any context inside her. That's why she keeps repeating the same thing over and over without being able to stop, no matter how many people are trying to help her do something different.

A result of this is that behaviors disappear as suddenly as they started, and she has no retentiveness that enables her to connect back to them later. The father can get Iris to stop doing certain things and start doing others. He places her next to him, plays with her arms and legs, steers them playfully where he wants them and repeats it over and over. He let's go and checks to see how much she manages on her own, and then repeats the cycle, and then once more. When she returns to the old behavior he repeats the new behavior practice again, and finally the old one has faded away.

Iris loves these practice sessions. They produce a substance in the emptiness and it feels like joy. When others do the same thing it hurts and is unpleasant, although the pain is better than the usual emptiness.

Iris hears the word "Iris" all around her. It is said in many different ways by many different voices, and it turns into different color-bands in the atmosphere. "Iris" is known, has substance, is about something that is close and which implies something definite.

Iris sees Iris. She can be inside and look out. She can be Out and see the Iris-body from the outside. She can be in between and see both views. She floats around in this state and moves freely in the world. This is calm and pleasant. Somebody comes and everything just shrinks and becomes small. There comes a bunch of words that she looks at and understands. This somebody expects her to do something with the words. The girl doesn't know what, and does nothing. There is nothing to do and nothing to emulate. The girl wants something to emulate.

Iris talks to herself aloud but it's not meaningful in a way that leads to any kind of feeling or action. It also doesn't have any coherence. Sometimes the father can trace what she says to reality and he tries to tie back to it, but then she is already into a new spiel and what she said before is unfamiliar to her. He never succeeds in getting her to connect to something that has happened earlier or something that will happen later.

The father has perceived that Iris doesn't understand that Iris is a person, a child like other children. The environment still consists only of different objects that Iris comes in contact with, and Iris is also an object, "Iris", and there is no consciousness of an I. He knows there is something that doesn't function in Iris' conceptual world, because she isn't developing mentally and linguistically like her brother. Sure, she imitates him sometimes, talks a lot to herself, but what she says has no meaning and isn't like what other children say. He figures he has to teach her that she is a girl. Give her an image of what kind of thing Iris is. How do you bring a person to that insight? How do others get that insight? What can you do to bring about the experience of the deeply human? He knows that it doesn't come from saying it, talking, explaining. He has done this many different ways and it has not worked. It was, as he said: "Like asking a blind person to look closer and then think that she can see."

The father sets up a mirror in the clothes closet and practices with Iris. At first she squirms like an eel to escape the situation, but he persists and holds her fast. He speaks soothingly and describes what he sees in the mirror until she quiets down.

The girl sees a typhoon in the mirror. It is gray and spins round and round. It is black in the center, there is a hole that is sucking in and sucking in. She resists him, fending him off. She hears "Iris, Iris, -- Iris, you look" and then he is pointing. There is an image of two standing there. She repeats, "Iris, Iris, hi-hi-hi …. ". The father's atmosphere is light and beautiful and she shows off in the mirror.

Then it's over. The girl comes out of the closet and again she is in the emptiness. The emptiness can only be escaped by losing herself and that is the most pleasant way she has discovered. She is constantly trying to lose herself and becomes very agitated when she isn't allowed to do it. Then there is an outburst and stimming and people around her get uncomfortable. She runs to the swing and sits there swinging and then ... Out.

Iris is Iris and not in the world. Somebody tries to make contact with her. Then that person dissolves. It becomes like any other thing and then becomes nothing and motionless and fairly quickly invisible. Then the emptiness again, and the pursuit of Out.

They say that Iris is cute and charming. She has long, streaked blond hair which the mother tries to tie into a pony tail or braids. Somebody comes and tries to grab her. She becomes very agitated, has a tantrum, she claws at her arms, and licks and licks; somebody tries to stop her, somebody feels discomfort, and it gets dark in the atmosphere. Then she scratches more and more until it really hurts and then the unpleasantness stops and she is laughing again.

Iris is Iris and not in the world. Somebody has feelings for her and the feelings come out in the room. They look funny and make shapes in a completely special way. There is a message which she doesn't understand. The message is an image, but she doesn't grasp what she is supposed to do with it. Then the person dissolves. It becomes like white milk around the girl and she is in the milk, alone. The person is like a statue that just stands there, immobile, and soon the image of the statue fades out. She is in her Out again.

The girl gets scared of a person when it comes towards her and wants to touch her. Then her whole body feels like it's on fire and she hears a sound that she recognizes. It's Iris herself who is screaming; she throws herself backwards to escape. In the girl's world this is unbearably unpleasant. It's like someone is smashing her entire world, like she is drawn into something full of terror images, like in a haunted house where any awful thing can happen anytime. She screams, hits, kicks, and runs as fast as she can. When she has escaped she sits down her heart pounding inside her, and her entire world a complete chaos of awful sounds and images. She hears words and laughter that penetrate her head, it is like a terrible nightmare, with images that are like neon signs with horrible faces that grin and grimace at her. The eyes are like big sucking holes that try to drag her down. She is shaking, teeth chattering and tears streaming down her face but she is feeling nothing. It's so awful that the girl only wants to get away, away. Then it is dissolved by the rocking and she comes Out.

The father thinks this is bad, because Iris gets far too little physical contact, too little touching and positive attention. He has noticed that she can get stuck in a single mind-state. For example, if somebody looks at her it gets painful because then she has to look back at them and then she gets stuck in the looking and remains there. She can't break it herself and almost has a tantrum. But the father has noticed that if he says: "Hear the birds", or "Feel how it smells", her fixation breaks and she is free again.

The people in the house are used to her so they also know the trick and use it, consequently the number of tantrums is greatly reduced but every time someone new comes, the problem reappears. As time goes by, most learn to help the girl steer away from her hang-ups and it gets easier and easier to have her together with new people.

The father told her that these things did not happen during the first three years. Then anybody could pick her up and have her in their lap, although without contact. Then humans were totally uninteresting to her. During those years Emma had been the only one she reacted to. Towards her the girl laughed and stretched herself; once in a while she might show some reaction towards the father. The girl had reacted to the mother's hands with some anxiousness and posing but it had been so limited that the father had ignored it.

Iris did not focus on taste, just on whatever was it possible to chew and swallow. Until she was about five you could serve whatever you thought she should eat, and she ate. She had no hunger, thus she never came to the table of her own accord, but she was very manageable. But when she was five years old, she got hooked on the taste of pancakes, and after this it was impossible to get her to eat anything else. For a whole year she was suffering from malnutrition because she refused all food except pancakes and all drink except coffee with milk and sugar. The mother's frustration was the greatest. She tried every trick she could think of. She starved the girl but it had no effect. The girl liked it because she could see the mother's beautiful colors dancing around in the field in a different cascade of patterns than she had seen before. She liked what the mother figured she would dislike, so the mother gave up. Or the mother tried to bribe her by holding back on the coffee and only give it to her if she ate a piece of bread, some vegetable, or something else that the mother had decided she should have. Then the girl gave up her interest in coffee and refused to drink altogether, or else she ate what the mother gave her and then chucked it up the next moment. The mother gave up.

When she got to about nine years old she didn't need as much supervision. She no longer went out naked or without boots, although she dressed with many items on backwards or buttoned the wrong way.

The girl was dependent on someone else knowing what day it was and what time of day, and what routine or ritual was supposed to occur next. The mother and the brother were good at this so she usually followed their lead to do what was supposed to be done.

She had no judgment of her own and could be scared witless by a small beetle, but on the other hand climb up in a tottering tower without understanding the danger.

She loved to jump from the diving platform at the pool, and she often jumped from the 10 meter level. It looked extremely dangerous because she didn't stay straight when she went in and people realized that it had to hurt. And it took forever for her to surface and this worried the people watching her. Little by little they got used to the fact that she always made it so they let her keep it up. The girl went up in the tower, stood on the edge, it pulled at her feet, she jumped out and laughed the whole way down. Then came the water: it was like a bubbling mass and it got dark, she sank and sank, then the bottom came and she bounced and shot up. The water touched the body and it didn't hurt like with hands. Sometimes there would be pain someplace afterwards, in an arm or a leg, it got red and stung, and that was also pleasant. She could sit there and feel it until it disappeared, and then she went up and jumped again. She could keep it up all day if no one stopped her.

The brother and his buddies would use her sometimes to try things out to see if they were doable, for example crawl out on a plank over a silo. If the plank supported the girl it was strong enough to support the others too. If not, they let down a rope to her in the silo so she could climb back up. Or she would jump down into the hay, and if it looked like it wasn't too hard, the others jumped after. She never hesitated, but did whatever they wanted. They didn't actually expose her to serious danger; that they understood not to do, maybe not for concern about her but they knew it would mean punishment for them.

The girl loved to do fun things like crawling across a silo on a plank, jump into the hay or straw, climb ladders, ride the lift line up to the ceiling and be let down, walk on new ice that is buckling and run quickly so you don't go through. She didn't think of these things herself, so she was happy when the others put her up to it.

It was also fun when it didn't work out, then the atmosphere got lively, the girl became happy and laughed delightedly. She didn't hurt herself often, but when she did, it was also fun.

In Iris' world it was one thing at a time. Something started, continued for a while, and ceased, then it was nothing and emptiness, then something else started, continued, and stopped. Sometimes she saw everything, every little detail, and sometimes nothing, only a bunch of happenstances. Sometime she could be staring at one thing a long time and when she touched it everything inside her changed. Then totally different colors and shapes came and the thing acquired a new meaning for a while, only to then disappear from her world, leaving only emptiness again.

Sounds could sometimes be what they were, words. The words also formed shapes that were familiar sometimes and unfamiliar other times. Some words gave her a push that made her do something, others just sat there floating around. The words could also be images or sometimes movies that were projected in front of her. They might bring out something she knew had happened and some things that hadn't happened but could happen. She had no idea that other people didn't see these things, for in her world they existed in reality, and she could sometimes blurt out thoughts about what she was seeing that made other people very disturbed. Sometimes, the mother tried to socialize Iris by taking her along to the minister's sewing circle. Iris could see that the minister fantasized about how one of the young wives looked naked, or in a bath with him caressing her. When she got up to go to the bathroom she saw how his eyes were following her rear end. And then she said it: "The minister is looking at the lady's rump when she walks." Then everyone became uncomfortably aware of what they all had seen. Iris' mother felt that Iris had once more embarrassed her. She excused herself with that she had to go home and cook dinner, and quickly departed with Iris.

Iris didn't realize that she perceived the others' thoughts

and impulses and that they didn't wish them exposed in front of others. "One doesn't say things like that, one just doesn't do that, you are an embarrassment for us, don't you understand that?" said the mother, and Iris thought what she saw when the mother said such things was even more beautiful. "Embarrassment" she thought sounded elegant, but she didn't know what it meant. The girl loved uncomfortable situations and she thought that others also loved them.

Nobody thought that she understood and even less that she could follow advanced discussions, and usually she couldn't or wouldn't, but sometimes she had her focus on somebody talking and then she could understand everything and often better than those who were preoccupied with the feelings triggered by the discussion. The men were talking about the difficulty of cleaning the milk pipes in the milking machine equipment. They got gummed up with fat and bacteria and it was impossible to get them cleaned. Then the girl said "Send a sponk, send a skonge, flop, chip chop". She repeated it several times and gesticulated with her hands. At first no one paid attention, but then there was somebody who said "Aha, that's it". The others wondered, "What are you talking about?". He patted the girl on the head and said "A sponge, thank you" and ran off. A couple of years later the idea was in common use.

In the girl's world it was men's words that became movies. The women's words became shapes and colors, like a piece of art, but those of the men had another meaning. In some strange way, the men's words opened the heavens and she understood that there was something more, something that was outside the present and she searched for it although she didn't know what she searched for. She found out that she could say things, and sometimes men became interested and started to tell stuff to her. Maybe not so much for her, but they talked often to themselves or amongst themselves, and then she could sit on the floor alongside them and be included in the play that became images and films for her.

The girl loved these occasions when some voices let out words that became films. Especially with certain gentlemen who spoke about serious matters: politics, economics, social problems. The girl sat there and followed along in their discussion. It became images and films. The films came out of the men's bodies and were projected in front of her. Then came the foreign words that she had never heard before: "rentability", "creditworthiness" "excise", words that were said here and now and flew out in the room and got the film to continue.

They talked about the fact that cars had been so expensive after the war that nobody could afford to buy them, but that now the excise tax was to be removed and that industrial workers had so much extra money that the factories were just spitting out cars. But there would be a new tax instead of the excise, they said. When they stopped talking the girl told them how she saw orphan cars coming out from the factory in a cascade. One by one they fell down at the homes of different families, children and adults and some old lady, and they celebrated, hugged each other, got into the car and cranked down the windows and drove off. She also saw a fountain of money, bills that squirted all over. Then she described how the bills were steered into the opening of a meat grinder and were taken for taxes, and a screw that screwed the money right into a safe.

Everyone looked at her and then came the white milk and they became statues, were dissolved and then they were gone. The girl was in the light, she was happy and was with them, her world was peopled by those who had been speaking, not as persons but as beings that were soaring around in the room. Then she was quite happy and could sit there for a long time.

This divided nature of the girl, that most of the time she did not understand anything but sometimes understood more than the adults, this was unfathomable for the people around her, and it was impossible to know how to react to it because it popped up so suddenly and so sporadically. One moment she seemed retarded and the next she seemed to understand the most complicated contexts, that lay far outside her range, and a short while after such a lucid thought process she would fail to understand the simplest instruction or correction and just stand there looking dumb and uncomprehending. What was it? Where did it come from? Why didn't she have access to this brilliance all the time?

The father figured that she was just sub-developed, that something didn't connect properly in her, which he didn't understand and even less what should be done do connect everything together, but he believed that there was a key hole to put a key in, but he hadn't found the key yet.

The girl's development did not follow any predictable paths. She could be stuck at some phase for a long time, only to prove able much later to do everything they had struggled trying to teach her. She could have hang-ups that he had worked on without result, and then suddenly they were gone without him having done anything special or come up with any solution.

She often had her focus on the finger tips, and let them slide over some object, often she would smell it, lick it, and touch it to create an image or movement in the atmosphere. This did often happen and it could turn into the most unexpected fairy tales. It was like tales that auto-played with lots of dramatics. She could stand still with the object and repeat the smelling, licking, and touching and thus continue the show. Sometimes nothing happened and there was nothingness, but sometimes it worked.

She sat playing with some gravel and pebbles. She perceived how there was something that was very small and how it grew and became huge and then became small again, and that it was the whole, whole universe, and that there was nothing outside of it. And this was somehow connected with the word creation, that it created itself, that everything created itself.

There was an oak by the side of the road. She sat down there and jiggled lose a piece of bark and held it in her hand. She saw how things had looked around the oak a long time ago, sparse "troll-forest", with grass on the ground and stones and moss. She saw how a stone opened up and out came a being that looked like a tree stump that had eyes and nose and mouth. And then other things also started to move in the forest. Hanging moss on a branch became hair and then there emerged a being, a wood nymph. All around in the forest there emerged small beings, small grays, children. Then, suddenly the calm mood tightened and there was an unease and all the beings became anxious about something invisible. They all sought cover and nobody knew what it was that was scary. The children that tried to find their way out of the forest to get home were the most afraid; they couldn't find their way and they stumbled over trolls and knobby roots. Flight, flight, flight. "Can't you hear when we are hollering for you?" Somebody yanked her arm. "You should have been home hours ago."

The girl did not try to achieve this in a deliberate way, but sometimes it happened by itself. The girl became exuberant, almost ecstatic and jumped and bounced and laughed. The father said a long time later that if it was autistic that she was, at any rate she was a happy autistic.

The girl loved to smell things. When little, she would pick at her rear end and smell the poop, but this habit the mother had got her to exchange for others such as smelling fruit or something else edible. Grownups, who reacted and admonished her to stop something, caused there to be beautiful light-color-ribbons in the air and she paid attention to their movement rather than the words. Often then, she would temporarily stop what she was doing because she found something more interesting to attend to.

The father understood that the smelling was a substitute for something. He often tried to out-compete it by holding her, hugging her, lifting her high in the air, playing peek-a-boo, wrestling, tickling her. Sometimes it worked. She lost the focus on the smelling and joined in the father's actions, but she often returned to the smelling as soon as he stopped, and then he became despondent and felt like a failure. He saw this behavior as an obstacle to making contact but at the same time he saw it as a help, since when he succeeded in making it stop he felt like he had made contact with her. He described her hang-ups as urges and desires that steered themselves from the inside, and he often took up the struggle to damp them so that they could be replaced by something else, usually intimacy and relationships.

During her school years the father taught the girl to finger something in her pocket and then smell her fingers, so as to not bother the teacher too much. It worked sometimes, but the teacher still had a tendency to get disciplining attacks and go to work on her. She couldn't know that things could be much worse, that they *had* been much worse, so when she brought it up with the father he would try to explain, but he saw that she considered the girl to be even stranger than she had first suspected, and that he also was strange who hadn't discouraged such intolerable behavior. He fought it hard to not turn cynical and cold by the teacher's lack of understanding and be just as mean back as he found her. He often mentioned an ancient Greek quote: "Against ignorance the gods struggle in vain."

The girl often put stuff in her mouth. In the beginning she would put anything in. The mother could find carpet tacks, thumb tacks, straight pins, and much else in the potty that had passed through the body. Often there were also small hairballs since the girl kept chewing on her long hair. The mother would put it up in braids to keep her from chewing on it but she got to it anyway from time to time.

She loved to have stuff in her mouth, not for the flavor, but for the feel of it. It could be a pebble, some grass, some hair, or something else that filled the mouth. She didn't put it in to swallow, but sometimes it slid down and then the girl had to find something else. It could also happen that the sores inside her lips were stinging her and that was nice. Then the girl felt that she lived and it got bright in her world.

Iris saw a pretty dark-blue jam in a jar on the table. She took a spoon and the jam was quite runny when she stirred it. She thought the color was so pretty that she wanted to see more of it. She crawled on the chairs with the spoon in her hand and put a little jam in each of the white cups. She put the jam on the edge so it would run down the sides in beautiful patterns. The mother turned and saw her activities and became extremely upset. "You nasty child. You know very well that you are not supposed to do like that."

The girl's uncles came in as they normally did that time of day. They heard the mother's agitation and saw what Iris had done. One of them came and grabbed the spoon out of her hand and put her down on the floor. "My God, how you always make a mess" he said.

Another said, "What can you do with her?", and they started excitedly to discuss what to do about the troublesome Iris. The Iris could see that the excitement caused them to become "one with themselves" and then it got calm and harmonic in the atmosphere.

Iris did not distinguish between irritation and frustration, disappointment, aggression and condemnation versus sadness, real fear, wrath and joy. She also didn't know any difference between the kind of feelings that people like to have and the kind they don't like. She thought that people were glad when they had feelings, no matter what kind they were. Happiness for Iris came from other's feelings, and others' feelings were equal to their reactions, and when those existed she was content. Then it got so unbelievably fine among them; there emerged a kind of order which still was not predictable. Everyone was preoccupied with their upset and no one paid attention to Iris. Thus there was space for her to return to the state of normality. She'd slink into her normal place under the table and there she was left alone. All their normal contact with her, criticizing her, trying to train her, trying to steer her was gone. Then there emerged a state in her such that the cramp let go and she could float out in the spirit that existed in the room.

The girl did not understand the word no. The word did not exist in her world. She heard only the other words and became focused on them, and thus did exactly what she was not allowed to. "Don't walk out in the street." Street, street, street, played in her head and she caught sight of it and was drawn there. Not to defy or misbehave, only because somebody said the word.

Then the mother got furious and grabbed at her. She came back quickly and the mother scolded her. There were almost white ribbons in the air and the girl stood still as a statue and held her breath. The mother shook her once more and screamed at her "You are a hopeless case for civilization" and dragged her along.

The girl loved school. First, to be able to sit alongside the brother day after day and be able to see all the pretty scenes that played out, images, words, music, calisthenics, and to sit in the cloak room and have milk and sandwich. She knew all the letters, she knew what they looked like and what they were called. That was all, she couldn't understand that you take the letters down from the posters and assemble them into something completely different. Where you were supposed to think in a completely new way than A as in ape, B as in banana. Nobody told her how you should do the thinking this other way, and Iris didn't get it by herself. In her world, images were images and nothing could change that.

The girl learned the words to hymns. They were written on the blackboard and they became pictures that she could look at. Even a week later when the teacher erased the hymn that was written below the words DON'T ERASE she could see it. She could see how the image looked if she closed her eyes, and she could have copied out the whole hymn if somebody had asked her to, and she knew both the words and the music by heart. She couldn't hear it on the inside when she herself sang, but when she heard the others she could follow almost correctly.

She played inside with the words and text, and when she got to go to church with her grandmother they would sometimes sing the hymns she had learned and then she could sing along. Somebody always pointed out that she sang a little flat. She didn't know what flat meant, but she thought it was something elegant.

She could recite the texts of many hymns but understanding this God in heaven and how he could be the father of someone on earth did not compute in her world. Symbolism wasn't her strong suit unless there were images in the atmosphere that were concrete for her, and that wasn't the case with God and his hangers on.

The minister liked her and her way of dramatizing the interpretations she formed in her world, and which produced entirely different actions than were described in the bible, as when she related how Jesus as a ten-year old came to a place in the city where sex trade was going on and stood among the women and berated the men and said that they were not to do like that, they should get married instead, and then he chased the whore mongers out of the temple. The grandmother, however, considered her blasphemous and said: "One must not disrespect the word of God", and wagged her finger and looked stern. The girl liked that very much. The grandmother then looked like a real witch that she had a seen in a children's book about Hansel and Gretel.

Iris now had a routine: get up in the morning, get dressed, eat, take a lunch bag along, take off her outer clothes in the coat room, and go to her desk. If the teacher changed something she would get lost, but usually she was left undisturbed and she could just be there.

The father had helped her learn something new. She had learned how to shake on the inside. Before, it used to be that her hands would come up to her face and flap around. The father trained her in front of the mirror so that she could get them down and let them hang along the side while they were shaking. She was able to do it after a lot of practice but the teacher was still disturbed by it and the father said, resigned: "Can't you shake on the inside instead?" And this, the girl found that she could.

The girl sat at her desk. Something happened that was incomprehensible and unpleasant. She got a spasm in her arms, her palms were stinging and she closed her eyes to concentrate on the inside shaking. Then it continued around the heart, in the breathing, in the head, in the arms and legs. The girl sat motionless, totally concentrated inside and this way it stopped and she looked around to see how things looked.

The teacher was concerned about her sitting stiff as a rod with her eyes closed. She spoke to the father, because she worried that the girl had epilepsy. The father knew she didn't so he calmed the teacher; he knew what the girl was doing.

The girl sat there and was aware of all that happened. Then the teacher directed a question to her. She heard the question and knew the answer but nothing came out of her mouth. This situation inside her, where things did not connect properly even though she knew exactly what they wanted from her, it was difficult. Her head was spinning and she wanted to whirl around and dance. Then there was a pair of eyes directed right at her. She heard her name. It got dark and painful. She saw the eyes and everything else vanished. It lasted a while and then the eyes and the question vanished and everything returned to normal again.

It was different when she got her magister (master's degree teacher) because he had the kind of atmosphere that she could be present in a different way. Not so that she could answer and be in that direct a contact, but she could say and do things so that he knew that she understood and that was nice in a completely different way.

To get an idea, think about it and tell it to the magister. To talk and talk without knowing about what, let it become any story whatever, saying it with words because somebody is sitting there writing it, that was so beautiful. It became like a special reality and the girl was happy. Then she got to copy what the magister had written and that was fun. She did it as carefully as she knew how. It didn't turn out exactly the same but it was good enough anyway.

Every day the girl was looking forward to school. It was like her life had got a new substance. The girl wanted to always be with the magister or near him, and she learned not to disturb him. She learned how to do what he wanted, for he said it in a special way so she got to think *how* she should do it herself.

When they had a test the girl got to be alone with the magister in a small room and that was very special. He talked and explained, and then she got to tell about it. He listened patiently and sometimes wrote something. Often he would think about what the test was about and she could see images and think of what to say. Afterwards she got to copy what he had written on another paper which he then kept. She often came to think of important things on these occasions, and these she would talk about with the magister. He always took time after school, and then she had to walk home because the bus left right away when class was over. When she walked she would talk with him even though he wasn't there. She could "hear" his answers and comments and it was so inspiring that she often gave out shouts of joy, and the way home took many hours. In many ways, these were the best years in the girl's life, both in the school and with girls and boys that she had become interested in.

The father lived his whole life in the normal world and the girl could tell quite early on that he was completely blind to what was inside other people. He struggled his whole life trying to get people who were different to be reconciled with themselves. But he did not understand the dark that was inside them because he was so light himself. The girl he accepted totally without ever understanding why she did what she did.

A man held the horse's reins in a tight grip, to all appearances just like anyone would do it. The horse was sweating and rose up on its hind legs. The girl said to the father "The horse is scared because the man is angry". The only thing the father saw was a horse that was up on his hind legs. He couldn't see the communication between the horse and the man that the girl saw, but he said: "The things you notice! Yes that may be the case." The girl knew that he didn't see this himself, but he confirmed that the girl did. He would often end with the words: "You certainly are one of a kind."

The next time the same man took the reins and the horse reared somebody said: "What could be the problem with that horse, the way it acts?"

Without thinking he answered matter-of-factly: "The guy is mad so the horse gets anxious".

Somebody else said: "Where did you get that? What kind

of nonsense is that?" They were afraid of everything that was supernatural, everything that wasn't concrete and tangible that everyone could see with their eyes.

The father found himself in a sticky situation and didn't know how to get out of it without exposing Iris and still back up what he said. "I just thought it looked like that" he said, but that was not how it was. He had not been able to see this himself, but accepted what Iris had said.

The father constantly protected Iris from the fear others had that Iris might be right in something she said, the fear that she wasn't just somebody insolent that should be locked up. He often said to her: "This you can tell me about, but don't say it to anyone else." But the girl could never remember which things she could tell and which she couldn't and of herself she didn't know the difference.

In the Lutheran world the girl grew up in, everything supernatural, everything occult and everything erotic was banned and was not allowed to exist – unless you kept quiet about it. It was terrible and a great scandal if it got exposed. The problem people had with Iris was that she constantly exposed the terrible and shameful in them. For them, it was first when their actions were exposed that they incurred the sin.

"You drag us all down in shame" somebody told her.

In the Lutheran morality it was also important to be good, calm, sensible and balanced. "Then you can rest with a good conscience."

But they couldn't deny even to themselves that Iris' actions several times a day drove them to rage and meanness. Her mother said and really meant it: "You drive me crazy."

Their method of defending themselves against these obvious breeches of their own moral code was to declare Iris peculiar, stubborn, insolent, strange. They assured each other: "You don't need to worry. It's just Iris." This way they could be cleansed before God.

They could not in the least take Iris seriously, because then their defense would collapse and they would be forced to examine themselves. This nobody was prepared to do. It was much easier for them to tell themselves that Iris was maladjusted

The father struggled his whole life trying to have understanding for all this ignorance around him. He didn't know what kind of wisdom he bore inside but he knew that adopting other's values and viewing people as they normally did was not his style. To divide people up into good and bad, worthy and worthless he thought such a simple-minded way to avoid wrestling with problems that he felt sorry for those who didn't care about life's secrets any more than that. The only comfort he received in his troubles was that the girl little by little actually was able to master the normal world, even if she did it in a complicated and unusual way, and he became more and more pleased the more he noticed her developing on her own terms and making it OK. And when she in later life started to work with addicts, criminals and psychotic people he was deeply gratified that she took up where he left off.

CHAPTER 4

Outside the ordinary, in the real
(Iris puts her internal experience into words)

The external life –what a person normally thinks of as her life, what most people agree on: eating, sleeping, going to school, having a family, and living in a society – the value of all this I was oblivious of for the first ten years of my life. I called this the ordinary reality or the ordinary world.

I had another habitat where I knew the world. This was a condition that was light and colorful and where I was everywhere myself, and which I called Out or the real reality or real world or the immaterial.

I was thirty-five years old before I started to put my experiences in the real reality into words. I met a friend, Göran Grip, who posed questions that made it possible for me to talk about the real world. The real world had been as self-evident as breathing, but now it became something much richer than that. He stimulated me to remember and describe and I will try to convey a fraction of the real world. I describe Iris' childhood from an additional perspective.

I sat on the swing. At first I went very high and speeded up and just flowed with the delightful swinging motion. I let the swing slow down and then the motion caused my self to be disconnected from Iris. When I had been freed up inside this way I just had to say the word "Out" to fly away and up, to come out in the atmosphere.

There were my two friends, Slire and Skydde. Like me, they were essences. They were sweeps that could transport themselves every which way. We were like beautiful silk fabrics that swept through the universe, light as feathers.

They were boys even thought they didn't look like regular boys. Slire was light complexioned and animated and could come up with all kinds of things that we could flow along with. He loved to play and draw us into the games. Skydde was dark, more serious, and very wise. He conveyed a lot of information and integrated it in the games. Me, I was just along.

Iris remained sitting on the ground while I myself was with Slire and Skydde, but at times, something, my attention, could be in between and I could see both. That was amusing. I, myself preferred to be in the sweep with Slire and Skydde, but there was always something that pulled me back to Iris. In Iris everything became so difficult. What was so easy in my self became complicated in the ordinary world's reality.

The real reality is like the wind, *is* the wind. When the wind is blowing you feel it or see its effect on the tree leaves, hearing them rustle; you can feel its draft on your face and can be certain that the wind exists. When it's calm you don't feel it but you know anyway that the wind exists and can explode into a hurricane at any time.

There is nothing that is true or false in my experiences, there are only phenomena that are perceived. No more than you can say that the weather is true or false can you say that perceptions of the immaterial – of the real reality – are true or false, they just are. It's possible to describe them to anyone with an open mind. Some can see the immaterial world and know something of it, others not.

Many said of me that I had to be mentally disturbed, having such fantasies, as they were called, but Father said I knew how to distinguish between what he called the external reality and what was inside me, and he urged me to do so. I didn't do it automatically, but I always knew if the world I was in was the ordinary world or out in the real.

This internal experience, the real world, differed from the ordinary world primarily in that I knew much more factual information there than people generally realized. My problem was threefold. I didn't know how to convey my knowledge from the real world to the ordinary world, secondly I didn't realize that others were not aware of the real world, and third I wasn't participating in the ordinary world. This led people around me to consider my experiences as fantasies that were incomprehensible and scared them. Father taught me that I couldn't talk about the real world any time and place, but that it should be and remain an internal world. I said "Out" about that world and he said "internal" about it, but I knew it was the same thing so it didn't matter that we had different names for it. I didn't understand in which context I was supposed to speak so I chattered away constantly and consequently nobody listened to me.

Most people considered my talk unreal fantasies you shouldn't bother to listen to because they weren't based on reality. Some also got scared and told me to be quiet and stop talking that way. I couldn't understand it. I couldn't grasp how this could be dangerous, something to avoid, so I excluded from my world those who reacted that way since they couldn't accept the real reality, which was my life.

Farmor said: "Stop talking about those crazy things. God hears and sees everything and he will punish you". But I knew that that's not how it was in the real reality. In the real reality there was meaning in everything, however right or wrong it might be in the ordinary reality. And this was nothing to reconcile with; it was about being in contact with the real world, and get help from it to be OK in the ordinary world. Even if a person was ever so black and did ever so many dumb things in the ordinary world, she still wasn't an evil person. She was blind, and desperately did the only thing she could to survive: steal, kill, lie.

The paradox that I had such great unconveyable riches inside while at the same time I was so ignorant and vacuous and unable to communicate them in the ordinary world caused me to seem strange to the people around me. It was for example hard to understand why I so often was laughing.

It is about the primary thought process. The primary that precedes the secondary. The primary thinking happens without words and sentences; it is a kind of knowledge that is already fixed and ready and which can appear again and again in different forms but which never is automatically translated into words. The primary is what counts when nothing else counts. To convey the primary thinking to the ordinary reality one must do it in a form which fits just that time and place where one happens to be. The ones you wish to convey it to have a language which is already established, they have social norms and cultural rituals, fixed opinions about right and wrong, of what is and is not. This causes the primary thinking when it is conveyed to them to become limited, truncated, and caught in a specific time-bound and culture-bound cage.

The primary is always the same even while it constantly changes. What is the same doesn't vanish even though it changes. Everything exists the whole time and is connected although it constantly changes. Nothing stands still, for then it's dead; everything is in motion because that's what life is like. That's what life is, what a human perceives as life, in spite of the fact that she continually aims towards the sterile; it's the sterile that has status and which she desires even though life, the vitality, then is lost.

In my world I looked at the story of the paradise. The paradise was what remained fixed, and what was called hell was nothing but what was in motion, it was like life, the incomplete which caused paradise to be alive. The paradise exists continually also, even if it is in a flurry of motion; in the motion is the incompleteness, the dissolution such as sickness and death. The struggle exists to make life vital and it can't be ended any other way than by waging it until there is peace, and then it starts anew on another field, for thus is the life alive.

Many fights are just about ego, and are waged just to win something in the secondary and have nothing to do with the real struggle. It was Sunday and the kids were allowed to ride their bikes to the lake to go swimming. As usual, a fight broke out about one of our bikes that was considered easier to ride than the others. My brother and one of the summer kids always fought about it. This was an ego fight, a status fight that was completely incomprehensible to me. The fight was not at all about the easy-riding bike, but about winning and dominating. It was a fight which had nothing to do with the real struggle.

In the real struggle everyone wins peace for a moment, in the ordinary ego fight there is one who thinks himself the winner and another who thinks himself the loser. When somebody wins at somebody else's expense both lose. It's like wetting your pants, at first it is nice and warm, but right away it gets cold, wet, and disgusting.

This dimension, the real reality, lacks a concrete anchorage in our civilization. It can't be converted to secondary because then it is lost. The immaterial plays catch with the ordinary reality and enjoys it heartily. People often have no thought about that world. They devote themselves to the material and what produces results. How many consider it a marvel, a joy, that there is something to eat? Most people think: what in the world should they have for dinner tomorrow, what should they choose. Often they choose based on cost and forget completely to ask what they would really want. This is a completely different process and that process does not nurture the immaterial.

It is great that in our civilization we don't have to worry

about the material, but at the same time it makes us shallow and limited, and that is not so great. A richness is lost and it can't be replaced with something else.

Different religions steal from the real world and take out patents on it, and this is not the right thing to do. The real world belongs to everybody and everybody can have contact with it, and it can't be earmarked such that one behavior means that you are Christian and another that you are Muslim, or Buddhist, or Sikh. You can't copyright the primary. Religions fool people into believing that life, the incomplete, is sin and misery, and that you have to wait until you come to God and paradise after death and that all will be well then. This is deceitful, since everything always exists, and the only thing that changes is whether my self is poured into a body so that I am alive here and now or not.

I sit on the swing. It's summer and it's warm. The sun glitters through the tree branches. The rays find their way through the leaves and I see water drops in the grass. There is dew this early morning and I get glad inside. None of the other kids in the house will get up this early and disturb me.

At first I swing very high to get some speed and I flow with the delightful swing motion. It feels like floating in air. The wind swishes around me and it tickles in my stomach. I hear the light creaking in the tree and the rustling of the leaves. I get warm all over and let the swing come to a stop.

Quiet, quiet, totally quiet. I feel my body. My fingertips and toes start to tingle. The pleasure spreads through my whole body. Soon I am in a kind of intoxication and loosen myself from

Iris. I go Out. I turn around slowly and see Iris sitting where she sits. It is calm. Iris is smiling. There is peace. She looks like she is sitting there deep in thoughts. I am Out.

At first I fly around a little aimlessly. I am floating a few meters above the ground. I look into the house and see the people in the kitchen. I fly over the yard and meet the world. I know and feel everything, and still I feel nothing. When I am glad I *know* it but I feel no joy as in the ordinary body. *I know about* all my feelings, no not just *my* feelings but all feelings, all feelings that can exist, but it is like I think them without feeling them. My physical body is by itself in some way and I myself am something else, something immaterial, but still a body. This immaterial body is like Iris, except transparent like a type of light. It has everything that Iris has but it is invisible unless it is materialized one way or other by the present. The immaterial body is like invisible ink that is there the whole time but only appears if it is warmed up. Even the immaterial body is separate, and I myself am the essence, and the essence can leave the immaterial body and be between it and the material that is still sitting on the swing. It is so pleasant to be Out, everything is bearable and nothing is threatening. I can't be lost no matter what happens. Here I am and it is eternal, unending, and everything at once.

After a while my immaterial body becomes a sweep, like a veil of silk fabric that can sweep through the real world. When you are in the real world you can glide unhindered through objects and living beings in the ordinary world. It is only people that you mustn't touch because they may get uncomfortable and scared.

Two well known figures appear. We meet. They are Slire and Skydde. They come closer and we are three. We look at each other, form a circle, glide forward and around, around, and just are. We don't speak in words like normal people for we can see the others' thoughts. We can juggle with thoughts every which way, hide them, turn them around so the others can guess them like riddles. We can twist them inside out and let them have a completely different meaning. Two wait while the third hides. Sometimes it gets crazy and hilarious.

~~~~~~~~~~~~~~~~~~~~~~~~~~~~

For me, the word pussy willow meant cats that pissed. I toss this word to Slire who turns and twists it: catpiss, pisscat, pussy cat, cat twig, twig cat, switch, sticks. He tosses the words to Skydde. Skydde gives out whole sentences: The cat pisses on the bush. The twig whips the cat. The pussy is in the shell. The shell is stuck on the twig. I say willow cat and see the hazel twig and the shell and the furry body. Slire and Skydde fly around hither and thither and bow to indicate I am on the right track. And when I see that the furry body *is* the pussy willow they stop and tremble and vibrate to show that it is finished. I have learned that pussy willows are not cats that piss.

~~~~~~~~~~~~~~~~~~~~~~~~~~~~

Anders, my uncle, comes ambling from the barn going towards his room. Little melodic snatches and a well dressed woman come out in the atmosphere. He is thinking of the dance last Saturday and is looking forward to the dance next Saturday. The dance is what he most often thinks about. Slire throws the word pussy willow to me and tells me to throw it on Anders. We fly over to Anders and wait for the right moment. As long as nothing comes out from him into the atmosphere, we have to wait. But just when bright gold-red, slightly glittering joy comes out from him it is time. I throw the word pussy willow into him. He is still in his image of the dance, but suddenly a bush appears. He pushes it away to return to his pleasant imagery. I wait for the next opportunity. A smiling woman who accepts the invitation to dance comes out in the atmosphere. I throw in the word pussy willow again. The smiling woman is blurred by the image of a bush. He gets irritated and sputters and mumbles. I keep this up until his thoughts are all filled with hazel bushes. The dance is gone and he has forgotten where he was going and the only thing left in him is a scrubby thicket. He stops, cusses to himself and tries to remember where he was going. He turns around and goes back to the barn.

The game changes form and becomes about what we should do. Slire always has ideas. He would like to do everything at once, but still it becomes one thing at a time. He is eager and impatient. He has light blue eyes that are always glittering. Skydde is dark and has brown, serious eyes. His eyes hold melancholy and wisdom, as if he knew all of life's misery but still believes in life. He is warm and secure and thoughtful. I love him because he helps me to collect myself. I know that when I am with Slire and Skydde life is whole and right. Then I understand everything and nothing is unpleasant. Everything is light, nothing is wrong and whacky, and it's as if missing and longing vanish. Everything that hurts is in Iris' body and is not here now.

I know myself that it exists, but it doesn't matter, everything is exactly the way it should be. Other people, especially those that are scared, have an ability to say and do things to me and with me that are painful in my body. It becomes like an unbearable fire, as if I am exploding, as if my whole body is torn apart. Then comes the hysteria, I scream, kick, bite, throw myself to the ground, bang my head, and try to make it stop in my body. It usually gets better if I can rock for a while. Then I come Out and then the world is good again.

We float around; tumbling about, play rebus with our thoughts.

I toss out "Nothing"

Slire grabs the word and says: "If you say nothing, there must be something that is around nothing otherwise nothing can't exist."

Skydde says: "Nothing can also be a result. If nothing is a result there is something one believed was something but then proves to not be something and then the result is nothing."

"The result is what is left when everything is finished" continues Skydde.

"No the result is nothing that remains. The result existed only just then. Then it disappears also."

"What's the point of talking about result unless that's what remains?"

"You can talk about it anyway, it's just that you stop something at a certain moment, and then you can call that result."

And then we start a new strand.

"Childhood."

"Childhoods."

"Hooded children."

"Behoove children."

"Child bearing."

"But what is that."

"The child is a burden when you bear it."

"No, no, no, child birth is that a child is born" Skydde corrected.

"To be born."

"To be born, what is that?"

"That's that you drop down on earth."

"From where?"

"Well, don't you know that daddy has one part and the mommy has one part."

"But then you don't drop down on earth, do you?"

We fly up high so that Iris looks like a tiny dot, and dive down so that she becomes gigantic and then back so she becomes normal size again. Up and down, up and down. We chase and catch each other, tumble about, turn ourselves into balls, and stretch ourselves into strings. Sometimes Slire catches a thought from somebody on the ground and tosses it to me.

My two uncles are walking across the yard talking about stars and planets. There had just been a solar eclipse. Slire dives down and comes back with the word planet and tosses it to

Skydde.

Skydde makes a bunch of balls out of it and tosses the balls to me.

I float away a bit and fling them away so that they create a show and ask: "What is this?"

Then I can see how the balls fly away and look like a moon, a sun and an earth. They move around each other. All three of us fly towards the ball earth and straight into it.

"*Here* is a planet" Skydde says.

I comprehend something I hadn't understood before and it is so much fun to just learn and learn and learn.

In the ordinary world I have seen a sign outside a house that said "For sale", and I had seen the same sign in Donald Duck. I misread it and thought it said "For Saul". I knew who Saul was because Farmor had told me about the king in the bible. But I couldn't understand why those houses were for him, and why it needed to say that on a sign. I had asked one of my uncles why it couldn't just as well have said "For Paul" on the sign, but he just got irritated and said: "What are you babbling about!"

Now Slire flies away and catches the word itself from the sign: "for sale" and flings it on me. I catch it and see the whole story about Saul that Farmor has told me. Then he gives me the impulse to toss the word to Skydde. Skydde sends it back to me and then it comes out correct. Saul becomes Sale, and Sale means selling. The house that had the sign "For sale" is for selling and I understand that anyone can buy it.

Everything is so clear and easily grasped when Slire thinks it. Skydde showed me the thought in a different way and I know there is only one answer.

Slire says, airily and childishly: "The sun warms and shines."

I become aware of the sun warming and shining.

Skydde says: "But there are more secrets. The power that comes from the sun, this people can capture so that they can use it when there is no sun. And *that* is called *energy*."

We are into science for a while.

Skydde points to Iris down there. The return is unavoidable. I am reluctant and try to remain, I don't want to go back, I don't belong there, I belong here. He pushes me gently towards Iris and shows me that the body needs something. He shows me that I am welcome whenever I wish, but now I have to return. Iris twitches and the world is ordinary again.

But before I return I have to tease a little. I jump into Iris' body and look at the other body, the transparent one. Then I jump back to the transparent body and look at Iris sitting on the swing. Sometimes I am midway between Iris' body and the immaterial body, and that is like a being a consciousness, an essence. It's not possible to remain in that state, it is only a transition, but in it there is a different comfort than in the body states. Skydde indicates that I must return to Iris.

There are several hiding places around the farm yard. In Iris' world there is a constant search for them. The swing, the outhouse, various seats on the farm machinery in the barn, under the elevator where there is a huge empty space in the straw, under the pastor's desk in the outer room, under the table in the kitchen, in the kitchen cupboard, behind the anvil in the smithy, in the opening in the church steeple.

These places have acquired a special meaning. They are protected places where I easily can come Out. I can go Out in other places also, but then a lot of rituals and preparations are necessary. I can also find this kind of permissive places in new surroundings I come to.

They constitute a map, a pattern one can follow and exist in. Going Out is not possible if somebody else is present, but then there is always some other place on the map one can get to. The map is a pattern, a list which resides in Iris' head and this I can get out and look at. At every occasion when it gets empty and nothingy in the ordinary world, the map comes out and guides the steps to one of these places.

It was often said that Iris was a peculiar child that could sit in the same place hour after hour and just look absent and not do anything. This was not normal. Children were supposed to be with other children and play, and not sit and dream.

It is fall. The sun is shining and it smells of ripe grain. Behind the barn is the old horse-drawn rake. The type they use to rake up the hay to make it easier to put up the hay fence.

Once when I sat in the seat driving it I went out in ... That's not what I was going to tell, but now it will be that story anyway.

The horse rake has a bowl-shaped seat at the end of strong seat spring which can bounce up and down. I love to sit on it because it bounces so delightfully. The horse is also good to sit on because it walks and then it rocks the whole time.

We have four horses, Svea, Doris, Blanda, and Cookedrye.

Cookedrye is so called because he got fermentation in his stomach when he was a foal and then they cooked rye and gave him so he could fart out the fermentation and the stomach wouldn't explode. It succeeded and he survived, but after that it couldn't have any other name.

Svea is the oldest of the horses. She is treacherous and is liable to bite at any time. None of the horses are fond of Iris and are apt to give her a bite when they have the chance, but normally Svea is the only one that bites. Blanda is the youngest, peppiest, and most docile, so they can put Iris on her without too much of a risk.

When Iris gets close to the horses they start to sweat, pull back their ears, and stomp their hooves. The field around them is pulled in and gets darker. Iris is not doing anything and still they react in this way. When Iris has been standing there a while the horses' reactions ease and then it gets back to normal.

It's the week before midsummer and baking hot. The hay has to be harvested; first it must be turned with the hay turner and then raked up with the horse rake. It is harvest time and everyone on the farm rushes at top speed. This creates funny figures in the atmosphere, because normally there isn't anybody that moves quickly in my proximity, except mother, but that is another matter. My existence is enlivened by a bunch of sounds and lights that move and twist around each other and form beautiful figures in the air.

Iris is sitting on Blanda's back and one of the uncles is on the seat. There is a jerk each time the rake is lifted to drop the raked pile of hay. Then I disappear from the ordinary reality ...

Slire and Skydde appear. We are sweeps that play "Whirl around horse leg while she is walking". This goes like: we try to float as close as possible to the horse's legs without touching them. This is not too easy, because the horse is moving the whole time and we try to get as close as possible. We know that we must not bump into the horse because then she'll get scared, start to sweat, and may bolt. Also, she is continually tossing her tail around to get rid of all the horse flies and bugs that try to feed on her. When we had enough of this game we move over to the rake.

The horse rake has long steel prongs placed close together and shaped like half circles, like a huge rake. They drag the hay into piles; then the hay pile is released by lifting the prongs high. We throw ourselves in front of the prongs and allow ourselves to be rolled around with the hay that is being gathered by the prongs. Then, quick grab onto one of the prongs and follow it up so you don't get left in the hay pile. Then let go and drop down again to roll around in the next turn. We keep this up for hours. It is so much fun. It can be varied in several ways, and we play a kind of "Simon says".

This time it is Slire doing the lead. I follow. But it is no fun to just follow after Slire. In the real world I can always see what Slire and Skydde intend to do, and they cannot hide their intentions from me. So, for the game to be exciting Slire has to deliberately avoid thinking ahead what he'll do, otherwise the game gets way too simple. Slire reaches up to grab hold and follow the rake prongs just as they are going up. I also reach up. In the last second he changes his mind and remains in the hay pile. If I follow the prongs up I have lost, so I have to quickly stop and also remain in the hay pile. I have to try find out how to do it, it is so much fun and I want to keep it up forever but ...

The horse stops. Iris feels a pair of strong arms taking hold of her and lifting her down. The uncle says: "Oh Iris, have you wet yourself again without saying something. Why can't you be like other kids and say something when you need to go, so I could stop?"

Iris answers: "I was playing with Slire and Skydde".

The uncle: "You and your fantasies; imagine, if you could learn what other kids learn we wouldn't have all this extra trouble with you."

Iris talks often about her experiences and uses all the words she has collected, and she feels that her experiences and tales are real, but she is often told that she has "her own thing", and that it is just a bunch of fantasies and that there is something strange about this kid's peculiar stories that you can't make heads or tails of.

As time goes by Iris is allowed to sit on the horse with the driverless hay turner behind. It looks like rain and every grown-up is needed to bring in the hay before the rain starts so nobody has time to be in the seat. The horse knows the route but refuses to move if nobody is holding the reins. But if Iris sits on its back then it starts moving. The horse turns by itself and walks row up and row down, and unaware of the service she is performing Iris sits happily on the horse's back.

I look out on the world. Beyond the field there is grain growing. It is green and billowing like water. I am drawn there. I flow along in the swaying motion. It is swishing around my ears, the wind caresses my face, lightly, lightly I float over the plain.

The air becomes shimmering like a mirage and is blue. It's like everything is silvery, shiny, glowing, and it glitters and sparkles.

Then my essence friends pop up. One comes from one direction like a little typhoon, the other from the other direction like a long sweeping strand. By the color I see which is which: the typhoon is dark, that's Skydde, the sweep is flax yellow, that's Slire. They come sweeping over the billowing grass and I hook up with them. We fly away all three of us and it is like riding a roller coaster. We fly side by side with spread-out arms and legs. We let the sweep touch the green grass and it tickles lovely. The world is open and we are in it. To be hoisted up and flung down, hoisted up and flung down in a tingling lovely motion that makes us howl with delight and so ...

A voice is heard: "What are you screaming for, you're scaring the horse. Did a horse fly sting you or something?"

It's one of the uncles who heard me and got worried. Iris quiets down and the horse moseys along with Iris on the back. It doesn't take long before something else comes into her field of view and then she enters into it.

The ordinary world disappears, and I am Out again. We fly up among the clouds. They are little tufts of wool and you can fly right through them. Inside, the light is different because in them there is no sunlight. Often we float on top of small clouds and roll down from them and float out in the sunlight.

Iris falls off the horse, rolls down on the ground and remains still. Blanda stops and stands there, scratching the ground with her hoof. An uncle comes. "What are you doing, falling off the horse? Did you fall asleep?"

I tell him that I just rolled off a cloud and it was so soft that I forgot that I should get up again.

"Sit properly now and don't tumble down again, we don't have time with this." He leaves and soon I am in the real world again.

Rocking, rocking along in a quiet trot, the world is transformed; it's like being carried away floating in air. Everything around me takes on a different meaning. Blanda becomes a shimmering thing. I see her walking quietly and securely, but it's like she is floating a bit above the ground. She becomes transparent like a fairy tale horse. I look at my immaterial body. It's dancing around, whirling around, around like a typhoon. It looks so funny. The typhoon starts like a little gray string along the ground and widens into a circle. I am in the middle of it. The immaterial body is like an immobile beaming face and has a thin sheer cloak around the body. The cloak is spinning around the same way as the typhoon. Everything else is still.

It is light, light and blue, beautiful and captivating. The typhoon sweeps along over the landscape and the landscape continually changes character. Sometimes the ground is flat, meadows and fields with an occasional birch grove. Then it turns into great dark woods, hills and valleys, with deeper colors and darker solemnity. Then come the sea and the cliffs, they shimmer and glitter in all imaginable red-violet colors. It is light inside and the body chuckles contentedly. Somebody shouts: "Iris, Iris, where are you? You look like a ghost, where are you? Have you disappeared completely?" Poof, and I am back in Iris. Somebody unhitches Blanda and she finds the way home by herself.

I remain sitting on her back. I hear somebody whistling and singing. It creates a bunch of light ribbons around me. It is beautiful and forms a lot of patterns. They disappear and I get taken down from the horse. "Go in the kitchen, food is on."

Iris remains standing, not understanding that what comes out of the uncle's mouth has something to do with her. When he has put away the horse he starts scolding her because she is still standing there. It creates darker more deeply colored light ribbons around him and she stands there looking. Then she wets her pants again. It gets nice and warm around the legs and it is like being hoisted up a bit. She just stands there and enjoys the sensation. The uncle gets very mad, and the light patterns get even more fascinating. He stops suddenly, grabs her arm and drags her with him inside.

He says: "We had an accident again."

Mother takes Iris into the wash room and undresses her roughly. She mutters the whole time that she can't do anything with Iris, that she hasn't even managed to teach her to let people know when she needs to go.

People are so peculiar, they carry on with a bunch of stuff, and they try to get me to do them too, but I never know what or how, only that there is a bunch of people who are there, who are in my way sometimes, who are funny sometimes, who make my world light up. The people, same as the animals, have a special dynamic, a force that moves and fills me in a different way than things. Things just remain motionless and also have a light around them, some pleasant, others meaningless, but they just sit there, motionless uninteresting images.

Around me there are so many colors that my existence is continually filled with new stuff, without me needing to do anything for it.

Mother is going to wash me before dinner. I often come in completely dirty. I have rolled around in mud, swum in the pond with my clothes on with pond weeds stuck in my wet clothes, burrowed down in the vegetable patch, or like now, wet myself. It pains her to see me. My hair is tangled and frizzy and sticks out in all directions. She puts me in the tub in the basement and pours water over me.

Standing there with the lukewarm water flowing over me makes the world full of glitter. It's like ending up among the stars. I sweep around and catch some, toss them away and, and ...

Slire comes riding a rocket and Skydde is drifting down as if he is hanging from a parachute. I catch some small stars, toss them away and catch them again. We start to catch and toss the little light bundles and, and they form ribbons across the sky. They become patterns. The beams are round and we can ride on them. Pull us up and ride down. Fling us sideways and we fly far, far out and come back as if we are riding on rubber bands.

Mother's irritation makes the atmosphere dark. I feel her rough hands and the brush she is using chafes my skin. Pain, pain, lovely pain, it carries me far, far away from mother ... it is like a long bright red tunnel, I flow along in it and it is fast, everything gets warm and feels breathtaking ... and we tumble out in a sea of glitter which spreads as if we fell into a deep, warm, pleasant ocean.

Mother's voice: "Can't you ever learn to do as you're told!" The voice creates light ribbons that sweep around; there come new ones that sweep into the old. They sweep around me and I catch them and tie them together. They become pretty rosettes with a lot of gaudy color bands.

They dissolve when new light ribbons come out of her mouth. I laugh, she gets madder and madder, and there are more ribbons to tie. Mother hollers for Father. She shrieks: "You have to come and take care of this damn kid before I do something terrible to her."

I stand naked in the tub. Father comes in; he looks at me with warm eyes, gets a towel and wraps me in it. He sits down on the stairs with me on his knee and whispers in my ear: "Little Iris, little, little Iris you need to have clothes on, so now we'll get you dressed. "

And so he does. My arms, legs and head twirl around in every direction. It turns into such funny figures and I love it when my arms and legs get all tangled up in the clothing and in Father's arms. He holds me, sometimes quite hard to be able to get an arm into a sleeve or a leg into pants leg. I laugh and whirl around all I am able, but he is always stronger. Sometimes he says: "Stop", and then I become a statue inside an iceberg. It is cold with a lot of icicles. Beautiful, and big, and it reverberates around me. It is so still and solemn, ice-blue, and a throne where king Bore is sitting, like in the fairy tale, and I am there as a statue. Then it was God that sat there, I knew. It was dead and beautiful.

Father takes hold of me and lifts me up, shakes me and tries to make contact with me. He says: "There, there, now you are here with me again, hop up on my back and I'll carry you into the kitchen.

Father sets me at the table next to himself, but I glide unnoticed down under the table and somebody else comes and sits down on the chair.

It's nice to be under there, with all the nice legs around me. I fly Out, up to the ceiling, look down at everyone sitting there. Words are streaming out of their mouths, words that go between them, which are sucked in by somebody and are transformed into other words that come out. It makes the atmosphere change again and again. I recognize it, and still it is like something new. It's like something is changed, but I can't understand what. Then I see a hand that comes down under the table. It's holding something and I see that I am supposed to open my mouth and take it. Sometimes I do it right away, sometimes not at all. The hand disappears and I am up at the ceiling.

There were many different kinds of animals on the farm and Iris spent a lot of time with them. There were pigs, cows, calves, sheep, hens, turkeys, ducks, cats, and two dogs. Iris' world was populated by those animals. They had their own personal atmospheres. First, each animal type had a special image, and then each individual animal had its image, in addition there was a changeable image associated with the animal depending on what was happening around it. When Iris was in the proximity the image looked different than if for instance the father was there. The animal itself meant no more than humans for Iris but the images were important. They formed patterns that flowed together and continually made new images and then the girl could be with them.

The humans did not have a type-image in the same way as the animals had. They each had a specific image and it didn't connect to the others as a type. Moreover, a human's image often crashed into that of another, and then there arose a bunch of strange conflicts that caused people to become unfriendly. Iris saw a bunch of different feelings that streamed out of the humans and formed beautiful light-colors in the atmosphere and mingled into pretty braided patterns, but sometimes they became like an explosive storm. The girl loved these light-colors, they were so beautiful and they captured her interest for hours.

Some people had such captivating light-images that it was quite impossible to lose them, the way it usually happened. It was as if she turned to stone and remained in that person's proximity as long as possible. Parson Karlsson, he who sat in the outer room and wrote his sermons every third week, was one and the teacher in the fifth and sixth grades was another.

It was like their spirit was of a different kind than the others'. It colored the entire atmosphere and everyone was pulled into it whether they wanted to or not, and couldn't leave as long as the person was near.

Iris sat in her usual place under the kitchen table and listened to a neighbor who sat on a chair by the door telling the latest gossip. "I sure did see Nilsson's girl come from the barn with that hoodlum from Margaretelund. And everybody can figure out what they had been up to in there. There you see what happens when honest folks think delinquents can ..." There was a knock on the door and he shut up instantly when the Parson came in. It was time for him to go to the outer room to write his sermon, and he came to ask for some water. Immediately the neighbor turned into a sham-religious sinner. His eyes shifted, he smiled self-consciously, and quickly changed topic.

"Nice weather today, Pastor", he said and the insincere goodness virtually beamed from him.

The Pastor looked at him a little surprised and said hesitantly: "Well, maybe you could say that about this rain."

Iris was able to see only the legs of the mother. They rush over to the kitchen counter and Iris heard her get the dean's water pitcher and run the water until it got cold. She got irritated because it went so slow. She rushed to him with the pitcher and the glass and at the same time the neighbor got up, scooted around the Pastor and swung open the already half-open door and bowed politely when he went past.

The only one who didn't enter that atmosphere and get affected by it was the father. It was like he was immune to this kind of influence. Not that he was unpleasant or antagonistic, he just didn't get pulled in, and therefore he could talk and answer from his own self in a different way than the others. It was fun to watch. The father had an entirely different contact with these people and a different significance for them. Iris could see that something came from the Pastor that resembled insecurity, but the word for it was respect, not fear. The father was a mysterious person to the Pastor. He didn't believe in God, and was therefore unquestionably ungodly, but he unfortunately fulfilled all the criteria for being a good person. The atmosphere that usually flowed out from the Pastor was stable without turbulence around the people in his vicinity and filled the whole room. But when he was with the father, the Pastor's atmosphere got curly and whirled around and around and returned to the Pastor and came back out and looked different.

Sometimes there could be a sound in someone's voice or from the radio that had the same effect on people. The sound filled the whole room and everyone became enclosed in the atmosphere that emerged. It was fun to be in it because then the other people became alive in a different way.

It was the same thing in the movies. In the film somebody would do something, talk, sing, or different things happened. The room got filled with the atmosphere that rolled out from the images on the screen and colored the whole spirit in the room. It was so much fun to see how one by one the people watching ascended into this spirit and eventually it was everybody. Here and there someone, maybe a couple wrapped in each other's atmosphere, were outside. They didn't know it, but they could have been included if they just stopped doing what they were doing.

The mother had a strange atmosphere. When she was at home on the farm it was strong and colorful, but as soon as she was outside the home it disappeared inside her and was not visible at all. She became invisible in a remarkable way, and sometimes even so that people didn't notice her. She met somebody she knew, her atmosphere came out and flung itself around the person so that she jolted and often exclaimed something or started laughing. Then their atmospheres mingled and braided together, but it was the other person's that dominated and if there were several people the mothers atmosphere disappeared fairly quickly.

When many people were gathered the mother sometimes could project her field so that everyone paid attention. Then words came out of her mouth and everybody got light colors in their fields, and this could continue the whole evening. Then everybody was happy, and they were aglow and smiling when they went home. They said it had been a successful evening.

The word "successful" floated in the atmosphere in a special way. Iris crawled under the table and held on to the word. She rocked with it in her lap and … Out.

My essence-friends came and I tossed the word up in the air. Slire caught it and let it grow big so that it covered the whole sky. They were red printed letters and they were unbelievably large. We flew up and around the stems of the letters and the stems became round. Successful, successful, it was successful, it was successful, successful it was, successful it was. It was singing with a peculiar voice, a peculiar melody, a little monotonous, but at the same time suggestive.

The mother took Iris by the hand and said: "Now that little enjoyment is over, now it's time to go home."

Iris' brother sometimes teased her when she sat under the table. He was able to provoke her outbursts with ear-piercing screaming, screaming until somebody took her and put her in another room and closed the door. The girl started to rhythmically go round and round in a figure eight on the floor humming, Out.

I disconnected from Iris, and was at her side as she continued to go round and round. She just continued at a steady trot and everything was as it should be. I swept away, out through the wall, and the wall disappeared. Then Slire and Skydde were there. We formed ourselves into different animals and guessed. Skydde's animals were easy to see but Slire's were more diffuse. My animals had shapes like the animals I knew on the farm so the others guessed correctly immediately. We switched to forming the spirit of animals we knew. First there was an atmosphere that said horse, and then there was an atmosphere for each separate horse, and then the trick was to see which. There were our horses to choose among but there were also the neighbor's horses. The closest neighbor had warm-blood horses with thin legs, long and slender. Somebody was sometimes riding on them and then it turned into a completely different atmosphere since then the rider's atmosphere got mixed with the horse's. I got better and better at guessing and seeing more and more of the different spirit beings there.

The door opened, the father came in, picked Iris up, went into the kitchen and put her in the chair next to him and put out food. She began to mechanically stuff her mouth with what was on her plate. The father watched carefully that she was at home in herself and he talked painstakingly about what she was eating. There was no taste sensation in the girl's mouth, only something soft that could be chewed and be diluted and flowing so it could be swallowed. Iris often tried to swallow big chunks if she could get away with it, but usually she couldn't so she had to chew it all runny so it made it to the stomach.

When Iris saw a puddle of water she could not resist throwing herself into it. Usually somebody was holding on to her, but as soon as there was a moment's inattention and the grip wasn't tight enough, she pulled her hand free, ran over and flung herself heedlessly into the puddle. The person with her got very angry, and it got very beautiful in the atmosphere, fireworks, beautiful.

From the outside it looked like Iris had a strategy and waited for the opportunity to trick the person. But that's not how it was in Iris' world. Inside her was a constant urge for motion, it was not something she was conscious of, but the minute she came across something that gave her an impulse and the possibility was there she followed it casually without the least thought of self preservation or judgment. She did it to come Out in the real world, and that the others could not understand.

In the puddle something cold hit her face. It seeped in through the clothes like shivers penetrating to the body. I disappeared into something and Slire and Skydde were there. We rolled around each other and Iris loosened. She remained in the puddle and rolled round and round. We dove down into the cold dark mud and went straight out into something else. It was red and looked like a round bubble. We swept towards the edges of the bubble and they moved as we moved. We tried to go through the walls of the bubble, but this wasn't possible; it was as if elastic and just expanded. We flew right at it and it expanded endlessly.

A jolt in the arm. Iris is dragged out of the puddle. Somebody scolded and there was again a light show around the person. Iris was satisfied.

In the autumn all the farm machines were put in an area in the wagon barn. There was the horse rake and other machines that had a steel seat attached on a long bent flat spring. Iris crawled in there. It was nearly dark, cold and dusty. She found the horse rake or the hay turner and got up and started bouncing.

I called on Slire. He came like a whirlwind and wanted to play "the transformation". We pulled ourselves apart and got super wide, we stretched ourselves out and got super long, we blew ourselves up and became big round balls, we pulled on each other till we got warped and distorted, and we formed patterns according to feelings we picked up around us. It was like the house of mirrors at Liseberg, but it wasn't the reflections but we ourselves that looked peculiar. Skydde came and joined us but it was like he didn't change even though he changed shape. We pulled him in opposite directions and he followed when we stretched him out but still he didn't change. It was fun, and we did it over and over again. One very strange thing was that in the real world I knew exactly how everything looked, how everything actually is in reality. But in the ordinary reality all this knowledge disappeared and I no longer saw it as it actually is—other people didn't do this either; what they saw was the image shaped by the concepts of their surroundings, and that image hid how it actually was.

While everything was clear inside, it wasn't possible to use that knowledge in the ordinary reality, because there it became so foreign and peculiar. It's hard to explain that at the same time it is and still is not. How can that be? You can't understand it and still that's the way it is. In addition, the knowledge from the real world doesn't result in me being able to perform conscious acts. I see and hear in the ordinary world, but nothing happens that gives me impulses to act.

One of the horses had a wound on the leg that had dirt in it. The driver needed alcohol to clean the wound and went to the neighbor.

"I need to get some alcohol from you for the horse."

The neighbor answered: "I don't have any alcohol."

The driver said: "Sure you do. You have alcohol hid away in many places, all over."

"No I don't *have* any alcohol."

"You are lying."

"Do you accuse me of lying?"

"Yes, you are lying."

"You're wrong, I am not lying."

"It's a sin to lie."

For me, in the ordinary reality, the argument between the driver and the neighbor was a meaningless discussion about right and wrong, about truth and lies. In the real reality I saw that the driver was right; there was alcohol hidden away here and there, in the dog house, in the barn, buried next to the manure pile; I knew all the places. But I knew that the neighbor also was right, that he told the truth. In the real world I could see that in his mind all the alcohol was committed. And therefore it was as if he didn't have any.

Iris went over and said to the driver: "It's not possible for you to have any alcohol."

The driver said: "But then there is alcohol. Then, can't I have some of it."

I said again: "It's not possible for you to have any alcohol."

Then the neighbor said angrily: "She is lying. I have no alcohol. It's the dumbest thing I have heard."

The driver said angrily to me: "If you know where the alcohol is I want you to go and get some for me."

Then everything I knew from the real world disappeared and it got all white and milky around Iris and she was alone in the milk. The driver and the neighbor became like statues that just stood there motionless, and soon the images of the statues faded away.

These generalities, these valuations and perceptions, for example that the neighbor lied and that it was a sin to lie, were not accepted by me, because they were not correct. But the generalities were correct for most other people and therefore they thought that my opinions strange. It was difficult for me to explain that both the driver and the neighbor were right, because that did not fit with the generalities in the ordinary world. Indirectly I knew that others didn't understand the real world, for if they had there wouldn't have been this argument about who was right or wrong. How could it be like that? Why didn't they understand?

That *was* incomprehensible to *me* and still it was a fact. In the Iris-world I couldn't apply the real world, and in the real world almost nothing agreed with what was found in the ordinary world. Slire, Skydde and I played with this sometimes but it was like they just shoved me into the ordinary and there I was alone and didn't want to be there. I wanted to be with them, but at the same time in the ordinary world. I wanted the two worlds to merge. But this I found impossible.

It took a long, long time before I could understand the paradoxical, that they actually do merge, that both worlds exist simultaneously, and that it's inside ourselves we make the shift. To make the shift is to see the real world's meaning in a context, and then shift around and see the correctness of the ordinary world's meaning. The driver was right: the neighbor lied. The neighbor also was right: he didn't lie.

To make the shift is to be able be in both worlds almost at the same time. I am in one, one at a time, but I can shift so quickly and so often that I can take advantage of both simultaneously.

The father's great joy—the others' also, but for them it wasn't as important—came when the girl behaved somewhat normally. It nourished the hope that she maybe, in the best case, could develop sufficiently that she wouldn't need constant watching. He was hoping that she wasn't finished growing and that they didn't know what could happen at puberty. He was happy with things as they were, but it still would be wonderful because she herself would have life so much easier.

For now, the father was glad that she was joyful and laughed a lot. Not that he always knew why, but in any case she was happy. When he described her to others he often said that she was fun-loving, but that was a partial truth for she seldom laughed when others were present.

I often floated about and was involved in my way in the environment. I could connect to whomever, see what heshe was involved with, what thoughts and feelings that were streaming out in the field, and let myself get caught up in it. That was fun. One of my uncles was almost always thinking about music, when he wasn't thinking that there might be little girls coming to ride the horses. I heard and saw this music in his field and danced along with it. I loved rhythm and followed at his heels.

Another was almost always thinking about the dance on Saturday. He often thought about the ones he would dance with, and that it would be great to have a snort. I didn't know what a snort was but I knew what dancing was. He thought about the girls and there were often images of him dancing. I swapped myself for the girls and danced with him and that was wonderful, we floated along as on a glass floor, or an ice floor if it was outside and cold.

A third uncle thought mostly about concerns for everyone and everything. There was nothing to play with in that, no sounds or images or people or happenings, just words, and sometimes it was words I'd never heard. I collected those to play with together with Slire and Skydde.

The father noticed at once when the girl connected to his thoughts and met her so she couldn't avoid being with him in the ordinary reality. He talked about a problem, hoof and mouth disease, and was speaking entirely non-judgmentally: "I wonder if there is something in the air or water, or what it could be." Since what he said was free of valuations and opinions I could follow, and I said: "When they breathe." My reply made him understand that I grasped what he was talking about, and that despite everything I was not retarded.

The mother just got irritated and wanted to get rid of her because she felt so bothered that she got aggressive and considered Iris insolent.

It was possible to connect to the brother and the others in the house, but they usually started teasing her and then it was spoiled. The Pastor and caretaker August were ok and so was Fil.

The family went to the Liseberg amusement park. The father took the girl on all the merry-go-rounds and she liked that. Up and down, up and down, round and round, round, round; it was a little like her world and she was delighted. They rode on the ghost train where there were a lot of screaming and flashing lights, almost like fireworks, and Iris thought that she was in the real reality. Then they came out, and it was over; she saw the cars and said "more, more"; the father bought another ticket and they rode many times. He thought that they would ride until she stopped saying "more" but after a few times he was too tired to continue. The girl was satisfied and left without the usual rituals.

Another time at Liseberg the brother disappeared. There was great consternation. He used to stick to the mother like a band-aid and never leave her sight but he had caught sight of the arcade and was drawn there and remained there. Everybody began running around like headless chickens trying to find him, hollering his name, questioning the guards, and all were worried sick.

It was exciting. Suddenly the atmosphere was filled with all the different personalities and a lot of crackling emotion colors. I flew out in the air and started sweeping around everybody. Most people were running around laughing, which was such a contrast to our group.

My brother's name flew out in space, loud and clear, it was like a red ribbon in the sky that formed a doodle. It came out, swept around, and faded away, came out again, swept around and faded away.

Somebody was dragging the girl along so she stumbled, and somebody pulled her up again. She tried to get away but she couldn't. Then she gave up and somebody picked her up and put her in some kind of wagon, and she felt vibration from the wheels. Out, Out, Out ...

Skydde came first; he came down and got me. We flew up a bit above the heads of the people and then Slire came. Slire took the lead and we flew to the ghost train. Dove in and swept around, hooked onto a car and hung on to it. The fun part was all the scare colors that came from the people in the cars. It was a new color mix with horror-delight. It spread around the whole room among skeletons and other light effects. We swished around among the emotion colors and tossed fire balls at them. This was a game that Slire often played. He shaped a color patch into a ball and threw it at somebody so it exploded and spread like rays in all directions. We did the same and then we looked to see how long the rays got, and when they disappeared somebody made a new light ball.

The girl was jolted back to the ordinary world. Somebody shouted: "Up girl! Hurry up! We found him!"

He stood by the entrance and cried. His whole face was full of tears. The girl had never seen him cry and it got so beautiful around him. It was like little stars, as if he had the whole sky around him with lots of stars. The mother scolded him and didn't see how scared he was because she was even more scared, the father picked him up and hugged him and then the star-sky around him disappeared and everything went back to normal.

It was over. Everybody went out and the mother held the brother's hand in a tight grip. She looked very angry, and he looked at her and tried to look like a good boy. It passed, and everybody went to the street car. The girl sat next to the father and the car squeaked and lurched. Out again ...

Slire and Skydde were outside the window and I flew out to them. We became long and narrow and swept around the street car. It didn't have square corner so we could sweep around it almost as if it was an oval, and we could sweep fast, fast, almost as if riding a roller coaster. We had our face against the window pane and inside sat a lot of people. Many looked out the window and we made a bunch of different faces and had fun. Then the brakes squealed and it became like a color spray to the back. We dove down in it and let it rain over us. We got a lot of color splotches around us and we spun around in them until they disappeared. Then the car started and we resumed our sweeping around it. There were a number of new faces and they had a different spirit around them.

"Don't sit there and dream, come, we have to get off, this is where we are staying tonight." It was the mother that grabbed hold of the girl's arm. She still had fear coloring around her and her face looked terrified. Otherwise the atmosphere around her was empty. If the fear hadn't come out with its color she would have been non-existent because she had no other atmosphere. The girl thought this was strange, but that's the way it was.

On other occasions on the trolley I crawled around on the floor. I lay down and followed along in the shaking and rattling. Suddenly the brakes squealed and I went Out in it. The trolley was a lot of fun, it shook and rattled and created a strange feeling, sometimes it screeched and it was a lovely sound. It became an image I could go into. I waited and waited, and poof, there was the sound and I laughed. The braking-light and the laughing-light blended and played catch. The braking-light disappeared and then the laughing-light.

The girl was picked up by a pair of strong arms. Sometimes she accepted it and offered no resistance, but sometimes she had an outburst for she wanted to remain in the lovely state created by the trolley.

Sometimes the trolley was filled with transparent veils. The walls got transparent and the space inside got bigger and bigger. Slire came through the roof and lifted it high, high up. It got so wonderfully big and spacious. Skydde sat with me just above the floor.

The word that was there was "ticket". It became a dark-blue figure when it came out from somebody's mouth. The one that said it was dark-blue, all of him, cap and all. The word "ticket" came laconically from his mouth every time somebody got on the trolley. The one who came on then started to dig through hisher pockets and sometimes there came a piece of paper that went click when dark-blue man clipped it with his pliers, or otherwise there was some money.

The father said it when we got on the trolley, "ticket", the conductor said it again "ticket"; it became an image in the atmosphere and then vanished. The mother and father talked with each other and the word came out again, "ticket". We caught the word, made it into a ball and tossed it among ourselves. We ran around and bounced from window to window. There were many and were placed in all directions. We stretched them so they got irregular, then we came back and they were normal.

"Get up, we have to get off." She heard the father's voice through her sphere and the girl leapt into the body again. She tumbled down with a loud crash, and at first it was unpleasant. The father picked her up and she hung over his shoulder like a sack. That was better and she relaxed. The rest was a walk to the Jarntorget place where we were staying; the air was fresh and invigorating when she walked by the father's side through the park.

Slire and Skydde came. We swept out over the banister and rode down with terrific speed. Up and down, up and down, up ... and we became like thin veils that floated down in the middle. The serpentine banister snaked along side of us and we let them caress our sides. Then we started to snake through the balusters. They were ornate and had many angles and corners. We played "Follow John" and created patterns. A voice came and colored the atmosphere: "Iris, Iris, you have to come in and eat. Iris are you there? Iris where are you? Come, so you don't keep the rest of us waiting."

The youngest son in the house came out in the stairwell and brought the girl in. She sat on a step with her forehead pressed against the banister. It was so cool and lovely. She got marks in her forehead from it. The mother asked the boy where he had found her but she didn't wait for an answer but turned to the girl. "Look at you kid! You are all red and streaked in your face, what have you been doing? Have you been sitting in that cold stairwell? Can't you understand that you'll get a bladder inflammation if you sit on the cold stairs? You are hopeless. Dumb kid that never can learn anything."

The family stayed a few days with some other relatives on the other side of the street. It was a fancier house and they had a huge apartment with high ceilings and plaster decorations. There was a grandmother who was an artist and who had a lot of strange paintings on the walls and a bunch of plates with patterns. The girl crawled into a corner and flew into a painting.

It was like a kind of suction. I was sucked into the painting and it was awful. It was a dramatic picture with demons and devils. It grabbed me and laughed hysterically in my ears. It was dramatic and traumatic. I hollered for Skydde but he didn't come. Not Slire either. I was totally alone. Terror and panic tore at me and I was thrown back into the body.

The girl rushed into the kitchen and crawled under the kitchen table. Her teeth were chattering and she trembled like a leaf. One of the mother's aunts was in the kitchen and she tried to take the girl. The mother warned: "Her imagination has run away with her again and scared the wits out of her so she lies there trembling. Let her be, it passes after a while. If you pick her up now she'll just get hysterical."

The aunt thought it was terrible that the mother didn't pick the girl up to comfort her, at the same time she was saying that the girl wasn't quite normal reacting in this way, and had they actually not sought help for her. The mother said that was something for the father to decide and the aunt started scolding her because she was so helpless and didn't "assume any responsibility." That hurt her feelings and she tried to get out of it by referring to the father, but the aunt just kept it up and the mother was destroyed in her field and disappeared into herself.

A short while later the girl was back in the studio. There was something magic about that room and she couldn't resist going in there despite the fact that she got sucked into its horrors and despite Slire and Skydde not coming there. The grandmother had a folding partition in the middle of the room and now she pulled it aside. Behind it was a young beautiful girl playing the piano. She played beautiful scales. The girl sank down by the piano with her back against the sound box.

It tickled her back. I detached and went Out and the whole room got bright and the sound formed new light ribbons in spirit colors. It was so lovely that my whole body became warm as if by a fire. The fire tongues licked the paintings on the walls and the images became nice instead of scary. They changed constantly like the music tongues that licked the paintings.

"Well, there you are! You are all red-eyed! Now, give it up and start behaving like a normal kid." It was the mother that intervened again. She felt Iris' forehead and realized that she didn't have a temperature, but said anyway that maybe there were after effects from sitting in the cold stair well a few days before.

There was an elevator in the building and the people lived on the fourth floor so they rode the elevator up and down. It was a fantastic arrangement. It made noise, it squeaked, there were several lattice doors that you closed, and then you pushed a button to go up or down, depending on where you started from.

Early one morning, nobody else awake except me, out in the hall, out through a heavy door into the elevator and push the button. It jerks and starts. It starts to move and it makes clicking noises. I sink down on the floor, below the mirror. The room gets nice, there is wood on the walls, the door with wrought iron scrolls, the mirror that reflects the wood on the other side. The ride is like a lovely motion and I sit there. Clunk, pause, clunk, pause, clunk, pause, I float around. Stop!!! The real world disappears. I stand up and push the down button, sit down quickly and go Out again.

I rode up and down in the elevator and went Out in the real world. I flew out through the lattice like a sweep. First it was pipes that folded and you could squeeze between. You had to stretch yourself so you became a flat ribbon. That way you could braid yourself all the way from one wall to the other. Then there was the lattice of iron with pretty flowers with leaves and stems and holes in between. There you could fly straight in and out. We had a fun game. Slire came up with the rule that you had to fly out of the elevator right before you passed the door to a floor and in again before it had gone past it, otherwise it was no good. You were supposed to make it through as many holes as possible in the iron lattice by each floor. Sometimes the rule was that we had to fly out at one floor and up the stairs and then fly in at the next floor. When we were going down we rolled down the stairs and when we were going up we floated up like waves the same as when you are swimming against the wind.

The door from the relatives' apartment opened and somebody ran down the stairs, went in again and so up. It happened a couple of times. Suddenly the elevator jerked in the wrong place, it stopped and somebody opened the door. "Are you sitting here, you can't do that, you can't be in the elevator, can't you understand that? Are you completely nuts, you're not allowed to joy-ride in the elevator, it is punishable."

Somebody grabbed the girl's arm pulled her to her feet and dragged her into the apartment. There came a bunch of light ribbons out of everyone and there came a bunch of words that looked like fireworks. The girl saw all the emotions, and I heard some words I knew: worried, not allowed, what should we do with you, never. A little fear, but that disappeared very quickly. The words became pictures that the girl could look at and play with. After a while they got tired of scolding and left the girl alone again.

The girl got confused. She didn't understand what was

wrong or dangerous about riding the elevator, why she couldn't do it. There was so much in her world that people denied her and she couldn't understand why, especially when they said it was something she ought to understand by herself. She didn't know that it was possible to understand something yourself, even less what. Why people didn't do something that was fun just because it was fun was incomprehensible in her world. She saw other people do things and she thought it was things they liked to do. Later she found out that one did things because of duty, not for pleasure, and that was even more confusing.

All the bags were packed and everyone went down to the station. It was close by so there was no trolley ride this time. Then we came to the train, it was a narrow gauge, which went to a little town where we had to change to ride to our local station.

I crawled in by Father and sat with my face pressed against the window pane. I went Out and started riding on the outside of the train. Slire and Skydde came and we clung from window to window. Let go your grip, fly up, dive down, hook up again. Fly forward to the front of the train, back to the end, whirl around and go the other way. We went in under the engine and hooked on to the connecting rods that drove the iron wheels and went up and down. The most fun was when the train braked. Then the connecting rod stood still or went backwards. We also hung back and let go before the train stopped and let it start and get moving again before we hooked up again. We left the train and flew around the trees that stood alongside, turned around and started the chase to catch up again. We knew we could, but we acted anyway as if we almost didn't make it. It was exciting to sit still and fly around outside. Everything moved and at the same time everything stood still. Sometimes we came to a road crossing. There were blinking red lights and loud ringing. We flew out and jumped from car to car, that were standing still, and then back again to the train. Sometimes we took off down the road and found a car driving towards the crossing. Then we latched on to it and hung on through all the bends and when it stopped we hopped over to the train and continued on our way. Slire and Skydde came up with a bunch of different rules how it all should be done to be exciting and we tested them to see if they worked and which ones we liked the most. I was sucked in again by a voice that said: "We are going to eat now Iris, please sit up." It was the father that gently straightened the girl up in her seat.

The father put a sandwich in the girl's hand and she stared at it. He took the sandwich and brought it to her mouth and said: "Open." Mechanically she opened her mouth. He said: "Chew" and she started chewing, the mouth moved mechanically. "Iris, eat now! Where are you? Be here now and eat, look at me." He took her head and turned it towards him. The girl landed in herself, looked at the father and the taste sensation came to her mouth and she could eat by herself.

The train stopped, the family got off, there was a horse and carriage waiting. It was one of the uncles that was there to get them. He boosted the girl up into the carriage and off they went. In the carriage, alongside the uncle, Slire and Skydde came again. We started playing whirling around the horse's legs and competing in wait and catch up. Skydde won almost every time because he was so calm.

At home in the house farmor was on the second floor. She had such a funny light around her. Today I realize that she was always nervous and worried. She believed she was sinful and that her surroundings would condemn her, she was afraid she wouldn't find time, afraid of saying the wrong things, afraid that someone would have something to criticize. It was fun to sit in a corner in her kitchen and look at all the pretty patterns. It became different if somebody came to see her. Then the pattern got lively, like snakes that twisted around each other. Sometimes it looked warm, sometimes cold. It depended on what got in her way.

The whole atmosphere was filled with good snakes. I flew around with them and we dove under chairs and tables, up to the ceiling, whirled around the lamp and round farmor's legs. Slire stretched himself into a snake also, Skydde and I tried to do the same but we weren't as flexible as Slire. The most fun was around the lamp and the radio. The lamp had a constant outflow of light ribbons, sometimes it was a star spray, almost like sparklers. From the radio flowed sound that became different color patterns that you could catch and tug along through the air.

I rocked and rocked and ... right among farmor's snakes. I whirled around and dove through. Suddenly it all changed and I went up to the ceiling. I managed to get caught in a light strand, and that was the most fun. Then I could hook on, and the strand moved slowly and sluggishly, but suddenly it went turbo and it was like whirling around in a merry-go-round that swings in all directions. To just ride along, to allow oneself to be carried, to not know what would happen or what shape it would take, this was exciting. I looked behind me. Slire and Skydde had also been caught up and were pulled along in an intoxicating jumble.

"You have to go downstairs and eat."

The grandmother took the girl by the arm and mumbled something about her being stuck in place and that she ought to obey instantly when she was told, that it wasn't good to sit there like a statue, that the girl should play with the other kids instead. The grandmother had a guilty conscience and was annoyed that the girl had put her in this situation.

The other children were very grateful to the grandmother when Iris was with her or when somebody else took care of her since then they could play in peace.

The brother came home from school every day with at least ten buddies, often more. They played great-games; games that could continue for weeks and that had very complicated rules. The rules were often worked out during the game. They played, something wasn't fun, the group got together and had a council, tried different strategies and junked most of them. When they had come up with a strategy that worked they restarted the game. The girl was placed somewhere she could be seen. She got to be a part of the game and they arranged an extra role for her in some way that didn't inhibit the play too much.

I twirled around all who were running around me. They shouted and there came images in the air which I could see. They laughed, tumbled, stumbled, and crawled. There were strange squiggles from all the bright-lights that sprayed out of the children, which I caught into myself and tumbled around in. We, Slire, Skydde, and I played our own games in the air and there were constantly new patterns to play with.

Slire hooked on to a running boy and snuck inside his shirt, hung on; bounced up and down, lost his grip and got left behind. Then Skydde came and took over, he stayed inside the shirt but he was careful to not touch the skin since then he would have lost the game. He fell out and I took over. We found different persons and it depended on how they were dressed which game we played, but just hooking on was our favorite. We also took out some word and flung it at some of the other kids. This often stopped that kid, which gave the one we were hooked onto a chance to escape from the one that was stopped.

To me this was really living: to sit crouched and wrapped-up and be a part of it. Everybody ran around me laughing, blundering, falling, crawling and slithering. It produced a cascade of light, sound, colors, and patterns in the atmosphere. There came beautiful formations and I was irresistibly sucked into them. Quickly I was there; I flew around, hooked on to the shirt collar of some running boy and was pulled along in a wild dance. It was so lovely to feel the sweep of motion and sometimes go around the boy to the other side and get into a new situation, back again, back and forth. I often threw myself between the boys. It was like jumping between ice floes, from one to the other, back and forth, over to the other again, fasten to the pants legs or hook on to shoe laces, the hair, arms, and spin around, round, let go and be flung away, dive back and fasten in a new place, and most importantly, getting inspiration from Slire and Skydde.

Once when we saw that the children were playing hide and go seek we realized that they would tire of the game very quickly and then we decided to play "disturb" and try to introduce a new rule for them, a rule that we had already figured out. *Our game consisted of getting one of the children to propose this rule for the others, and we also made bets about which one we would be able to influence. We couldn't do a lot of influencing. Some children were completely un-sensitive while others were easier to steer. My brother was the easiest so it was no sport to do it to him; we decided to pick one of the others. It required that they not be focused and aware, because then our attempts had no effect; only if they were in a state of intuitive reaction was it possible to affect their impulses. There were a few that radiated sensitivity, that had long tentacles, and there we could spread our impulses. It was an exciting sport. Among the twenty-five kids that used to come and play at our house there were three who were suitable candidates. We waited for the right opportunity, when something came out in the atmosphere from one of those children, and then we tossed in the idea for this new rule. We kept doing it until one of the chosen kids stopped the game and said: "I have an idea. Can't we do like this instead. When the one who is IT has found somebody that was hidden he can't just run and tag for him. First he has to run to him and touch him and the one who was found can't run and tag for himself until IT has touched him." This was the rule that Slire and Skydde and I had figured out. The other children went along with the new rule, and suddenly the old game had acquired a totally new and more complex strategy.

"Where is Iris?" The brother stopped and looked around. He had long since forgotten about the sister. He looked at a bundle lying in a pile under a bush. "There!"

Father told him to get the sister and bring her with him to eat. He hated this, that it was always Iris that ruined all the games. He threw dirt clumps at her and she came roughly back to reality. When physical pain intruded in my reality and I didn't know where it came from I got scared, and then the atmosphere got black and threatening and full of terrible masks that grinned menacingly at me. It was so horrible that Iris screamed to high heaven and had a serious outburst that took time and effort to get her out of.

Nobody understood what Iris had reacted to since nobody saw what was changed in the atmosphere, but if the father came and the girl heard his voice she could follow it and then she calmed down inside.

All the children played in the hay barn. When it was Iris' turn she went and hid so nobody could find her up on the loft in an air pocket between some hay stacks. I went Out and then Slire and Skydde came. There was a lot of straw moving towards the straw chopper which was running full speed. I and Slire and Skydde slid down the straw while turning backward somersaults. The rule was that just before we got to the wheel cutting the straw we had to turn around and go back up. We were doing the usual sweeps. At one point Slire happened to accidentally fall through the wheel and got chopped into pieces that flew out in the air outside the barn and tumbled to the ground a few meters away. All three of us were astonished, for this was something completely outside the normal. I and Skydde stood there and stared at him where he was lying in pieces on the ground. It took a while before he had collected himself from the surprise and gathered himself up and started moving again. I knew he wasn't hurt despite the fact that he had lain there cut to pieces, but it still got me thinking that people in the ordinary world could disappear. I had heard about someone who had been gored by a bull and died. I ran into the kitchen and hollered: "Slire fell down from the straw chopper and killed himself, but he didn't die anyway."

Father listened to such stories from me the same way you listen to history programs on the radio. It was a tale or a story from a distant planet that didn't belong in reality, but which still was interesting and fascinating. He was so convinced I was mentally OK that he never worried about my story; knew that I could distinguish between what to him was free fantasies (and for me was the real reality) and what was real (and for me was the ordinary reality).

For me everything was real, but I was clear on which parts of my reality that he and the others called real and what they called fantasies.

The grandfather got the task of keeping track of the girl. He had as his assignments to weed the vegetable garden, rake the gravel walk, pick the fruit, get the potatoes and do other practical things for the kitchen. He also made brooms to sweep the stairs with, repaired clogs and darned socks. When the girl was with him it was nice, for he often forgot about her. He was in his world, humming and singing and ...

Slire and Skydde were around me. We sweep away in the melody colors, the humming colors and Farfar's movements. We ran round, round and formed a single sweep around him. From the ground, up in the sky, down again, up again. It was such a lovely feeling to land in soft cotton, turn and sweep up ultra fast, end up among the clouds to stay and then turn slide down again. Over and over again ...

"Iris get up, you can't sit here and dream." Farfar talked to her, she saw his lips moving. He pulled her up, she stood up and mechanically she began to walk behind him.

Farfar also had his own world. He was light and always had a warm field around him. He often went around humming some sad melody. He was never angry or irritated, but sometimes he was afraid, although not in some scary way. He was the most afraid of farmor. Her words to him were sometimes so hard and stinging that they smashed all his love to bits. It was left lying around his feet a long while after he had been scolded. He looked at the girl with a heartbroken look but as soon as he saw her face, all the broken pieces got put back together again and he beamed with love again.

He was a grounded, contented person, happy to have lived his arduous life, to have had farmor by his side, to have seven surviving children round him, to have worked the farm so the family had never starved, to have made a place for some other poor souls as well. He was glad that he got to be old and retire, that his sons took over from him, that he could continue puttering in the soil, that he got to sit and smoke his cigar and blow the smoke on farmor's flowers to kill the lice. That he could have a "clear" when he had a cold or to toast a guest. "You understand my lass, that's living, that's the joy of life."

The girl often sat under his chair when he sat and "pondered". The others thought he was thinking when he sat so quiet and absent minded, but that's not what he was doing. He sat there and floated in his emotional space which I could share with him. He didn't notice me but I could see him the whole time. He was like a beautiful being from a fairy tale. Chalk-white hair, dark eyebrows and light-blue eyes. He was thin, almost skinny, gnarled and bony, but strong and sinewy. He had transparent, light orange cape on. Sometimes it changed color and got pale yellow and the he was even more beautiful. He was so different, because there didn't emerge any thoughts from him that you could hook onto, and you couldn't toss any to him. You could only be with him, and that was very ok. Slire and Skydde and I could be around him, sweep through him, and we often tried to get him with us, but it never succeeded. He just was there and floated around like on a flying carpet.

When Farfar died, his spirit atmosphere remained long after him. I could float around in it sometimes when I sat under the chair he used to sit on. By that time I had understood the difference between ordinary world and the real world, but I couldn't comprehend the fact that he was dead since he was still here and I could see him. That's how it was with farmor too. She had died half a year before farfar, and her voice could be heard anyway when somebody did something she used to say was forbidden.

Farfar used to pilfer plums for us kids. Farmor ordered him to not give us any because she wanted them for preserves, compote, and marmalade. He promised, but when he was raking the grass around the fruit trees he bumped into the tree and lots of fruit fell down. He ducked behind the raspberry thicket and raked the plums to himself and stuffed them in the big pockets of his overalls and went whistling behind the bunk house and hollered for us kids.

The people in the real reality could change any minute. I could look at farmor and get her to be a young girl, or a child, or the mother of a child or someone milking a cow, or an old hag. She could also be a feeling --rage, fear – but she still was recognizable as farmor. I was the one who evoked these changes in her, but all of it was farmor, it was only as if I picked out different puzzle pieces of her. I could do that with people in the ordinary reality. They never changed.

Sometimes it was possible to see the changeable people from the real reality among the ordinary living people. They could be dressed completely differently without anyone remarking on it. Their old fashioned clothes were sometimes just rags, sometimes beautiful silk dresses. Father asked about this and I described and described. Usually he was satisfied and didn't ask any more.

But among the ordinary people there were some that were different. The teacher in the fifth and sixth grade was as constant as other ordinary people. But when he said, for example: "I understand that there is something wrong with you Iris but I have no idea what it is. But I will do everything in my power to make sure that you learn everything that all the others learn", when he said "wrong" I noticed quotation marks around that word and saw that he was a middle-person. Without him knowing it himself, he was coupled to the real world. When he was with me he opened the real world for himself in a way that we could meet.

Sometimes the girl hid in an arbor. It consisted of lilac bushes and was very dense. She had found a cavity in the hedge that was like a hut and the ground was thick with old leaves. She sat there burrowing her bottom down in the leaves like sitting in a hammock. When she had settled herself she began staring at a twig that was waving in the breeze now and then and soon she disappeared through the greenery and away ...

First Skydde came. He took my hand and we swept around for a while. It was so funny. First you don't see anything, or more precisely, everything is seen as a picture, then if you focus on something it gets real. It emerges, assumes shape, and becomes actual in the real world. We fly up to the chimney and see the crows that live there. It is fun to be with them, and land on the edge next to them and see when they follow each other. They have movements and patterns in their beings that they read amongst themselves. There is a continuing exchange among them the whole time. They are never alone. Their atmosphere never looks like it does in normal peoples' atmosphere when they are alone. That's also how it is with the people visible in the real reality; they are never alone either, like lonely people on the earth.

We sat in the opening in the church steeple, Slire, Skydde and I. I was the swallow mother and they were the swallow chicks. I taught them to fly by pushing them over the edge. They flapped their wings and tumbled around and got lopsided and fell to the ground ten meters away. I flew down to get them and then we went up the steeple steps and continued practicing our swallow flight. Skydde got it first. He's the one that figured how to hold his wings so you could soar. When both of them knew how to fly we needed to catch some food. We spotted a butterfly and dove like swallows, like thrown darts. At the last moment we dove under the butterfly. We were not allowed to fly through live beings because then we would affect them. The sport was to miss the butterfly with the smallest possible margin. As the mother, I didn't let my chicks pass if they didn't get close enough to the butterfly that they could have caught it.

The crows didn't care about us and we imitated them and acted the same way as they. We moved back and forth among each other, Slire, Skydde, and I and played crows. We flew like them, cawed like them, nodded and minced like them and laughed. It was so much fun in the crow world. We walked on the roof ridge and played caw-caw and let it be colors that we made into shapes. Our caw-caws at first looked like the ones from the crows, but then they got different. Theirs were like balls and stars and such that came out of their mouths. They changed to wet streaks which plowed a path next to us which the crows then wiped up. Skydde had a special ability to catch these, whatever they were, and change them into crackly spots. We tried to do the same but didn't succeed.

Splash!!! Shucks! The girl got soaked. There was a sudden downpour and the rain gushed through the thicket like a water fall. The girl got up and began to roll around in the wetness. She loved to be soaked, loved the wetness that created such a fun experience in the body. Hardly anything else could get her to be so present in the ordinary world.

The mother got angry and thought the girl was ornery and got wet only to make extra trouble for her. Especially if the girl resisted undressing so she could put dry clothes on her. Then she got punished by not being allowed inside or outside, depending on what the mother thought was the most attractive at the time. The girl liked that about the mother. Her atmosphere was full of emotion colors which formed the strangest gyrations and ended up as images. The girl played with them and then there came even more curlicues from the mother and the girl laughed.

Emma was mine. We were in the same world. She called me her little golden heart and it got so nice in the atmosphere. She never tired of me or tried to get me to change. We were in the same field, in the same atmosphere, simultaneously in the real and the ordinary. She was something different than anything else I knew. She was a moving substance, she was like Slire and Skydde but she was also one of the ordinary who could talk with the father and the mother. She was big and warm and held me with her one arm and squeezed. She was like a being that occupied my world and that I could remember the whole time. I could play with her. She picked me up, put me on her lap; it was like being in a tub with warm bubbling water. I rolled around in it, her hoarse and husky voice enveloped me, I rolled round, round, and clucked for joy. It became a special sort of music.

The whole world got filled in a special way. Everything got filled, both inside and out. It was like everything was one and I was part of it. It was completely different than anything else. We were in a ... what? ... just in a one. Emma saw me and laughed when she saw me, we met and she was included. I rolled around in it, her voice enveloped me and it was like waves that I floated in. her eyes looked at me, I looked into them, blurry but still so clear at the same time, I threw myself into her gaze and it was like going through a long transparent beam. Suddenly I fell out of it and straight into a sea of hands that picked me up as on a bed of roses, with velvet and silk, and tucked me in.

I saw arms and legs that flew around, that took hold of me and brought me back into my body and then I flew away in another beam and had new experiences and the arms and legs brought me back. Emma sang something and there came a starry sky, like sparklers, like fireworks, and I saw her mouth where it all came out. I went in it and was thrown out by the sound and flew away into space. I turned, pushed back, dove in again only to be thrown out again. Emma teased me in the air and I laughed. From that sound there came bright flashes that spread and blended with Emma's and became something else again.

The girl flinched. She heard Emma say it was time for eveningy. She didn't know what eveningy was but she knew that Emma would take her by the hand and they would walk over to the other house. She knew something very unpleasant was about to start and she didn't want to go to eveningy, but Emma guided her gently there and she had to submit in the end.

Somebody took hold of the girl and began tearing off her clothes. She screamed and defended herself. Somebody thought she should be grateful she had been able to stay with Emma so long. The girl didn't understand what it meant to be grateful, and even less that it was possible to not scream when the scream was there. The hands got harder and harder and the voice shriller, it got dark. It was like entering a dark cave, cold and inhospitable, there was salt and wet-warm in the face, on the hands and feet. Something rubbed around, harshly and unfriendly, it was like drowning in darkness. After a while it got all empty, nothing, and still and then it was nice to just let it be, flap the hands and go, go and then the girl was Out ... Slire and Skydde came and surrounded me. We flew into a cloud and tucked ourselves in so that we didn't see or hear anything, only were, then everything was back in order again.

Warm hands embraced the girl. She was in an unknown lap and was carried away. She was completely satisfied again. Now everything was as it should be and the girl began sounding and waving her hands in front of her face again.

A great unease came into me. Emma was gone. She wasn't where she always used to be. It was like empty in the air. No voice to float in, no hands that felt special and everything else that was connected to her. No voice to float in, no beam to follow, and no hand that took me and which constituted its own world.

Emma was sometimes in the atmosphere, but not in the same way as before. Before, she had been in both worlds simultaneously. Except for Father, there was nobody else who was with me in both. It was so peculiar, as if there now was something empty in life.

It was so strange, as if something had got empty in the world. It was new to the girl and she got restless. She began to whimper and shake her head, wave her hands and crouch and bang her head on the wall. Then it got calmer in the girl and she could return to the ordinary.

The church was an exciting place for the girl. She loved the old twelfth century church. Its uneven stones were so nice to sit by and follow with her gaze. And inside the church there were such beautiful windows. Once when the girl was little, a man came there and knocked down some mortar. The sound was nice, and under the mortar there were pictures. He said they were red-lead pictures and that they were painted in the fifteen hundreds. The girl went inside and crawled up in a window niche. The niches leaned outwards but the caretaker had placed a wood platform in some windows for flower pots or candelabras. It was possible to sit and rock there.

The glass made prisms and the sun made rainbows, and the world resembled a moving mass that came and went. I went into the moving world. It was glass-green and beautiful, like crystals in all directions. Then Slire came first. He whirled around and made long silver-green ribbons that formed figure-eights in the sky. He hollered: "Come, follow me." Then Skydde came and he waited for me. I flew away between them. The world got colored, ice-colored, all hues, transparent like ice although not cold, we could go straight through and there were lots of crystals, which melted together again after we passed and formed new patterns. Out, in, through, new-formed patterns and colors, backwards and forwards. Slire grabbed me and threw me through. Skydde was on the other side and threw me back. There came silver-green ribbons out from the glass on both sides, one ribbon for each time I went through. We all laughed, halted, made a new run and, threw ourselves away and through again, many, many times, until I felt a pair of hands taking hold of me.

A pair of hands took hold of the girl and brushed the mortar dust off her. "Come now, I am going to dig a grave now. You shouldn't be sitting here in the dark when it is such a nice day outside."He put the girl down on a couple of planks he had placed by the edge of the grave. It was the head end he said where the stone would be and he wasn't going to throw any dirt there. The other planks were to put his hands on when he was going to climb up after he had finished digging.

I sat crouched and rocked back and forth. There was a nice atmosphere around him. He was thinking the whole time and his thoughts and fantasies were so clearly visible. He was a happy person inside, but he didn't fit in too well in society. They said that he was an awful liar and that he believed it himself. Somebody said: "Lying and lying, that you can't quite say, but he abuses the truth somewhat." He was also a sneak-drinker. In many nooks and crannies around the church, in the stone wall, in the cabinet in the sacristy, in the tool shed, and a few other places he kept little flasks. After his wife died he had lived with his son and the son's family, mainly the daughter-in-law, had taken it upon themselves to "take care of him", which meant keep him from drinking. That's why he had his flasks stashed all over the place. He took a swig of the communion wine now and then also, but nobody knew that except me.

He often told his stories about those lying in the graves, and we entered those stories. They teemed with animals, places, and people. The people were transparent in a way that ordinary people weren't, and more alive. They talked with each other and I *saw* their meanings. We were there, although invisible to the others. A lot of things were happening in front of our eyes and we stood on the side and watched. The dramatics were strong. It was like a film, although not exactly. We were in the film but only as viewers. I recognized the community, all the houses that came, but they looked different both inside and out. I recognized the people also, although they were not any that existed in the ordinary world right now. There were love-triangles, forbidden love affairs, sudden deaths, and other horrors. Often there were gypsies who showed up with their fiery dancing and seduced young well-born girls. They became pregnant and were sent away, and it got dark around them. Everybody ate a lot of food and drank a lot. Parties, parties, and lots of adventures. The fate of everybody ended with foul sudden death and with funerals, which were also occasions for conspiracies and partying.

His stories could assume any shapes whatever, and it was so easy to follow and watch. I loved these occasions. I was present there in everything, without anyone attacking me, with Slire and Skydde by my side.

His voice came through to me. "I am done now Iris. You're supposed to come in with me; your mother asked me in for coffee and you are supposed to eat."

The girl was lifted to her feet, he stroked her hair gently and said: "You are indeed a little angel, you. But the others say you are so much trouble, but that I can't understand."

Another day the girl sat at the altar and gazed at the painting above. It was a man that hung on a cross. It was a carved wooden image suspended on a cross, painted and attached to a painting with a mountain motif and a city in background. There were suffering people around the cross and there were painted streaks of blood on the figure itself and on the painting also.

I rocked myself into the painting and heard all the whimpering. It was a deep wail that echoed in the mountains. I went into the lamentation and was swept into the people's inner. There was so much warm suffering. Some were relieved – it wasn't they who were hanging on the cross – others wanted to hang there instead of being on the ground, some clung to each other and felt elated, but all, all were in the lamentation. The ones who wanted to hang on the cross were black inside and empty; they wanted color and movement. Nobody saw them or listened to them and they suffered. They had empty holes with suction in them, and those I used to watch out for. If you got too close and got sucked in it was scary and hideous, and I did not wish to be there. Inside them it was as if wild animals could get to me and rend me to pieces, and when that happened it was difficult to put yourself together again afterwards.

Every time I went into the altar painting I experienced new things that lasted a long time afterwards and occupied my thoughts. I was gone inside in a different way than when I was Out. It was as if somebody else's life was happening inside me. Sometime somebody would push inside and make contact with me and that was confusing, because then came feelings in my body that were foreign and scary and which I didn't perceive as my own. I perceived that the other's will forced itself on me and that I couldn't understand it. Somebody in the painting was trying to get me to bring back a message which caused discomfort, another type of painful discomfort involving the body. It was something I was forced to accommodate myself to, but that I couldn't accommodate myself to. It was as if wild animals were attacking me and I couldn't defend myself. I got crazy and began strike, kick, bite, scratch, scream, and tried to get away.

The caretaker heard her and said: "Now she has an attack again!" and took her and held her. For no reason she fought and screamed like it was something dangerous she was involved in. On the outside there was nothing scary so the caretaker did not understand what it was about. He was just baffled.

When somebody had died and was to be buried the coffin was put in the morgue. There it was left with the lid open until the burial. The morgue was locked, but often there was a small window open. The window was on the long wall back towards the church bulwark, by the tool shed that stood a meter away and blocked the view so nobody would observe it. Since I often was with the caretaker I had seen this and knew that when the window was open there was a coffin in the morgue. Somewhere inside me there was a cautionary impulse. It wasn't that I thought I needed to keep from being seen but I generally still avoided being seen.

There was a small ladder behind the tool shed. The caretaker had used it for putting up the hymn numbers for mass, but he had gotten a new more beautiful carved ladder, so the old one had ended up behind the tool shed. I dragged the ladder to the window and climbed in.

Slowly I crawled up to the edge of the coffin. I sat down and looked at the body. Sat there and looked and looked. Then I began talking, long words and sentences, they just gushed out of me, all the words I knew and I played with them in every form. They changed place and became new patterns. Inside me new meanings came incessantly and it was so delightful. The person in the coffin got spirit life, looked up, smiled, became transparent and was with me. A life was rolled out, the life that the person had lived. I was in the other's presence in hisher experience, and the situation was like a film being played. I and the person in the coffin were spectators of the whole rhapsody of events and at the same time we were in them. I viewed the film as a friend of the person. First, as a small child. The person grew up and got bigger. We wandered further in the life film and new events popped up. There were confirmations, weddings, parties, and funerals. There were all emotions, joy that was expressed certain ways, sadness that was expressed other ways, some rage, but it often turned around inside without expressing itself, and fear. The fear was special for it formed ghosts, the most hideous images that didn't belong in my world of perceptions, but which still pervaded everything and everyone. Then a sound from the ordinary world penetrated.

The girl jolted, became conscious of where she was, snuck out as quietly as she had come in, crawled along the church wall and didn't stand up until she was at the house. She knew intuitively that she was not allowed to be there and she kept out of the way so nobody would detect her.

She often went up in the church steeple. There it was gloomy and there were lots of bats. They flew around and swooshed around her head. She opened the hatch and crawled up in the window niche. Then the bats suspended themselves from the roof beams. They hung in bunches like gray-black balls. Sometimes a wing flapped in the air.

I released and floated up among the bats. They were my friends and they didn't mind that I was there. They were like a big gathering. They were my friends and I had names for them. I talked to them and after a while they began flying around with me. They became like little dark clouds that twirled around me. All the bats formed a carpet that I lay on. Slire and Skydde came. The bats became like a grate. They hung together with holes between them. We flew in through one hole and out through another. We pulled colored threads through the holes so that they made a pattern. Then the bats broke out of the pattern and flew away. There were only the colored patterns left that constituted the carpet. We balanced on them. We crawled around knots and snarls in through openings and snared each other. We braided the colors together and wrapped each other in them, pulled some thread, and one of us spun like a spool in the air. The color threads turned into new patterns and swirls.

We rose with the carpet high up and saw the ground beneath us. The world consisted of colors that ran into each other and little dots and squares that stood still below us where the carpet passed over. We played, took something out of the air we called visions, threw them at each other, let them change and threw them back. Then came new visions and we continued until it was full of visions and we could assemble them into patterns you could understand.

Bang ... a door closed. I jolted and was back in the steeple.

The best game in the steeple was to sit in the hatch and look over the landscape. It was so high up that it sucked at my feet. It looked so tempting and I swept my gaze up and down, up and down till I drifted out. Slire and Skydde came and we sent out thoughts. "Let's play rolling down the church wall." That was the best game there was.

We rolled out through the hatch and rolled down the wall, the more turns the better, with the most complex movements that you could imagine, and then we floated out in a soft circle and up again. One of us first made new patterns and the others copied. Then we changed so that another took the lead and the others copied, however many times. We gathered in a pile on the ground and flew up again, parted, made pirouettes in the air, back to the hatch and rolled down again. Sometimes we made it all the way to the top of the steeple and rolled from there. There was also a lightning arrester that ran across the whole roof down to the ground. This we slid down on and spun around like spirals.

The stairs creaked, the father came up, he stroked the girl's cheek. "You're sitting here! I am going to ring the bells so you can help me catch the tab." The tab was a piece of wood that kept the clapper in place so that the bell wouldn't chime but strike complete strokes from the beginning. Then he put her down and took her inside.

On the way in the father had some things to do and when they passed the swing he put the girl there.

The evening sounds came like a serenade, the swing rocked and I was Out. The rustling of the wind formed drops of light that played catch, a dog's distant bark became blue light, like ribbons in space, the crackle under their clogs when the men walked across the yard became sparks, and their words were like a red shimmer. All was like a light show and a serenade in my world. It was like an essence, a consciousness that enticed and enchanted my mind.

The father came to get her and they went into the kitchen. The mother told her to wash her hands. She looked down at her hands. They played catch, turned and twisted. She said: "Hands, hands." They looked funny. The mother grabbed the girl and shoved her into the wash room. Her hands were hard and her words were like sticks that struck the air. The soap lathered and formed pretty bubbles. I patted them and tried to push them down in the water but that didn't work, they always popped up. The water ran over the hands, became rills which were like   glittering pearl necklaces. I followed them and they laid themselves around my feet. The bubbles also followed the glittering pearl necklaces. More and more water came on the floor and I stomped around. It was fun.

"See, what a mess you made!" The mother grabbed her and wiped the floor. The girl sank down on the floor and crawled under the table.

After the meal, the father took the girl with him to bed to rest a while. He lay down and laid the girl at eye level.

His eyes burrowed into my mind and I was carried out into something I normally wasn't in. It was like another reality. It was like seeing with different eyes, hearing with different ears, smell and taste in another way and feel …. It was both pleasant and unpleasant. The body became like something else, not only something that was, but something that was felt. Fathers hand touched my skin and first it burned, but then it went over into a pleasant sensation, like wind blowing on your skin. Father's words reached me and got me to see things, tangible things like chairs, tables, clock. In my world they were just substances that floated around without meaning, but just in the moment I was in Father's eyes they became firm and tangible, like material, that got a meaning in a different way. It was like seeing with his eyes. The father called them realities. He said: "You need to understand realities; otherwise you can't make it in life."

Every day the father spent time keeping the girl in the reality world and conveying knowledge. He got many good laughs at her way of interpreting the world and explaining what she saw and understood.

He told her about Luther nailing up his theses on the church door. For the girl, theses were the same as letters and words and she didn't understand that the words were on paper. She talked with him for hours about how Luther could first get the letters to hang together as words and then how he could get the words to stick on the church door without glue, and how he could find place for all the words on a small church door. The mother heard the girl's explanations in the kitchen and made up a funny story about how dumb and untalented Iris was to think something so dumb which she told her friends at their coffee klatches, and the they all laughed and thought it all was very funny. It wasn't intended in malice, more in amazement.

Such stories created a certain amount of interest in the phenomenon Iris and they contributed to her development in the everyday social world.

In the morning when it was totally quiet it was easy to disappear up in the ceiling. I twisted around and looked at all the familiar things. I swooped around and touched every thing. Nothing could break and nothing was forbidden. It was only people you couldn't touch because they were apt to be uncomfortable and scared. There were plenty of decorative knick-knacks, fancy small figurines that children were not allowed to touch otherwise, but when I was Out I could fall on them, swoop around them, go through them, do anything, anything. I got little and clung on them like climbing in a tree, I danced around them and went in and out through all cavities and looked out through their eyes.

Slire came and took up the chase. He raced before and behind, over and under me so I would lose my concentration. He teased, disappeared, and came out from the most impossible places and I was startled. Skydde came and stayed by my side. He showed me a bunch of words that played in the atmosphere, words that came from people, but also words that just were there. There were words I had heard people say and other words I had seen them thinking. It was strong words like "dead, sick, abandoned, imprisoned, shot" and there were warm words like "love, happiness, warmth, care", there were angry words like "damn, the devil, hell" and a bunch of exclamations that people used when scared.

When people uttered words a substance radiated out from them. It might be pleasant but it could also be poisonous. There were lots of different mixtures and Skydde helped sort out what was what and how I could think about the different substances. It might be something dishonest and then it got sooty and covered with something bad. Skydde made forms of the words and hung them up in pictures. It might be a meadow, and there he stuck a horse. It could be a stove and there he stuck a log of wood. It could be plot where a person was lying motionless and on it he stuck a churchyard and a coffin. It could be a big hospital and on it he stuck white coats running in the hallways. It could be a building with window bars and on it he stuck prisoners. I had heard a lot about the war in Algiers that was going on but I didn't understand what war was, except that it was miserable and terrible. Skydde showed me uniforms that were running and shooting. He showed how some on the other side fell. He showed me some in the own ranks that fell. What had only been miserable and terrible became more tangible and he showed me how they dug a mass grave.

The girl jolted. Somebody leaned over her and spoke to her. "Are you having a bad dream, you are soaked with sweat and you were screaming bloody murder." Life got normal again.

The girl seldom slept. She didn't fall asleep until everyone else was asleep, and awoke before anyone else. She had a small green night light and if it wasn't on she whimpered continuously and the mother could not bear that sound.

I fixed my gaze on the lamp and sank into the light green shimmering, and so I was in another dimension. There everything was like water and air, like wind and movement. I just soared in it and floated along as on a carpet. It was full this green and also it was nothing, it wasn't empty, but it still wasn't anything firm, but it changed shape the whole time, and I was there in the form so that it was gently soft around me and I was pulled up in lovely whirling eddy.

My gaze fixed on the window. It was black at first, then it got grayer and grayer and little by little light. I was drawn to Father who was awakening.

The father went out in the kitchen and put on coffee. He lit the stove. The girl tiptoed after and crawled up in the corner by the stove and sat there rocking.

When I entered puberty the whole situation changed. For one thing my whole world got much blacker and scarier. There came black demonic images and scary sounds and lights. For another, Father's working with me to get me interested in the outer reality had lured me to it. Father asked me to be in the ordinary reality instead of in mine. He said unless I was in the ordinary reality I would seem so strange to other people that nobody would want to associate with me. He said he couldn't struggle with me if I continually disappeared into my own world. He wanted me to cooperate and he would teach me all he knew about the ordinary reality. He told me that there was so much excitement and joy in it that surely with time I would get a feeling and experience of it.

That didn't happen the way he painted it, but I have received much else and I am glad that he continued the struggle so long that I could go on and work my way into the ordinary reality on my own.

CHAPTER 5

On the church wall

When she was twelve years old the girl discovered what death was. Before, there been no distinction for her between the material and the immaterial. Emma's body lay in a coffin in the churchyard, but Emma herself was still around and was with Iris sometimes. Some time before she had heard about a person that died from being gored by a bull.

Death was that a person went Out from the body and never came back to it. That she was buried in a coffin in the churchyard and didn't live in her room anymore. Gradually came the awareness that there was such a thing as a beginning. A beginning was when a calf was born; it was new, then it existed, and then it was finished when it died. The animals were butchered and eaten, but people were buried without anything done to them. Iris' farmor and farfar died half a year apart and four elderly neighbors also died around this time. This caused Iris to become interested in the subject of death. That some people stopped walking around was perplexing. Those around the dead person cried and became black on the outside and you weren't allowed to laugh or scream or speak loudly for a time. Then it was all over, as if the person had never existed.

She was preoccupied with death for a long time; she talked about death, sat and looked at the churchyard and the tombstones, and tried to comprehend it. She became increasingly conscious of the human, that human beings were something different from all else, and that you needed to think in a different way when it concerned humans. This insight puzzled her; she didn't know where it came from and how to react to it. It was difficult and painful and unpleasant and still she was drawn to this special world.

From time to time there was a funeral in the church and then she was often there. She loved it. Partly because the caretaker August was there. She had often been with him when he dug the grave and she remembered his account about the deceased. Partly because people at a funeral became at one with themselves, became distinct and cried in a lovely way. The pastor allowed her to be there. He felt that she probably would benefit from it in the future. The grandmother, on the other hand forbid her from attending the funerals of other families. She was afraid of death and thought that the girl would be sullied and it was abnormal for wanting to be included in such sad occasions.

The girl lay on the church wall and observed everything happening during the funeral. There were many people gathered around the casket which was standing on two trestles. The opaque ones were always dressed in black and stood still. The transparent ones were dressed in different colors, had their hair put up, and walked around together with the dead one. They paid no attention to the pastor and the people in black.

The people in black were in the pastor's atmosphere. This was a precious moment for the girl, since they were crying and thereby became comprehensible.

When the funeral was over and people were on their way home the girl sat by the gate and observed them. Surprised she noticed that only a few were left, the people in black, and she wondered where all the others who had been there had gone. She ran down to the father in the barn and asked: "Where are they?" He didn't understand what she was referring to. He looked at her kindly and said: "You certainly are one of a kind!"

So one day she understood what death was. She sat on the church wall. Behind her were all the graves, and there all the dead ones lay. In front of her was the farmyard and there were her father and all the uncles and they were alive. Then she had the realization that the dead ones lay in the earth and moldered and were no more, and the living on the other side of the wall grew up and aged and changed and could move and talk. And she thought: "That's it. The ones who lie in the earth can't move and can't talk. But the ones in the yard can and they can understand each other." She understood that when you are alive you can change but when you are dead you can't. And then she understood that all those who were Out, the transparent ones who had been at the funeral together with the dead one, they didn't change; they had no substance that was grounded and changeable. When she saw that she thought: Aha, That's the difference between life and death, that the physical part ends up in the earth and can't move anymore. Then one is dead. As long as you are on earth and can move you are alive.

And immediately she thinks: But why are people unfriendly and refuse to talk with each other when they know they'll die and lose that contact.

She discovered acrimony all around and was amazed that most people had somebody they were enemies with, sometimes constantly, sometimes now and then. They said words that she could see hurt the other, sometimes so the person became all black inside, sometimes red, and sometimes nothingy and absent. She understood that both the speaker and the hearer got sick inside from this.

Sometimes it got black for someone unintentionally and hostility started from that, but often there was something that you were supposed to be unfriendly about from the beginning, and that's what was so incomprehensible.

She thought about the time when two of the mother's siblings had come from Göteborg with their families to visit and leave their kids for the summer. The girl's aunt, Tuttan, came in to the mother in the kitchen, exuberantly cordial and gracious and bubbling. She talked about her hair, which she had dyed in the same colors as the mother's, who had naturally beautiful chestnut brown hair. The girl who sat in a hidden corner of the kitchen to avoid being the subject of effusiveness saw that the aunt's cheerfulness came out in the atmosphere level with the face, but further down, about level with the stomach there was something dark that radiated and pulsated and was mean and just looking for somebody to be mad at. The dark pressed up against the light around the face. The girl saw that the light and the dark created a tension in the mother, a discomfort, and she thought it was fascinating that their conversation was so ambiguous, that there were several things going on at the same time.

The mother was making pastry dough. She took a big hunk of butter from the churn and put it in the dough. Then she went into the cool room and skimmed lots of thick cream from the bowl of morning milk that she also added to the dough.

The girl saw how the dark blew all the light from the aunt. "Shame on you" the aunt said. "To be using real butter and cream in dough. It's unfair that you farmers can use butter and cream by the pound in your food. Look at all the hungry children running around on the streets in Göteborg and don't even have salt for the gruel. And consider that people in the city have to buy margarine and maybe an ounce of cream for the coffee after Sunday dinner. For the whole family."

The girl saw that the mother was considering if she should let this pass and she knew the only problem the she had regarding the cream was that she would get criticized for not using all of it. She said: "But it doesn't help those kids if I make my dough without butter and cream."

Actually the aunt agreed with her about this. She was too smart to think that it would help the children in Göteborg if her sister stopped using butter and cream in her cooking. So she changed the subject. "You should be ashamed, having such luxury that you can cook and bake like that. *We* other siblings had to get out in the world and work. But you got spoiled, got to lie in a hospital, and was cared for by grandfather, and by the way, it was thanks to you that we all became mother-less. And to top it all you married rich. You ought to realize how tough we have had it and not get up on your high horse."

The girl saw that the mother's atmosphere disappeared and it got gray around her. She was, as usual, completely crushed and couldn't get a word out. Their brother Otto came into kitchen, attracted by the excited voice. Tuttan held her forehead and said: "Oh, I can't be here, I just get a headache!"

Otto said accusingly to the mommy: "Have you irritated Tuttan again.

They left the kitchen and silence returned.

The girl had no sympathy for the mother, but it was such a baffling curiosity with these quarrels that were in the atmosphere even before there was anything to be mad about. And it amazed her that words could have such power over people, that the mother could be completely destroyed --just by words.

The mother had stopped the baking and stood completely still and quiet. She went into the pantry and closed the door behind her. When she didn't know how to act, when her atmosphere had turned black or disappeared the mother had the habit of going into the pantry. It was a small room with neat shelves, insulated against the summer's heat and the frigid cold of winter. The door had a regular handle on the inside but only a nail on the outside to keep the children from getting in and raiding the cookie jar. She stood there looking at the shelves, organizing and enjoying the sight of all the good food, nice and orderly. This was her kingdom, here she ruled, here was nobody else who decided and nobody who attacked her. When she was glad again she came out and continued with the baking.

There was actually no reason the girl thought, why people should be unfriendly and not talk to each other while they were alive. It is such a short time, such a small part of eternity that they can be in contact with each other. Eternity for Iris was where you came from and where you went. Eternity was the real reality that was behind the ordinary reality.

Right then the father came to her on the church wall and said: "What are you thinking about?" She asked, why are we born, when we have to die anyway, and then the father laughed and said there is a long life and lots of experiences between these two irrevocable states.

You come into being because two people love each other and they have children, and you leave because the body doesn't have the strength to renew itself anymore. In the meantime you are a human being made of flesh and blood, and have the possibility to think, feel, and do things to feed and house and clothe yourself, and above all to be together with other people like we are here on the farm. That is happiness" he said. He sighed and continued: "I wish you could stay here in the ordinary world and not be inside yourself so much. Because then you are so strange for other people that they can't make contact with you."

Then Iris told him she had figured out what death was. He understood. Iris asked: "But why then are people enemies and stop talking to each other? Why aren't they friends and talk to each other *when they know that they are going to die?*"

The father answered: "Because they don't understand that.

If they understood it then they'd know there is no reason to not talk with each other. That *you* understand we have to die doesn't mean that *they* understand it. Why don't *you* explain it to them?"

He walked away and the girl remained sitting on the church wall. First, she thought about what he had said: that *you* understand doesn't mean that *they* understand. It was a completely revolutionary thought. Up to then she had thought that everybody understood what she understood and in addition much, much more. They were regular so they knew everything. That she would understand something that they didn't was totally outside the realm of possibility for her.

Then she thought about the real world, which was known to her and where she could always be, and where everything was calm, and everything was as it should be. It would be much simpler to be Out than to engage in people-thinking, and she sat there and thought that she could choose to remain in the real world, and not care about the ordinary world, with all the death and all the people.

In the real world everything is clarified. It can be hard and complex, but it is clear and visible, and there are no hidden agendas. In the real world, together with Slire and Skydde she had what she thought of as real togetherness. To play the whole time, to fly around, that was life, the only reality. When she was in the real world it got harder and harder to return to the ordinary. It was like being asleep and not wanting to wake up. And in that state it got more and more painful to let go and tumble down in the ordinary and to get up and go to the toilet and get involved with all the physical. The transition to the ordinary world finally became nightmarish. It was like she flew into a cone and landed in her body. And when she was in the ordinary world, the real world became like a dream, something that was completely different.

At the same time the ordinary world had taken on a great attractiveness because it was so unpredictable and full of shocking surprises. People reacted so unexpectedly, they said such fascinating things.

Her father had said that he wished for her to be in the ordinary world rather than the real world, and associate with people there, and choose the ordinary world because she had a task there, to tell people that they should not stop talking to each other, because there is death.

It wasn't at all tempting for Iris to be in the ordinary world. It was too difficult, she didn't understand how it hung together, didn't understand its values. It was perplexing, like a coat that you had to put on the right way and with the right side out, and you were supposed to be somebody other than yourself, somebody that fit in, and it was difficult and awkward and complicated. She struggled with that thought and weighed the known easy, against the difficult, complicated, messy, awkward, and incomprehensible. For a long, long time.

She sat on the church wall. She felt that she had a task. Finally she thought: "Well if he thinks it is good, it must be good so then I'll opt for that.

She decided to remain in the ordinary reality for as long as she would live and not bother with the real anymore. She bid farewell. She thought about Slire and Skydde and their games and how it had been. She was thankful for that: it had been a lot of fun, it was vibrant. And now it was over.

She decided to talk to people and tell them they were mortal, so they could stop shutting each other out, because they could do that soon enough when they died. There was no point in doing it while they lived.

She had a mission. To become ordinary in order to be able to talk with ordinary people.

CHAPTER 6

To become ordinary

To be forced to be in the ordinary world had been tedious, awkward, and painful for Iris. She had to change her clothes, and she had to *like* changing her clothes. And she had to like that clothes smelled clean and not of Iris. Iris couldn't understand how people could like the smell of newly washed clothes. To Iris they smelled strange. She liked when a person smelled of sweat, because sweat smells of a human being. She discovered that if she ironed her clothes they smelled ironed and at least didn't smell clean then. Consequently she always ironed her clothes. All her clothes: underpants, socks, wool sweaters.

Iris' skin was very sensitive to light touching, which could sting or burn like fire. Therefore she always used to put her flannel shirts on inside out so that the nice soft side was next to the skin. She also didn't want the buttons on the front because the fabric gapped between the buttons which she didn't like. Therefore, she used to wear them backwards with the buttons in the back. Then the collar was on the front of her neck, which had the advantage that she could turn it up and hide her head behind it to protect her face from the coarse sweaters, and also to hide from the world. And there, behind the collar she breathed the strange smell of new wash away and filled it with Iris smell.

Iris often induced some form of pain in her body to feel that she was alive. She scratched her skin till it bled and licked the wound to make it sting. She pulled up her lip and sucked it against her nostrils and picked on the skin inside her lip till it bled. Then she rubbed the wound with lemon or salt to make it really sting. She put soap on her finger and rubbed her eye with it so it stung and the eye teared up and got red.

Iris had difficulty sitting at the table like all the others. She preferred to sit under the table, but when she did sit on a chair she would lean over almost with her face in the plate to avoid noticing if the others were looking at her. And she would hum continually to drown them out. The humming gave her a form which kept the forms of the others at a distance so they couldn't invade her. She didn't want to eat with a knife and fork, only with a spoon. At home this was ok since the others ate mostly with a spoon too, but when they had company this wouldn't do.

Iris engaged in a lot of rituals. When she and the family were about to leave to visit somebody, for her it was something new, strange, and undesirable impending. Then by going to the toilet —even if she didn't need to, drinking some water —even if she wasn't thirsty, taking out her boots —even if it wasn't raining, and walking up the stairs four times she got ready to leave the known and venture out in the impending unknown. Only then could she sit down, put on shoes and coat and go out.

All this she had to give up if she was going to be ordinary.

It wouldn't do to put the shirt on inside out and backwards. It wouldn't do to sit under the table. It wouldn't do with a bunch of rituals. It wouldn't do to rub soap in the eyes or salt in the wound inside her lip.

The first thing Iris did in order to adjust and become ordinary was learning to speak casually. She had seen that when ordinary people were talking with each other it was often about something different than the thoughts they had inside them. Iris was out on the town with her mother. They met an old acquaintance. Mother asked enthusiastically: "How are you doing these days?"

The acquaintance answered: "Fine, thank you. How about yourself?"

Mother said: "Everyone is out planting now, since it is spring."

Iris asked herself how you talk casually like that and wanted to learn how to do it. She tried to stop thinking and repeated to herself every word they said so it would sound exactly the same and be equally thoughtless. But she didn't have a lot of success with it.

She also practiced conversation starters. A good starter is: "Where are you off to?" or "Do you want come along ...?" or "What do we do now?" or "How do you like ...?"

This worked much better. Because once she had spoken the starter she just had to stand there and let the other one talk.

The problem was what if she got a return question. She learned to duck such questions by starting to tell about something, anything whatever. She had also figured out exactly how long she could talk before it started to bore the other one. She used to ask if the person was in a hurry because then she had to shorten her story.

When the other person in turn began to tell her about something Iris didn't understand a thing. Everything in her thoughtless talk was without substance to Iris with no fixed points to focus on. Then she would wait until she heard a word that meant something to her. Then, when the other stopped talking Iris posed a question about that word: "You said something about..."

People loved to flaunt their knowledge and a good starter was to say: "Do you know anything about ..." In this manner she could milk the other person for talk. Some people didn't fall for it but on some others it worked very well. She started to seek out people she could talk with this way. She gathered up everything she learned and combined it with the old stuff she knew and created images and films in her head that she could call up when needed.

If the other kept talking too long, it got awkward and then Iris used one of her pre-learned enders: "It was nice to see you" or "Apropos of nothing ..." or "By the way I have to ...". That way she could put an end to it.

To become ordinary, Iris also practiced general knowledge: what you should say "ugh" and "gross" about and what one should say "good" and "nice" about. Almost everything the other one said that contained the word tax, or politics, or the neighbor lady you could say "ugh" or "Oh that's awful" about. Anything that had to do with science, "they have come up with" or "medicines" you could say "good" or "isn't that fantastic" about. Iris became expert at getting people to talk about things that you could say "ugh" or "gross" about.

Iris had the greatest difficulty with casual talk. If she started talking about something that was not casual, something that was meaningful for her, the other one got bored, discovered she was in a hurry and disappeared.

Iris thought a lot about where the first thing one says to another comes from. When she met someone she would stand there and look at himher and wait for some word or sentence to pop into her head that she could say to himher. But no word came and she just stood there and looked at the other one. After a while the other got irritated by Iris' silent attention: "What are you staring at?" And then she could answer that question very concretely: "I am staring at you because I think you are an interesting person." Then the other might answer: "You are crazy", or sometimes interestedly: "Really? And what do you see?" And then the conversation was off and running.

If the person didn't pay any attention to Iris' interest heshe would remain in Iris' mind for hours afterwards.

In general life consisted of Iris trying to be social, trying to go out with the girls she had grown up with, meeting boys, going to the movies and dances. She handled it very well, but she was so insensitive to all the unspoken assumptions that she often put her foot in her mouth. Jokes and irony were totally lost on her. She never even noticed it but her friends were sometimes ashamed of her and scolded her. Physical touching was also a problem. She had learned that she was not supposed to run away, but to stay and talk, which she did. As soon as somebody got too forward she would start to discuss all kinds of issues, and often the boys tired of it so she escaped.

Iris also struggled a lot with what you should like. She had learned that you should like different things. You should like being cute, and you should be delighted and smile when people said you were cute. You just had to do that. On that subject there was no choice. You should not like when young girls used make-up or wore long pants and one should not like parties and pleasures. But Iris had no opinion on any of this. The difficulty for her was that you had to express your feelings with your face and whole body. But Iris always looked unchangeably contented. So when she, in order to be ordinary, said she disliked something at random nobody believed her. She wasn't received as skeptically when she asserted that she liked something. The big problem was to like and dislike the correct things. There she missed constantly.

To be ordinary she also had to learn about the clock. Little by little she was able to figure out the hands: ten of four, five-thirty. But she had trouble connecting what appeared on the clock to the fact that it was time to eat or go to school. She got no impulse to go to school even though she knew that she was supposed to go to school at "eight o'clock". She failed in this and for a long time it made her feel stupid or failed as a human being. If you can't tell time you are not quite normal. But she saw to it that there was always someone who told her when it was time to do something.

The Iris-world was in a way, very complicated especially

as seen from the outside and still in another way very simple inside. This is a difficult paradox to understand; how something as simple as life itself can get as complicated as it did for her. One the one hand she was physically well developed, looked quite normal and was able to handle most things, but on the other hand she constantly got snarled up and frustrated by the simplest actions that all normal people seemed able to handle.

She could be cleverer and come up with better solutions than anybody else and at the same time she could be hopeless and not understand the most elementary instructions. Sometimes she knew about things before they happened and could prevent and react to them with exquisite brilliance. At other times she was liable to climb into a situation in the most tactless manner imaginable.

She could sometimes have a deep understanding which helped people make contact with their deepest soul and actually extricate themselves from difficult problems, and at the same time she could laugh and joke about somebody's ill fortune.

A neighbor was at the kitchen table talking about her son soon having to start school. He wore glasses and was a little late in development and was very dependent on his mother.

"What if he gets laughed at by the other children" she said. "He has no talent for sports, what if he can't handle gym." She worked herself up more and more and was soon completely hysterical.

The girl was listening and said: "But is it dangerous now?"

"He probably won't learn to read and write, what a scandal that will be" the neighbor continued. "But is it dangerous now?"

the girl asked and held her gaze.

The neighbor hesitated.

"But is it dangerous now?"

"Yes, but ..." the neighbor said and lost her concentration.

"Is it dangerous now?"

"No" the neighbor said and relaxed a little. "Actually not. I can always talk with the teacher. And I can accompany him if need be. And, besides there is the whole summer before he starts."

Everything was simple in the girl's world. The only thing that existed was what existed just then. Nothing else interfered so everything was just exactly what it was. The girl thought that everyone knew everything, that they knew more than she, so she could learn from them. She liked to learn, to find out more, to collect information and make lists. To place different things on her internal maps and then follow them. She thought that whatever she knew everyone else also knew, so there couldn't be any reason for her to tell about something unless somebody asked. Also, she could never recall her knowledge about something if nobody thought about it or said something that was included in her lists. If it was there, she could surf backwards in her head and pick out the film, or image, or list and see everything it contained, like the search engine on the PC.

The older she got, the more she collected, gave words to, could talk about, and added up, so completely new insights were created. She loved to listen to the radio, especially if it was something about science or human problems. There was the Radio Doctor and Liz Asklund's mail box.

It was not just a matter of listening, it was something more. When certain persons were speaking it was as if they had a giant library with them that so they could open a book and look in when needed, and then the girl could see what was in the book, not just what the person himself registered but also some things that he was not conscious of. The girl thought this was fun and played with it and tried to capture as much as possible from other people.

Many people, often the ones in her proximity, had a lot of junk in their library, meanness, trash talk, sensationalism, naked ladies. They were uninteresting. Others only had stuff that was available all around, and that was also not interesting. But a few had something entirely different.

The church caretaker August was one of those who had a lot of exciting things inside him. When he was digging a grave Iris would sit on the edge and watch. August glanced at the tomb stone and saw the names of the ones who had been buried there before. Or he might pick up a bone or a skull and start to speak about them. He talked about their life. There was drama, poverty, hardships, unhappy loves, how things used to be in the old days. The girl saw that he didn't have personal knowledge about the things he described, but she also saw that he absorbed it from the atmosphere and it flowed through him and got its form from the fact that it was he who was doing the telling.

The girl would then repeat these stories to the father and anyone else who wanted to listen and then they said: "That

August, he sure tells some stories."

"That is one who has a doubtful relationship with the truth" one of the girl's uncles said. The girl did not understand this for she had seen everything he told about so she knew it existed in the real reality.

Then came summer break; the children that used to be on the farm had grown into adolescents. The summer kids came from the big city, and the ones who were a little crosswise with the law also came. The girl looked at them with different eyes. She saw a person, an individual, a human being. She had learned how people talk with each other. She had learned a number of starters so she could begin, the other one answered and the conversation was started. It was a lot of fun, and everything else she used to do got put aside. She had practiced a thousand different ways to say "hi", she had stood in front of the mirror and practiced until she got it to look pleasing to her.

The girl loved to practice different things. She didn't want to sit alone anymore, she constantly wanted to try the new things she had learned and practiced. She wanted to be with the others and talk and talk. Sometimes they got very tired of her and thought her a tedious pest but this didn't bother her for there were always new ones to hang out with.

That summer wasn't like the other summers. There were not the same kind of games and play as before. Inside Iris the world was new, not such that the old world was gone but like it somehow was renewed. She didn't know what it was, but it got muddled and confused in her. Before, she had sought some corner, or a swing, a place from where to observe in her way, and be with them in her way, without being engaged, but this didn't suffice anymore. It wasn't interesting. It was as if a magnet was pulling her closer and closer to this confusing, muddled, painful state which was unbearable and impossible to stay in but which it was also impossible to escape from.

Some youths were sitting in small groups talking and they were up to something the girl couldn't comprehend. Before, everyone had been in the same atmosphere but now it was like they all had their own atmospheres. The girl had been able to see the patterns, and had been in them, sitting on the milk platform, in a haystack, or on some machine. But now this didn't work anymore. They were all around her, each in their own atmosphere, and she didn't know how to deal with it. Before, she was together with the people working in the fields or with the father in the barn, but now it was like the old just didn't exist anymore.

Then the girl discovered two atmospheres that met. It was two young people standing by the church wall. The boy looked at the girl and his atmosphere came together towards hers. The girl looked back at him and her atmosphere gathered and was directed towards him. Then words came out of them and they walked back and forth and seemed to understand each other. They laughed together and became serious together.

This was totally new for the girl. Where did the things he said come from? And how did she know how to answer? Suddenly the world was all changed again. There was something that was entirely different from what the girl had known before.

Time after time Iris came to the barn and asked the daddy:

"What are they doing?"

He didn't know who "they" were, and not at all what she meant. And she herself couldn't explain.

It took him a couple of weeks to realize what she meant. Once when she stood by the church wall and uttered her laconic: "What are they doing?" he followed her gaze and saw two young people in love that stood there talking and joshing with each other. Seeing that made him very pleased, he realized that she had discovered something about life, the life of people which she had been totally uninterested in before.

The daddy got eager and started telling about the birds and the bees, about sexuality and relationships. But in the middle of his discourse Iris said no less laconically: "What are they doing?" Then he understood that he was talking to her at the wrong level. He hesitated and thought for a while.

Then he said: "Look at the girl, how she looks. Then go inside and look in the mirror and see if your face looks the same way as hers. If you don't there is something missing in the mirror and then you can change that."

What she had seen was that there was something between the two young people --their love. The boy said something and then something happened in the girl. She answered and then something happened in the boy. And then they ended up in a common field, an emotion field.

Iris had discovered emotions.

She became happy. She stood in front of the mirror and

stared at herself until she saw something different than Iris. Stared until she looked into the eyes and saw a person. She got scared. It was strange. She remained sitting on the floor a long time, shaking.

Then she went in front of the mirror again. Looked, stared. Then suddenly she saw that strange image of herself again. The familiar Iris disappeared and she saw something else. What this was she couldn't say but it was something different.

The father had said she should look at other girls, how they looked and that if what she saw in the mirror didn't look like other girls then there was something wrong with the image, and that was what she needed to change. This was concrete, this she could understand.

She saw that she didn't look a bit like the girl by the church wall, but it wasn't primarily a question of looks. She understood that she could change so she would look like the girl. This was the first time ever that she made a comparison.

She had seen how the girl in love had smiled and how her eyes shone, and how her face blushed. There in front of the mirror Iris tried smiling to make it look like hers but it became an ugly grimace. Then she understood that there was something special in the girl that caused it to be a smile and not a grimace, that her eyes didn't look like watery pig eyes, and that her color was so alive; it looked like velvet, and not like Iris who just looked like she was warm. The father had said that if she practiced how she looked she would get this feeling, but no matter how much she practiced she never got any feeling. Finally she understood that it was a special state inside her that would make her look like the girl, and that it had to be possible to find that state within herself.

For one year she continued to practice. As soon as she saw a girl looking at a boy she ran over and started looking at them. They got very irritated but she got a glimpse of how the girl looked.

Then she went to her mirror and practiced. She practiced looking at her hair and brushing it. She practiced looking at her mouth and it was not beautiful with a bunch of sores under the lip.

She had to stop pulling off skin. It was a difficult practice, but she got it. She could move her mouth and smile. It often looked like a grimace, but it was also possible to produce a smile.

She practiced several hours per day. She had fun and her world became completely different. Everything that had interested her earlier was past and other people, other humans, talking with others became overshadowing.

Before she had seen every person's atmosphere, but it had not been essentially different from a cat's or a dog's. But now it was the person herself that was interesting, all the different people, that they were wholly distinct persons, and that they could change any minute and that anything could come out of their mouth and that the trick was to see in the atmosphere what they meant and to answer that. The girl was totally entranced by all this.

After a year the father figured it was time to go out and try it in real life. The girl got the assignment to try it on boys in the neighborhood, and she did. They just groaned and wondered what new kind of craziness she had come up with. Once, a family came to visit. There was a young man with them and she played out her whole repertoire. He became interested and they "played" for a while, but then he wanted to grab her and kiss her and then all the stereotypy behaviors came back. She had learned one step, but not what to when that step worked.

So she didn't find that feeling by looking for it.

A new buddy of the girl's brother who didn't know her came to the house. He said Hi to her the way the young people by the church wall had talked with each other. She went over to him to see what this was. Then something happened with her body. It suddenly became filled with something she didn't recognize. The normal tension that was in her released and she got warm all over, and her whole body was pulsating. Suddenly she felt her body in a way she had never felt before. And in the same moment she understood that this is what she had seen in the two young people. She turned around and ran into her closet where the mirror hung and, even before she got there she knew that now her face looked like the face of the girl in love had looked.

She stood before the mirror and looked to see if her eyes glittered and her smile was a smile and not a grimace, and how the color in her face looked. The only thing that she saw as different was the smile. Her smile had suddenly got a new meaning; there was something in the smile that she had never seen in herself.

She was very pleased and walked around with the smile on her face a long time. Her brother saw it and asked: "What are you smirking for?" But for her this was not a smirk.

Forty years later I was at a reunion in my hometown. A man with gray hair asked me to dance and asked: "Aren't you Iris?"
   "Yes, that's right. Have we met before?" I asked.
   He said: "Yes, but you probably don't remember."
   He related how he as a twelve-year old had moved to my town and on the first day of school my brother had brought him home to us. When he came into our kitchen I was standing there. He turned to me and said a normal "Hi". And then my whole look suddenly changed. I went over to him and said "Hi" back he said and then he got all perplexed and didn't know what to do and just stood there. Suddenly I turned and disappeared and he couldn't understand what he had done wrong.
   "And you have no idea how many nights I dreamed of you" he said. "You occupied my mind for very long time. I didn't dare approach you and got shy and tongue-tied. And you didn't notice anything." And in fact I hadn't. He laughed and said: "You were actually my first love.."

Iris was beginning to see that a person could say something --that Iris didn't comprehend—to another person and that the other person responded with something –that Iris didn't comprehend either—and what she then started to discover was that there was something that distinguished people from animals, that there was something specifically human. Then she became fascinated with how humans were on the inside, what distinguished her from the animals, a fascination she has to this day.

She started to discover a whole new world, and the big difference for her was that the thing with animals and plants was a given, not alterable, except that one can nurture or destroy it, but that humans were constructed in a different way. And this led her to become totally fascinated by this new thing. But she still couldn't observe herself in the way she was now beginning to observe other people. She discovered consciously that communication exists. Somebody said something to her and it affected her whole body. She saw a bridge and actually entered into the small field, in the ordinary world, without feeling like she was drowning.

To her it looked like life actually was. She had no reference as to how it should be or used to be, she couldn't make any comparisons with others, or even see any commonality. The way it was in her world is that she stood still without thinking consciously of anything and thoughts just came and somehow steered her so that's what happened. Sometimes it was in the atmosphere and sometimes it was focused on something specific. It could be some little detail that absorbed all her attention, and then it was in that detail she found herself unable to shift her focus to something else until it vanished by itself. The people surrounding her were just the environment, she was not present in it but she was at one with the atmosphere surrounding her and them, and which for her was the real world. This caused her to define situations differently from others and consequently she wasn't predictable and could react totally unexpectedly to almost anything.

A man came from the social services in Goteborg to bring a summer child. He said to the father: "So nice to meet your daughter."

Iris answered: "But I am always like this!"

The man blushed and got embarrassed and said something apologetic to the father. He didn't understand that the father didn't know what Iris had responded to. She hadn't responded to his words but to the thought he had while he said it was nice to meet the daughter: "Ugh what an annoying and ugly kid. Can this be a good place for a summer child? She really should learn how to behave."

A neighbor's wife came to visit. The daddy said to her: "I see you got a new hairdo." She answered: "Ugh, yes my hair doesn't look at all like what I had imagined."

Iris could see that she didn't think that the hairdo was a disaster at all, but she said what she said because she wanted a more flattering response from the father. But Iris had begun to learn that you shouldn't respond to what people thought but to the words they uttered. So Iris answered: "Yes, it does really look kind of bad."

But that was wrong also.

The girl got confused. She went to the daddy and asked if you should respond to what the words were or to what people meant in the atmosphere. The daddy said she should try doing a mix and responding with something that was in between.

It took the girl a year and a thousand mistakes to figure out how she should answer. But, slowly she got better at it. She couldn't go beyond what the other person said but had to stay within the field that was delineated by her words. Any urge or wish of her own to talk with somebody about something she did not have. However, if somebody asked her about something it was easy for her to answer, otherwise she remained silent.

A bunch of people sat around the kitchen table and talked excitedly about how deceitfully a man had behaved. Iris as usual sat under the table and listened to the others. The young man had asked a girl if she wanted to marry him and she had said yes. After that some time had passed and he had not contacted her, and at the next dance he had danced with others and gone home with somebody else. How could he propose, and then just ignore her?

Iris listened to the conversation and realized that they were describing a situation she herself had witnessed when she had been hiding behind the church wall listening to a group of young people that used to sit there. She had heard the young man ask the girl if she would like to marry him, and she saw the context in which he posed his question and she also saw that the girl had heard something completely different than what he meant. But it never occurred to Iris that she should try to straighten things out, she just registered it and as usual did nothing.

But now that she heard how this whole group of people around the kitchen table were all upset over how mean and irresponsible he had been and how much he had hurt the girl, Iris crawled out, laid her chin on the table and said: "But he only *asked*."

"Yes, that's what we are saying."

They didn't understand what she was saying but she didn't

know any other way to say it. "He only *asked*" she said again.

"Yes he proposed."

She said again: "He only *asked*."

Then there was a man in the group who understood what Iris meant: "I see, he didn't mean to propose, he only asked if there would be any point in proposing to her." It got totally quiet around the table. And that's exactly what happened. Finally somebody remembered that the girl had actually mentioned that the boy had said: "Could you imagine marrying me?"

A few years later a teacher was talking about the delinquents in the Margaretelund reform school. He said they were reprobates who didn't obey God's commandments and that everyone who came into contact with them was sullied and that that they had no right to live and should be eradicated from the earth.

This caused a conflict in Iris. One evening on her way to the station she had seen how a friend of hers got dragged into an alley by two regular boys who were going to rape her. One of the Margaretelunders, that the teacher was now denouncing, was coming in the opposite direction and she said: "Help" and pointed.

He saw what was about to happen in the alley, beat the boys up so they ran, and accompanied Iris and her friend to the station.

This didn't square with what the teacher said about them. It was two regular boys who had been bad and the margaretelunder who had helped the girl. She saw that even the teacher was stuck in the small valuation field and couldn't see the big valuation-free field. And his view that they should be eradicated from the earth also conflicted with what she had learned: that life should be revered. The daddy had taught this to her to get her to stop her sadistic playing with animals. Finally she said emphatically to the teacher: "You are wrong."

And then she saw how his train of thought got all disrupted and that he realized how it looked in the atmosphere and that he had got into a situation where he was ashamed of what he had said but that he couldn't take it back.

It resulted in him getting mad at Iris. He sent her out in the cloak room followed by her desk and then he slammed the door. She righted the desk, put things back in order and went home.

It was experiences like this that made her realize that people saw only a narrow slice of reality and that they didn't see what lay behind the situation, that they didn't see the larger context. But she knew if you just waited you would see what was behind it.

As time went by she learned to demonstrate the big field as a reality to people stuck in the small valuation field until their fixation on it let go and they could see the big field. Their concerns, what they were stuck in, eased off and suddenly they could speak in a wholly different way and actually solve the problem.

She learned little by little that it was a question of two dissimilar fields. One, a small near-sighted one where some people find themselves and where all events are disconnected from their larger context and one set of valuations obtains, and a large valuation-free field where the larger context is found and where the explanation for events is entirely different than it is for people stuck in the near-sighted field.

The natural is to be in the large field – in the real world – but when a person's ego or values take over she sinks inexorably down into the small field –in the ordinary world – like the teacher had done.

In the case of animals and plants there was no gap between the material and immaterial, but in humans there could be gaps in many strange ways. It was like there were empty holes inside people, and out from those holes came destructive things. She could see that it was the body that got scared and that it started a reaction that wasn't controlled by reason and might take on any kind of expression. And she could see that the body did this -- as wrong and desperate as it might be -- in order to survive. She could see that what was in the head wasn't in accordance with the impulses steering the body.

What she saw was that the gaps could be closed if only the person was prepared to be playful. She knew that then the person would be able to change inside by words, or by play, or by something that dislodged the little field she was stuck in. It never occurred to her to tell them this. But if somebody had asked her: "Iris, what should I do?" she could have shown them.

The mother, who had grown up in a sanitarium and not met her maternal grandparents until she was seven years old, had a father who lived in Skåne. She had met him once for about one hour when she was sixteen. Then he had had a confrontation with her grandfather. They had argued and the father had bolted away. She had heard from her siblings that he lived alone as a hermit not associating with anyone. He did day labor on farms to earn his living. She got a letter from him asking her to come down for a visit.

When the mother and father were newly married they had biked down to see him. He started by totally crushing the mother for her looks. He insulted her and told the vilest stories about her mother. When they had been there for about two hours they turned around and rode home again. Many years later he sent a letter and apologized and wanted the family to come down for a visit again.

The whole family rode down on a tandem bike, the father, the mother, the brother, a cousin and Iris. The father had reinforced the frame, the package carrier and the front seat. When they got there the grandfather was grouchy and petulant and criticized the mother and again told vile stories about her mother. They were not even true, but the mother broke down. Then the father cut it short; they rode their bikes to the house of an acquaintance to spend the night and took the train home the next day.

The third time Iris went there was when she was twelve and her grandfather was in the hospital. He had had a blood clot and was in very bad shape.

When she saw him she saw a shell with a black center. It was dark inside him and strange demons came out from all his holes, eyes, ears, and mouth. He was like a Swiss cheese with holes all over discharging talk bubbles. She saw how the others got angry and hurt and were ready to erupt. She saw their urge to strangle him to shut him up. Nobody could see how bad it was for him inside, and Iris who saw it couldn't convey it. She did in fact know what he needed and how you could get him to brighten but she had no impulse to say or do anything.

She believed that the mother also knew something but that she was too scared and the father was too angry because the grandfather had hurt and scared her, so he had no sympathy for this nasty man.

Iris was not interested in the fact that he was her grandfather and in fact she wasn't interested in him as a person either. She was interested in the phenomenon, that he had so many holes in him in a way uniquely human. Animals could be angry or scared or curious and they were always whole. There were certain people who were whole in the same way as the animals, but most were more or less perforated. There were a lot of peculiarities that apparently came from people's life style and how they had been affected by others and the values they lived by, however wrong they might be. And the strange things they were afraid of: afraid of themselves or afraid of pain, afraid of things Iris knew to be harmless, but they lived as if there were deadly dangers and that's why they had holes in them.

Iris sat on the floor by the hospital bed and concentrated on trying to make contact with the grandfather. She saw that his atmosphere was dark and threatening and scary for him. She said and did nothing but let her atmosphere blend with his and this caused his darkness to lighten. He got calmer and stopped accusing, criticizing, and scolding everybody. She didn't know then that he was driven by and struggling with what is called angst, but the condition eased and he became calmer and kinder.

It was significant for Iris because she got to see that people could be so different. Some as black as the grandfather and others as light as the father. This amazed her. She couldn't let go of the thought that this man had such a terrifying inner life and that it was possible to change it. She hadn't understood before that there was something inside people that caused them to behave so differently. She was also amazed that the mother reacted so strongly to his words. They were just words. Sure he said mean things, but what was it that caused her to be crushed by them? What did those words strike and how could it make her cry? Why did the father get so terribly angry that he quickly took her out of the room and sat holding her while she cried and cried? It was a powerful drama, which Iris observed with wonder. This was a mystery for her, something she didn't understand at all, but she was very curious and wanted to explore the matter.

During the trip home on the train the mother told the father how it had been to not have a father and then get one that was as horrible as hers was. With a shudder she thought of how her siblings had lived with him during their childhood, until she was born and her mother died. She understood that they were damaged, but she still had difficulty understanding why they took it out on her what they should have taken out on their father. The closer they came to home, the more the mother's mood lightened, and when we were all the way home she was herself again, practical, humorous, and in control of her domain, the kitchen.

Iris didn't understand relationships, inner ties between people, that you could feel something for others, that it made a difference if somebody responded to you kindly or unkindly.

The father had taught her to program a list in her head. She could keep it only for a short time, otherwise it stopped working, and then she had to constantly make new ones so she always had a list to follow. It was not easy and she often made mistakes, but now she could associate with others in a different way, and they all had lists that she could easily go along with and follow. Especially the girl who often had a fight with her best friend and then wanted to be with Iris instead. She always had good lists, fun lists, and then Iris didn't need to have her own. This was pleasant.

Fall came and school started. Everything was familiar but still not. There was something all new inside her, something incomprehensible that always pulled her into other people's fields. It got ghastly and frightening. Her world which had been light became full of demons, black and scary. She acquired new behaviors, another type of outbursts, and became difficult to manage, again stripped of the possibility of controlling her behavior.

The teacher's field was so nice, so secure, so uncharged. He stood there and words flowed from his mouth, words that formed the most beautiful images and patterns and filled her essence. Words which also meant something to her, but where the substance was meager and sometimes erroneous. Now she acquired nuances and depth, insight and wisdom.

Recess had become different. Everybody still went outside,

Iris too, but now there were these girl-boy games where the girls preened and the boys teased and it got very difficult and black for her. Then she went to be with the younger boys. They still played as a group, played handball and football and she could be with them and "participate" in her way by them playing around her. The boys had discovered that she was good at shooting goals so when they were playing handball they placed her strategically by the goal and passed the ball to her and she shot.

The teacher asked the girl: "Do you know where my glasses are?" The girl heard the teacher's question and she knew where the glasses were but she didn't know what she was supposed to do with that information. The teacher had asked: "Do you know where my *glasses* are?" His focus was on them, not on her and therefore it didn't occur to her to answer. If he had said "Do *you* know where my glasses are?" she could have gone to fetch them, but she still couldn't have said: "They are in the supply room."

If somebody said something to the girl she needed to know the context in order to be able to answer. The other person needed to be present in what he said otherwise it was impossible for her do anything with it.

The father had learned this. He would say for instance: "Now it's cold outside and then one needs to dress in warm clothes. Let's see what kind of winter clothes we have that might fit. Go and get your outerwear." This the girl understood, and could even ask: "Which jacket should I take?" The father answered: "it would be best with the dark one." Then the girl went and got it. He thought aloud: "Now we'll get the car and drive to the village and get a bag of feed."

The girl got better and better at knowing how to answer and she loved doing it. But sometimes nothing came out of her mouth although she knew what to say. Now the girl realized that it involved taking in what somebody said, tossing it up in the air, bring out what the memory   already knew, toss it up also, and let it fall down through the head and out through the mouth. It wasn't always the most direct answer but she could ramble away and get it out anyway. The teacher understood.

One way to learn how one should be, how to act, was to go to the movies. There all possible human behaviors were played out on the screen. The girl sat up front and followed one actor at a time. This actor had read the script, had rehearsed, and then exaggerated what she wanted to express. This was easy for the girl to see, to comprehend, and to carry with her in her memory and practice in front of the mirror. The girl had no resistance inside her, nothing that got in her way; it was just new and fun. She often saw six films per week. There were four theaters in the little town and two of them changed film mid-week.

Iris became known to the ushers and they often let her in without paying and then she would pick up paper and other litter afterwards, while the ushers sat in the office and drank coffee. The girl enjoyed biking into town, seeing the film, picking up the trash, talking aloud about what she had seen without anyone listening, going home to rehearse and then using it in practice.

Her brother and his buddies clutched their foreheads at her

theatrical showings, but she learned things and little by little she gained a whole new spectrum of expressions.

The girl had entered a transition time. Partly she had grown physically, developed breasts and started menstruation, partly grown mentally and acquired an expanded consciousness. The father was worried that she would be sexually abused, because he knew how boys are in that age. He prevented it by arranging to always have somebody with her.

The girl wondered how you would know when you should sleep with somebody. She had gone around asking and received a lot of unsatisfactory replies. "You just know, it goes without saying, it is obvious in the situation, you can just feel it." She didn't understand any of it. She could never just feel something like that, she would not be able to figure out when it was right time, she didn't know what to use to figure it out.

The mother came up with the solution. "When you meet somebody that you can imagine sitting on the other side of the kitchen table for the rest of your life, then you can start thinking about the subject." This was easy to relate to, she could do this as soon as she met someone. Quickly the mommy's words were played in her head: "Can I see this person on the other side of the kitchen table? –No" and then that decision was made.

When she later met one that she could imagine living with she asked the mother what you do once you know that. Then the mother told her all about sex, childbirth and everything she could think of that would be appropriate. Then she asked her to invite the boy home so that she and the father could meet him, then they could in a nice way explain to him what her problems were.

That's how it was. He accompanied her home once. The daddy took him out in the barn and they stayed there talking many hours. After that there was no problem anymore. He was killed in a traffic accident one year later so, tragically, it didn't turn out to be for life.

Iris understood that one should have a best friend and one should think it was fun to have secrets and whisper and love certain types of music, and that one needed to learn generally what goes in the ordinary world. She spent a lot of time going around asking, but some people got angry and thought she was making fun of them and others thought she was stupid and some thought that she was trying to usurp their place and position.

Once when Iris was a bit on the road to ordinariness she and her friend got a ride home by two boys. One of them made a comment in passing that the other boy's beard looked like that of Eric IV. Iris didn't understand that the idea was that you should laugh at that, but she knew her history so for twenty minutes she held forth about King Eric IV and Karin Månsdotter. The others were almost exploding with laughter and just sat there waiting for her to realize that the comment was meant as a joke. But she never did.

The girl was not preoccupied with sexual feelings. She understood what it was, that it was something you did for fun and later you did it to have children. She heard all the girls who worried about getting pregnant and then she knew they had had sex. That was not important in her world. On the other hand it had become important to be with some boy and talk with him and exchange sweet nothings. It got so nice in the atmosphere and the girl laughed and talked a lot. As soon as the boy got too close she pulled away. She had come up with different ways to stop when it got too intimate. Usually, she had to bike home, or go find her girl friend, or meet her brother because they had planned something, or go to where the others were.

When Iris was nine she got a little brother, who the father was taking care of. When he was a baby Iris had wanted to bite him, but the father had put him in her lap and held her head until the discomfort and stereotypy disappeared. She didn't get any direct feeling of contact with the child then, but she was beginning to be interested in the phenomenon in her lap. The child grew and Iris imitated him. In a way she was a twin to this little child; she was in the same atmosphere, saw him in forms and colors, and this opened something new in her. Later she could pick the child up, carry it, sing, play and this was also something new. The girl got interested in children and this interest has never left her.

Her consciousness began more and more to be directed towards others and social life in a different way than before. She understood in a different way now that life was about emotions, about feelings, which she was not able to generate. She practiced trying to feel, but it just got empty. Knowledge-emotions she could generate and she knew the expressions for all the different emotions, but feel them she was not able to do. Nothing emerged. She could see other peoples' feelings and she could get others to express their feelings, both in words and reactions, but she herself remained unmoved.

When her little brother was four he contracted blood poisoning. He ran a high temperature and suddenly he got fever cramps. Strange sounds came out of him, his eyes rolled back, and his lips turned blue. His whole body shook and trembled. The mother took him and started shaking him and screamed "Help me, help me, he's dying, he's dying" but didn't do anything to help him.

Iris understood that he could die and that it would be terrible for the mother, but for Iris it had no greater significance. If he died, he died.

Iris said calmly: "Get the telephone and call the ambulance." She didn't know the number or how to look up it in the phone book herself, but the mother just continued to scream. "Go and get Father in the barn" said Iris. The mother left Iris with the stricken brother and rushed to the barn. At the same time one of the uncles came through another door. Equally calmly Iris said to him: "Call the ambulance."

She picked up the child and went out in the cold. He was gasping for breath but got no air and then she blew in his face to help him. Finally his breathing started. Then she stood calmly on the stairs until the ambulance came.

She understood that the others' reactions were normal and that it was she who was standing outside something she didn't know about. By this time she had understood that one could die other ways than being gored by a bull, but she didn't understand the hysteria, the terror, the distress. If you died, you died.

She forced herself to be present. To be here and now,

instead of in the inside-world that she used to call Out. For the first time she got a direction in her life, a direction that wasn't guided by others, but that was her own. It was something new and she noticed that she was transformed in her understanding of the world and reality.

Through the years she had developed her ability to see the atmosphere. She saw peoples' feelings in the atmosphere and she thought that everyone could see the atmosphere the same way as she. What she now saw was that other people always wanted something, always were going someplace, and that it was feelings that steered their choices. "Oh, *that* would be fun to do", or "Ugh, so boring." She searched and searched within herself to find some joy or longing. But she didn't find anything. Instead she had hooked onto the will and wishes of others and thought for a long time that that was to have emotions. But now she understood that instead of feeling-emotions she had acquired knowing-emotions, emotions she knew the name of and that she knew how to express verbally: "Yes, *that* would suit me" or "If there will be *food*, I'd love to come along." Sometimes she even tried to act out the emotions, but then the others just mocked her and thought her ridiculous so she gave that up.

Before, she had lived completely unconsciously and then reality had time and time again hit her. But now she found knowledge-emotions and with their help she could be with others in some form of togetherness in spite of the fact that she couldn't feel like the others. Thus began a new phase in life for Iris.

CHAPTER 7

A full life, in spite of all the defects

When I decided to become "ordinary" I realized how much I didn't know and resolved to somehow educate myself. It started with mother and me taking a correspondence course in conversational English. She did the reading and writing and I talked. We practiced together and I learned the basics. We took continuation courses for a few years and gradually I began to understand spoken English. Spelling was a problem and it still is but understanding it I managed.

After that I took courses in "everything" from different institutions for a period of three years. There was sewing, knitting, crocheting, weaving of different types, lamp-shade making, batik, drawing, wood working, wood carving, blacksmithing. Each course was ten weeks, two hours per week, and I thought that was the time you were allotted for learning it so I practiced diligently at home in order to know it perfectly before the course was over. I took four different courses per week, one each evening Monday through Thursday; I took Friday and Saturday off, and all day Sunday I did the homework from the previous week.

Half a year after I finished school I started as a trainee at a hair dressing salon. There they let me hand out curlers and watch for several years before I needed to produce results of my own, which was an ideal way for me to learn. Mother had found out everything that a trainee was supposed to do there, and she came there evenings and helped me practice those things, and wrote notes for me to look at and remember how and what I should do.

It's a hellish situation you're in when you are expected to do a job and you have no idea what you are supposed to do, you just stand there like an idiot staring straight ahead without a clue. I had by this time learned a number of strategies for resolving this dilemma, and I succeeded more often than I failed. Father and mother were well acquainted with my difficulty and they assisted with a lot so it wasn't apparent to the casual observer that I wasn't quite with it.

It was up to the trainee to make sure the place was neat and clean, and mother knew I couldn't tell clean from dirty; I just did what I had been told, but was not able to judge the result. One Sunday each month mother and one of her friends visited me at the salon and did a general cleaning. They swept the spider webs from the moldings, scoured the floors, and washed all the chairs, mirrors, and windows. They also washed all the towels and brushes. Everything was so clean and shiny before they quit that the salon could have been used as an operating room. They used to joke about that and say that I should remember that the cleaning was not done until it was like an operating room. After two years time I actually came to some kind of understanding of what a proper cleaning meant.

One advantage I had was that I only needed four hours sleep per night, so I had quite a lot of time to practice. I had long days at the salon, from nine to six on weekdays, eight to four on Saturdays, plus an hour and a half commute. I spent the train ride reading or writing so I would not lose those skills, and when I was riding the bike I told the wind what was in the different books I had read. I also repeated in my mind everything I had learned in the course during the week until I had placed everything properly in my lists.

Father had taught me drive the tractor when I was twelve. He figured I needed that long a learning period to be able to pass my drivers license tests sometime in my lifetime. Also, I inherited farfar's old moped and rode it. One problem I had was that I didn't know right and left, but he solved that by putting a red handle on the ditch-side of the handle bar.

When I was fifteen I took over my brother's slightly more modern moped, since he got a motorcycle then and got his driver's license with it. He read the driver's license handbook aloud for me and I tried to understand what it said. It was very difficult because I couldn't understand what the practice questions meant, especially when there was three, four, or five alternatives, where none, or all, or one, or a few might be correct. This was a hard form for me to master.

When my brother was finished with the driver's handbook I took it with me to my teacher and asked for his help by explaining it so I could understand. This he did. We kept at it for half a year. He explained braking distances, why the traffic laws were what they were, and why you needed to learn them whether they were wise or not. The road signs were the easiest for me, they were pictures and once he had explained what they meant I wouldn't have missed a single one. The hardest was when you had to calculate the height of a bridge relative to a truck height, axle weight, etc. Eventually I knew the book by heart and all imaginable variations on the questions, and you couldn't fool me with tricky statements. It was the hardest thing I had had to learn up to that point, but I managed and I got my driver's license when I was eighteen.

I practiced driving with Father because he figured that there was no driving school that could have taught me without costing a fortune. He figured he'd rather pay for several drivers tests instead. I passed the written test without a single error, but I failed my first driving test because I turned left when the examiner said right and by using the heel-and-toe method, when I stopped and started on a hill. Most people used that method, but you couldn't do it on the driving test. The second time out, I passed. That time I had an examiner who only looked at the technical, that I wasn't a menace in traffic, and he passed me.

When I was twenty-four I dared to begin studying in adult education programs, designed for those of us who had not taken full advantage of their normal schooling. It was a tough time. I completed twelve subjects in a year and a half, and got a certificate corresponding to a middle school diploma. After that I took a two-year high school course with focus on finance and bookkeeping, plus typing and short-hand. Short-hand was too difficult so I never learned it. In the evenings during those years, while I worked full-time at a youth center, I took three-year courses in Swedish, English, Mathematics and History so I could gain admission to the university. It was open evenings and weekends which made it possible for me to attend classes while working there.

Little by little I learned more and more about everything that could be taught, but unfortunately, to experience life through feelings, that was not possible. I began therapy, first regular psychoanalysis for two years, then gestalt therapy for two years, then transaction analysis for two years, and I learned how to understand the world in psychological terms, but to develop feelings and contact on the inside, that was not doable. Inside me there was still the same quiescence and, even though I had filled it up with a bunch of lists that contained everything between heaven and earth, I could get no feeling for the human.

I was able to meet many interesting people during this period. Many who have had the greatest importance for my development although not always in the way they themselves could have imagined. The most important, Göran Grip, who many years ago described the origin of this book in his book "Allting finns" (Everything exists), has been a cornerstone in thinking about what I called "Out" when I was a child, and which is about the atmosphere and the immaterial.

Since I started my university studies I have never quite stopped. I constantly learn new things and discover interesting perspectives, but I have had the difficulty that these courses never provide the time and space for reflection but require a type of accommodation that I can't handle.

Since I rarely had time to read much literature because I am such a slow reader I asked some class mates if we could look at the table of contents together and they would tell me something of what they had grasped when they read the book. When somebody relates what they have read, it all comes out in the atmosphere, and quick as a flash I can read that and get the gist of it. This would take about a minute instead of forty hours of reading. Then I went home and looked at the table of contents again, wrote down everything I could remember, and then I could rehearse the notes I had made. In this way I could keep up without having to read too much.

When you have my kind of learning difficulty you can get permission to take your tests orally or at home, and this is what I did. In those tests I made use of a sophisticated method of cheating. I asked the teacher to pose the questions in a different way because I didn't quite grasp it the way it was written. This caused the teacher himself to think of the answer and then it came out in the atmosphere and then I knew immediately how to answer. It was important to not answer verbatim what the teacher had thought because then heshe might get suspicious, so I took my time and formulated the answer in my own words. One time the teacher was bored so he just sat there thinking about what wall paper he should choose. and that time I flunked.

This cheating of mine was never detected, and I don't even know if you can call it cheating. In my world I find it strange to have tests where you can't help each other, where you deprive people of the possibility of cooperation by calling it cheating.

It doesn't fit with my concept of the most quintessentially human, connection, which is the basis for security. What is gained by that?

All through my university studies I have been searching for the kind of knowledge or insight that counts when nothing else counts, what I call the primary. I have read and learned a lot, but it is not to be found within any faculty. There have been fragments built into some of the courses I have taken, but not delved into by the instructors. When I have asked I have found a deep interest in the concept, but also been told that it is not something they have focused on; that it is a different kind of knowing, not science, and that it can't be transformed into academic knowledge. This has induced me to devote myself to this unstudied field and I have become convinced of its importance, especially at a time when our civilization is based solely on the secondary, and that the language of the primary, which precedes the secondary, has not been developed at all. The result is that people are helpless in situations when they have conflicts within themselves, or trouble in their relationships, or when they have to care for dysfunctional individuals who are dark inside.

Since several of the people teaching at the university were interested in my awareness of the primary they looked to me for guidance in solving common human problems, such as conflicts, relationship difficulties, bullying. That's how my work as a mentor started. Later it expanded to companies and eventually to institutional work with addicts, psychically burdened individuals and other dysfunctional persons, where communications difficulties have been the primary problem.

One day in 1982 I stood staring at my watch. For me there has never been any coupling between what the watch face presents and reality. I have not had any feel for clock time, only for about-time, morning, noon, afternoon, and evening. I have managed quite well with this, but when something has involved an exact time I have a friend who always called and reminded me when it was time to get ready and make my way to the right place.

The clock on the wall was ticking, I was supposed to go to a meeting, I looked at the clock and it was eight. "Eight, right, it must be right now that I have to leave to get there in time." A remarkable feeling. I took off and got there on time, and my entire essence understood that I had connected up something that had been incomprehensible for me before. It felt like the world had opened up for me.

In the evening I met a friend at the school where I studied and told her about my fantastic discovery. She clutched her forehead and said: Oh no, I had hoped there could be one human being on this earth that is unaffected by time and can function as a nature child in our civilization. I was confused for a while, but then she shared my happiness.

The calendar was a bigger problem. I couldn't grasp that the date on a piece of paper had something to do with a specific day. I could not prepare myself unless somebody told me that it was today that something was supposed to happen. Life is a flow for me, a fluid condition, and it has nothing to do with demarcations.

I began practicing by looking at the calendar every day, and read the date of the day, day of the week, month and year. I tied it to the weather, to sunrise, to vegetation on the ground, to the birds I could hear. Eventually I developed a kind of structure so that I could look in the calendar and connect the day to reality, but I had no feel for it, it was just technical knowledge. It is sufficient, but the problem is that I have to write everything down, because I can either live calendar-free and function my old way without predetermined times when things should happen, or I can follow a calendar point by point without any flowing time.

The problem is that people in general function both ways. Their working time is well delineated in the calendar but in their leisure time they do what they have planned in their head without having it written down. It is more or less spontaneous. When I use the calendar I write down every meeting, every date, and every notification I am supposed to give somebody. This means that I frequently check my calendar and that I pin things down very meticulously. This is not a burden for me because I love to check my calendar to find out what will happen next. I focus on that with the attitude: "it will be fun to see how this meeting turns out". Sadly, some of my friends are offended by this. They don't want to be an appointment in a calendar, they think that spontaneity is lost, that I never call them spontaneously, or visit them, or am accessible unless we have booked time. Many find this cold structuring unsociable but for me it is fantastic to be able to follow a structure and it doesn't prevent me for a moment from being present in the here-now in a meeting. I am never in past time or in future time but always in the present. It's only during that short moment when I am checking my calendar that I am in a kind of transition phase.

My perception, which I see others suffering from, is the opposite, that they usually live in the transition phase to "later", or have gotten stuck in some old history and have difficulty being present in the here and now, in togetherness and intimacy, in being contented and in having access to all their senses in the here and now.

Nowadays I generally manage both time and place, even though I sometimes miss completely. It may happen that I leave an hour, or a day, too soon or too late, or that I hit the right day, but wrong month or year. Now, these occasions become quaint incidents in my life and people are often able to laugh indulgently with me afterwards. My colleague Lennart is superb at continually updating my calendar and confirming that I've got it right, so there are very few misses and this I am happy for.

What characterizes a person with communications difficulties is that she has to actively "trigger" the intake of other peoples' emotions and impulses. I have practiced so much that I no longer need to actively think: "I am now going to reach out and take in the other"; it's like driving, when you have practiced long enough and driven long enough, it becomes automatic to do what you are supposed to when you sit behind the wheel. Usually it functions without difficulty but now and then I forget and then problems occur. People sometimes feel rebuffed by me and feel hurt, sometimes I don't hear what they say and they get insulted, sometimes I forget I should be polite and then I screw up.

I don't automatically make contact with other people and much passes me by, but I have trained my powers of observation and my capacity for reflecting on things, so once in a while I can beat well functioning people by a mile.

On the other hand I am very uninhibited. I don't have a bunch of preconceptions and values that inhibit my capacity for intimacy. I have learned what obtains in the ordinary reality but I am free to follow it only so long as it suits me, and I am able to adjust my norms on a moment's notice if needed. A sort of immorality, you might say. It's not that I live lawlessly, or repress myself, but just that I simply adapt myself to the smoothest way of functioning.

I often notice in others that if they violate some code or norm they develop a guilty conscience, and feel like they can't live anymore. Simply said, they feel like villains. That's not how it is for me. I don't feel anything except "Oops, I violated something sacred".

According to my mother I am the most uncouth thing walking in a pair of shoes, and I believe that is true. I didn't absorb any information about polite and well-bred behavior until I was so old that I absorbed it in my intellect rather than deep in my marrow, and consequently I could rationally decide what I should keep and what I should toss out. However, it is easy for me to conform to somebody else's will. I am seldom in contact with any will in myself and find it practical to want what others want. I have to carefully feel out what the others want so that if they ask me I can say the thing they want as if it were my own. Otherwise they'll get upset that they always have to decide and unnecessarily think it unfair that I don't take any responsibility.

I have struggled a lot with the common unstated norms about what you are supposed to do and not do: that you are supposed to greet people when you arrive, that you are supposed to say "How are you?" before you bring up your actual errand, and other rules about how you behave around people. One day mother had decided that I should join her and her friends for Sunday lunch. They had already gathered in the lilac arbor. Just when I was about to go out to join them Father asked me to ask mother where the prescription was that he was supposed bring with him to town. I went to the arbor and stood there waiting for a lull in the conversation so I could bring up my errand. I had learned that I should not start talking before there was silence. But it never got silent, because tongues had already been loosened.

Finally somebody slowed down for a moment to take a breath and then I quickly snuck in my question about the prescription.

"But Iris, you must apologize when you interrupt like that. Also, you are supposed to say hello when you come in."

Right away I went around and shook hands with everybody, and then one of the neighbors said angrily: "It's not worth anything to do it when you have been told. It should come from yourself. Besides, you should have apologized for not greeting us."

"But I did say hello", I said confused.

"And don't *talk back* to me" she said and got even angrier. "Do you have anything to say for yourself?" she said testily.

I understood nothing. In the silence that followed mother told me where the prescription was. I took a cookie and turned to go to tell Father, who was waiting. Mother said "You don't help yourself before you are told."

I put the cookie back

"And once you have taken it don't put it back on the tray."

I took the cookie again and started to leave.

"And when you leave the table you say thank you!"

I said thank you.

"But it should be spontaneous."

I never understood this. The troubled youths that came to us were also "uncouth", but quickly and without visible effort they became full-feathered toadies and learned how to follow the rules that were so mysterious to me. I could see that they didn't mean anything with their "Excuse me", "Thank you", and "How are you", but the adults accepted these worthless words as if they were for real. I didn't know if they were too blind see through the toadying, or if they in fact were aware that they also were dissembling.

Justice is another such concept that I have struggled a lot with. I used to ask people what reference they used in deciding if something just or unjust. I often received the answer: "Common sense tells you what's just or unjust." I don't have any such common sense that tells me that and I don't know where I should get it. For me, everything that happens is what it is, neither just nor unjust. If you figured out a system with gradations, maybe you could decide if something is just or unjust based on those gradations. But only if the gradations apply.

During one period of my life I was active in the labor movement as a union representative, and I needed to negotiate pay rates. I carefully studied how the system was structured and found out that there was a hierarchy and that in the hierarchy it was important that each rate group had its distance from the next group so that the status of some group wouldn't be lowered. In general, there needed to be intergroup separations for it to be fair. In other words, there needed to be *differences* so it would be *fair*. And then there were pegs, a few wage rates that were floating, and they were supposed to be distributed fairly according to merit. This meant that we had to discuss and come to a conclusion of who deserved them and it had to correlate in a way that everyone thought fair. If we couldn't reach a conclusion, the only thing to do was to make a majority decision and go with that.

I assumed that there would be something in Stockholm similar to the meter rod in France, which is the standard for all the world's meters and constitutes the norm. Based on that reference point the system can function, and if everyone agrees on that base-meter you can see that it makes sense.

At one occasion we had a labor category which had not been centrally negotiated so it was supposed to be "inserted" at an appropriate level. I called Stockholm to find out what would be fair and was told that we had to decide this locally. I called different communities and asked what "suitable levels" they had for these positions. Nobody knew. I called Stockholm again and asked what the template looked like because I wanted to know what the wage reference was based on. I thought if I got those criteria I would be able to figure out what level it belonged in.

First I had to wait because they didn't know what I was talking about, then I was transferred to somebody higher up, and higher, and higher. It finally became clear that there were no such criteria and that the rate was determined based on "responsibility". The one with the greatest responsibility should have the highest pay. Then I asked about the criteria for responsibility. They did not exist either since "everybody understands what is meant by that and who has the most responsibility".

I could not understand how in the world folks could know what was fair and unfair when there was no reference to base it on, but people often objected to unfairness and felt hurt and offended and wanted redress. Same thing with responsibility. In my world, everybody took the responsibility they could handle and nobody was thought less of because heshe couldn't grasp the difficult things, but here a kind of ranking governed, that responsibility should be divided up, making sure that the one with most responsibility got the most pay.

I called around some other places and asked if they had inserted the new work category and finally got hold of a man who answered: "Let's see now, how about we take a stab at XX. That's midway between *leisure guide and social assistant*. That ought to be about right." Others had later called each other and they placed the work category at the same level and referred to each other: "This is the level for this category in all the counties so it is fair that you too receive it."

Catch 22: When somebody has arbitrarily come up with a proposal it is used as a fairness template, and the argument is that that's how it should be everywhere, because then it is fair, and if you deviate from this it is unfair.

Somebody explained to me that if there was something that everyone couldn't have, then nobody should have it, unless there were some special reason that legitimized that unfairness. I thought then that since not everybody in the world can have ice cream then nobody should have ice cream, if it is to be fair. I argued for that viewpoint and everybody thought I was ridiculous. That's not the way to reason; you need to confine the argument to Sweden. Then I maintained that since plums don't grow in Norrland, then nobody should have plums, or the ones who have them should at least share with the Norrlanders. That's not the way to reason either. What is fairness?

I discussed the issue with Father, and he said that for him fairness was relative. That it was based on how you value different things, and that's why the feeling of unfairness was different for different people. He said that it wasn't possible to be completely fair. Better to try to ascertain what others valued and try to accommodate that as far as possible. Then the injustice wouldn't be too great, at least locally. He also said that the concept of fairness is on a secondary level, and has no meaning for our survival on the primary level, so he suggested I shouldn't take it too seriously, not let it trouble me too much that people are always fussing about fairness.

I continue to have problems with fairness. I almost never feel unfairness, except if somebody has promised me something and then withdraws it in front of my face without any good   reason. I used to drive the argument ad absurdum when somebody appeals to fairness, and if there still was an issue, then I could discuss correcting the unfairness. Otherwise, I usually try to empathize with people when they feel aggrieved and unfairly treated until they get over it and can feel satisfied again.

Also, this peculiarity of isolating responsibility from life itself and put a price on it doesn't exist for me. To me that is a misapprehension. To me responsibility is a privilege. If I am good at assuming responsibility and others have confidence in me and I can live up to it, I gain something from it and grow as a person. I am the privileged one.

Children get rewards when they take responsibility for taking care of siblings and get a reduction in their allowance when they have failed to take responsibility for making their bed. Each time they show they are capable of doing something the bar is set at that level and then if they don't meet that, they get demerits. Then they feel conned and cheated out of their time, time when they could have been playing. Many children resist learning everyday tasks because it entails theft of their time and the gain is too small. Valuations are introduced in a context where they don't belong, and this leads to problems later in life.

For many years I thought about how to sort this out and

clarify the distinction. I had no instrument, nobody who could show me how I should think. After many years at the university and contact with smart people I concluded that there were two fields, one primary and one secondary, and that they are not in opposition to each other, but follow each other; that the primary is essentially different from the secondary but that both, each in its way, are 100 % important. Responsibility belongs to the primary and is not to be valuated but always implies some form of freedom and privilege in itself. But in our civilization the relationship has been distorted. That we want to use it as a criterion for paying people is one thing, but that is secondary and should not be mixed in with the primary, because then it gets fishy.

Security, what is it? In our country we are so anxious that we need a guarantee in order to feel secure. A guarantee means that you won't be exposed to life as it is but that everything will be rectified. In my world, the key is to give people the ability to feel secure amid the insecurity, not to create a world that is so secure people become incapable of surviving in a state of nature. To gain the inner security I have concluded that people need to learn "crafts". That each of us knows enough about the natural world that we can survive if we become stranded, that people know enough about communication that they can find the solidarity needed to form a group that can make it in hard times.

Communication, how does it work and what is it based on?

When I first noticed that other people were into something that I had no part in I realized that I was different, that I lacked a capability that seemed to be natural for everybody else. There is an atmosphere around us, a kind of immaterial connection, and it guarantees a kind of trust where you can give and take, receive and give, and in that moment have an exchange with others. With that comes the engagement, the intimacy that fills our basic need for connection and attention.

When one wishes to communicate with a particular person one gathers up this atmosphere and directs it at the person one wants to make contact with. The other does the same thing and so they meet in a mutual atmosphere. In that moment the total atmosphere changes and the situation is redefined.

In my childhood world I was very familiar with the total atmosphere. It contained so much and I spent as much time as I could trying to be in it. At the age of eleven I discovered that the atmosphere among other youths had changed. Their atmosphere was totally oriented towards each other, and around me it got like a colorless vacuum. I got scared and tried to find out what it was. I went to Father and asked what they were doing.

After practicing for quite a long time in front of the mirror I learned to function like the other girls and it worked eventually, but I made many mistakes and I always had to think about how I behaved, how I moved my hands, how I stood, how I looked, how I listened to the other person, how I responded, and the expression on my face.

The hair styling salon was an ideal school for me. I got

to stand there and pass out curlers and listen and watch for two years before I got to try it myself, and by then I had programmed in every detail so that I could behave properly. I learned communication, how it's done and how it works. First, communication has to be established, preferably by first creating a good atmosphere. In the salon this was done by extending a welcome greeting and seating the lady in her own booth. There one asked briefly about how she was feeling that day, talked about the weather, about the season, about work, or something else in the news.

The advantage for me was that I was standing behind the customer and that we only fleetingly looked at each other in the mirror and I could concentrate on the hair and not be too affected by the directness. Such directness usually caused my thinking to be blocked and I lost my impulse control which triggered my stereotype behavior.

I worked a lot on being able to handle direct contact and it caused a lot of pain inside. Eventually the pain receded into discomfort and with continuing practice I was able keep my thinking on track and not get lost.

I had learned earlier in life to see auras. Especially on calves. I knew when a calf had viability and when it did not. I couldn't tell what the difference consisted of, but a difference there was. During my time at the salon I learned to see this difference in humans also, and learned that it was possible when it was thin to coax out and enhance the life force. I applied myself to this and the women liked it and requested me; not because I was the best hair stylist but because it was so pleasant and stimulating for them when I did their hair.

Many years later I have reviewed the experiences I collected during the ten years I worked at the salon, but it took a long time before I realized that communication-atmosphere and communication-field were concepts unknown to others; that they have been taught that "that's just fantasies" and that fantasies are not real, and that it is a waste of time to be occupied with them, that it is better to learn something proper, real and substantial.

When I had discovered that humans are something different from everything else and that they had a special ability to use the atmosphere, my mind became totally occupied by that insight. I began to take in interest in children. Children were easy because they are so pliable and intensely curious which made it possible to play with them in the immaterial.

When my little brother was born my father placed him in my lap. At first I reacted with discomfort, but after a while he captured me and we made an immaterial play-contact. This was before my discovery of what young people did together with each other. My brother had a thin life force around him so I coaxed and coaxed him. He was sick many times during the first years of his life, and each time his field got thinner, but as soon as he came home from the hospital we started over again. This uneven struggle continued until he started school.

After the hair stylist years I started working in the children's ward in a hospital. There I discovered that gravely sick children were often quite secure and that they didn't have a fear of death, that they thought their life was what it was, as long as it was, and that they didn't feel cheated even if they had to die in childhood. It was only their loved once that were desperate, who felt that the children were cheated out of something. Parents and other grown-ups acted as if the life ended for them when the children were sick. I devoted a lot of time to make the negative atmosphere of the adults more positive to make it easier for them but also so they would be more reachable and accessible for the children.

I came in contact with an anorexic girl on this ward. She was so thin she seemed transparent, but she was cheerful and capable. She had been on an IV for a while and then she had to drink a nutritional drink and eat protein enriched ice cream. It was our assignment to look after her periodically to make sure that she consumed these items and then sit with her for an hour to make sure she didn't go out and throw it all up.

I noticed that she was very afraid and that she thought nobody liked her. That her kind and loving parents were disappointed in her and that she didn't know how to satisfy them. She thought she was mean and nasty under the surface and that she had to keep it secret because if it came out her world would crumble. She was compelled to repeat a lot of rituals over and over again, otherwise there would be chaos inside her and she would go under.

I saw that she had a very sensitive field around her and that she was easily invaded by the fields of others, especially if they had a need for something. She would immediately feel responsible and try to cater for that person's need, and when she did she lost own self. In this way I saw that she was a nonperson when she was together with other people. I decided then that my field would be uncharged and that from me she would not sense any wishes or opinions about how she should be. After some practice it worked fine. When I sat with her after eating she became a somebody-person and then she discovered completely new things. New thoughts came to her and we could talk and laugh and she dared to try out her own opinions.

We sat in a little room with two easy chairs and a table between us with some magazines. Sometimes she had the protein drink at her side and I had a cup of tea. I made sure that there was nothing in me that she would need to accommodate herself to. No wishes, no expectations, no demands. Only warmth in the entire room.

She was an expert at twisting situations into something she could accommodate herself to, and it required total attention to avoid sliding into it.

She said a little annoyed:

"What are we waiting for? What are we going to do now?"

"Waiting for?" I answered a little vaguely and let the warmth return to the room so that it got totally calm around her again.

"How long are you staying?"

"We have all the time in the world. That's just how it is", I said equally vaguely.

She caught sight of the glass and expected me to then be pleased and wish for her to drink the whole thing. Instead I gave up interest in her glass and devoted myself to distracted stirring of my tea. Then she could drink or not drink. And then an urge popped into in her head.

"I feel like going for a walk", she said. She checked herself. "What did I just say?" she asked, surprised.

"You said you felt like going for a walk."

Then she started with her accommodation again: "But I don't know if it is OK. And I don't know how long you are staying. And maybe they want me to be included in something here."

I moved the focus back to her. "But if you feel like taking a walk then you feel like taking a walk. And then you have that urge and it doesn't matter what becomes of it. If you feel like it you feel like it."

"Yes, I feel like it. I do feel like it. I feel like taking a walk." And slowly she dared to have something that was entirely her own and could hold on to it.

I taught her how to think in order to be a somebody-person even if others felt threatening. We left the room and a nurse came and asked: "Have you finished your drink?"

In that moment she was on the verge of accommodation mode again, and became anxious and couldn't remember if she had finished the drink or not, and she forgot to bring back the glass, and she should have put it back in the kitchen, and it was deadly unless she accommodated the nurse's wishes totally so that the nurse would be completely satisfied with her.

I saw all this play out within her and put my hand on her shoulder and said: "Hold it a little. Let's look at this thoroughly. Stay within yourself, stay with your consciousness and in your body." The nurse saw what was happening and left, without irritation.

"Look around yourself and think. Is it about life and death?

No. If the other one gets hurt or offended, is it dangerous? No. If I make an error, do I dissolve? No. Basically this is not dangerous. It feels deadly, awfully unpleasant, I get confused and almost paralyzed, but it is harmless. Ignore the time; take as much time as you need to roll this around in your mind so that your body can feel that it is not dangerous."

It took eight weeks for her to learn this. Then she was declared cured and she could go back home.

A couple of years later I met her in town and the she was radiant. She was attending high school and getting good grades and she was svelte but not skinny. She told me that she still closed her eyes and did what we had practiced together and that as soon as she got into a critical situation the eating problem would threaten again, but now she could handle it. She had also gotten over her fear of not being loved by her parents. During her sickness they had let go of their expectations and stopped praising her for everything, so that now she didn't always have to keep getting better and better. It taught me to understand the difference between affirmation and praise.

Some children came in with bruises and had been involved in strange accidents. I often detected that the parents had large gaps in their fields, and that they reacted violently and hard. I saw that they were scared and constantly felt compelled to defend themselves. I sometimes established contact with the child and helped her find a protected place within herself and taught her to be on guard. That accommodation of course made the child feel dissatisfaction with her home environment, but at least she could find some moment's feeling of security and be contented being together with me.

After my time on the children's ward I held a job in long-term care. I was on the long-term ward where most of the patients there were in the final stages of cancer. The clinic was pervaded with the fear of death and most of the staff found it depressing. When there was somebody that kept calling continually they were irritated and considered the person "difficult". There was a different atmosphere here and I saw that it was contagious. Everybody was constantly running around doing a lot of things whether they were needed or not. Eventually I was assigned to the night shift and then I had a lot of time to spare for the patients.

When a patient was restless or anxious I stayed with her after I had done my rounds. I sat down, held her hand and talked about the immaterial. I asked the ones able to talk how it looked in their fears and got many descriptions of hell and all sorts of horrors that humans can imagine. The worst anguish was that so many thought that they hadn't finished living, that their life hadn't been good, that they hadn't gotten out of it what they wanted (as if there is something special to be gotten out of life, as if it could be completed in the sense of "finished product"), that they had been too scared and too bound by duties. That feeling easily shifted into bitterness which they took out on the staff. They were well and had time left.

That envy was dreadful for the dying. They couldn't help being mean and difficult, and at the same time felt more and more guilt feelings. I realized the hamster wheel they were on and that the patients really wanted to talk about their lives, have some type of connection, and work through their fear of death. I sat down and quietly asked them to tell about their life. I asked them to talk about both the light and the dark. They were often stuck in the dark and it took a long time and many turns before they got through it. I asked them what experiences they had had, what the agonies had taught them and if there was something rewarding they could find in it all. Often then they thought of something and little by little their mood brightened and we began to have a nice time together.

I also did something I today call "primary-thought work" with them. It amounts to me gathering together all they have told me and making a story out of it. Then I ask the patient to close her eyes and listen to a story. What happens is that her whole life gets played out, the patient comes in contact with her life spirit, and she can live out the feelings that arise and talk about her life in a different way than before. Sometimes I did primary-thought work on dying and what it's like after death so that their fear of death disappeared.

Before they were born everybody has been in the state that death entails, so it is a question of being guided back to that state and re-experience it, and then the fear of death recedes. However, the fear of suffering could still remain, but it was possible to absorb the pain in the same way so that it became bearable and an ally of the life spirit. In those days it was still thought that you shouldn't give too much pain killer for fear of addiction. This was absurd, since no-one left the ward alive.

Then I came back to the children's ward again. About that time a regulation was issued to the effect that you needed to have caregiver education to work in the hospital. When I heard that I was ready to quit immediately. I hadn't learned to read and write during my school years, but I had eventually reached the point that I was able to struggle through a text and write somewhat readable, but to manage a course with eleven weeks of theory, that I felt was impossible.

The supervisor of our ward told me she was the instructor in the course and that she was very familiar with my skills. She thought I was very capable and knew how to "take" both children and parents in a superb way, and she wanted me in the course. She applied for me and said there would be a place for me if I changed my mind.

This was the most agonizing dilemma of my life. The day the course started I walked back and forth, walked halfway there and then turned around and walked home. Finally, two hours late I was standing outside the door. It was recess, and my supervisor saw me and came and got me, showed me my place and introduced me so naturally that I responded immediately. We studied anatomy, micro-biology, nursing, and psychology. I often didn't have time to read at home, but the others told me about it and the teachers knew about my problem and took a lot of care to explain things for me.

I discovered to my surprise that it was easy for me to learn. Everything I learned got stored and was easily retrieved when I got a question. Unfortunately, this didn't work in written tests because then I didn't get any associations and it was like my brain was dead. Fortunately it was permissible to take the exam orally if you are dyslexic, so it worked out. I passed the course.

This strengthened my self-confidence enormously. It opened a whole new dimension in my life. Something I had never even dreamt of being possible.

I also discovered that people had different degrees of learning difficulties. Before I hadn't had any clue that there were individual differences among people, and I discovered that I was good at explaining what I had learned in a simple and understandable way. The result was that our group got the highest grades that had been awarded in the course.

I also developed another ability. When I didn't know how to answer an exam question I asked the teacher to rephrase the question and while she was thinking how she should reformulate it I caught an impulse from her and presto! I knew the answer. Sometimes too well, so much word for word that the teacher got suspicious and wondered. I learned to not use this method except in an emergency, and that's how it's been in all my studies.

During my time as a hair stylist I became conscious of my appearance. I learned how to combine colors, how to look at things and understand style, what is appealing and what is "in" and what is "out".

My hair changed character, both color and style, my clothes changed character, became modern and with a very personal style. I still didn't have an innate feel for clothes, hairstyle, make-up, and such when it concerned me, but I developed a great sense for it when it concerned customers. By partaking in their context I could give them a satisfactory answer on what suited just them.

Preparing for some event people often came to ask for advice about hair color, eyeglass frames, style of dress, and I found it incredibly enjoyable to be allowed to help them with my ideas or fancies. I never knew where I got them, but I knew they would work and that satisfied me and the customers were also satisfied.

My boss, a beautiful young woman, with the prettiest hair I had ever seen, thought I was good looking enough to be the town's Lucia and applied for me. I became one of the candidates and that led to an improvement in my self image. There were more than one hundred girls that appeared before a jury, and from them they would pick seven. We had to walk back and forth and be checked out. Eventually the unselected were sent away with a lie that if they were in the running they would be contacted in a few days, while those of us who were selected were sent to another room to wait until the unselected had left.

There was a conservative dressmaker there who dressed us up in identical blouse and skirt outfits, a hair stylist who did our hair, a photographer who took our portraits. We got stars with numbers and had to pose with them by our face for the local newspaper.

As a participant in this contest I traveled around and appeared at different events, helped collect money for charities, served as a model for the clothing firm, the photo studio, hair stylist association and others. I gathered that this was part of modern life, standing outside a store and being pleasant, greeting people and selling raffle tickets to them. I loved it; I was enchanted and felt valued and important.

It was a new experience to be feeling acknowledged, have significance: how intoxicating!

This made me conscious of how much looks are valued, how you are observed by others and evaluated as capable or incapable, as beautiful, charming, pleasant. I began trying to learn how to know if something was one or the other. I had no feel for what was ugly or pretty, in or out, I asked what others thought and then put it all together so I got an idea of what the majority thought. In this way I could be reasonably sure that I behaved correctly and looked OK.

Earlier, my mother had made the decisions regarding my appearance and she had an excellent, well developed taste, so I was not too far off the norm. She got very dramatic about being scandalized and hurt if I didn't have the sense to choose appropriately myself.

For me to become a person in reality and not just a parrot it was crucially important to enter this external world. The problem is that you so easily can succumb to it and let yourself be seduced by it and get the idea that it is something primary and think that it has something to do with your value as a human being, something to do with contentment, that you can have some kind of external security which somehow will protect you from the inner struggle you have to constantly wage, that laziness is possible. But that is not how it is. The only thing you get from succumbing to the external is that you lose your self-confidence, and that leads to war, the bottle, or the bed.

In my case I was brutally prevented from entering symbiosis with my mother. When I was born she rejected me ruthlessly, and I became so afraid that I sank into emptiness. And since I had a tendency to autism I couldn't emerge by doing what a child with a lesser tendency to autism would have done: scream to high heaven without let-up until somebody responded. Instead, for the first three years of my life I remained in an emptiness state where people were just surroundings, not relationships.

The mother and the newborn baby enter naturally into partnership where, in an important sense, they are equals and where both are autonomous. It means that the child *is* capable of satisfying its needs itself if the mother is truly capable of putting the necessary wherewithal at its disposal. The child feels a need, the child makes use of the resource it commands; it cries. The need gets met and the child is satisfied and grows in self-reliance: the child has itself made sure that its need was satisfied. Symbiosis in the sense that a person lives her life through another person is not needed in this process, and has no place here. Symbiosis may be created, for example, when the mother has a need to be validated through her child in order to feel like a good mother, when she wants the child to stop crying and be satisfied for her own benefit. Then the mutuality and independence in their relationship are compromised and the mother makes the child dependent on her in a way that didn't exist originally. The child notices that it has to be passive in the meeting of its own needs, and has to accommodate the needs of the mother. This leads in turn to the fight during the obstinate age to reacquire its independence.

With Father it was entirely different. He observed me with wonder and he played with me and made up his mind to try to make contact with me. Not because he had a need for it but because he found it fun and exciting, and because I really was his darling child, as unconditionally as my older brother.

Because most of those who have been drawn into unneeded symbiosis always suffer from separation anxiety, our civilization is characterized by over accommodation. It is a complicated pattern of guilt, shame, conscience and morals that characterizes people's lives and relation to themselves.

People evaluate themselves, what is good and what is bad, and are terribly afflicted by it. What is good you have to preserve and build on; else you are a bad person without legitimacy and have to dwell in shame with a guilty conscience. Therefore it is hard to find anyone who is unaffected by this contingency.

In girls this can lead to anorexia/bulimia and body fixation. In boys it can lead to prolonged adolescence and concentration on body building and violent sports in order to achieve an external manliness. The entire youth culture of today is filled with compensation for what the symbiosis has robbed young people of, their autonomy. When I attended hair stylist school I learned the difference between my personal style and the prevailing trend and I learned how to follow it selectively so that my personal style didn't disappear. Every time a new trend appeared I had to see how the opinion of others changed and adapt my style accordingly. I developed two ways of seeing: one, what I actually thought and two, what fit with the prevailing trend. I carefully distinguished between these two so that I could give my customers the choice to be brave or safe.

I also used this parallel way of seeing in my work at the youth hall. Lelle, an untamed youth who constantly lived on the edge of sudden death, tried to belong by always being the toughest, coolest, most adventurous and he was always taking breakneck risks. One disco night I grabbed him and sat him down in the cloak room where I worked and confronted him about what he was doing in order to belong.

"Do you understand what you are doing, and do you understand *why* you are doing it?" I said. "Do you realize you do what you're doing to gain status, one way or another? You think it is about fighting and drinking and driving like an idiot. But that isn't you at all. What you are is something entirely different. You think if you acted like who you really are, if you were yourself, you would be nobody. And that's where you are wrong. If you really were yourself you would get the position you are seeking but not getting now. Can you understand that? Can you understand that you have the position you want but you think you won't have it unless you behave the way you do? And there you are wrong. Absolutely wrong."

"How can you know that?" he asked, suspicious but also curious.

"I can't prove to you that I know it. But I do know it. You can try to prove me wrong if you like. But that you can't do, because if you tried you would discover that I am right. And then you would have a problem, you'd have to agree with me. And then you couldn't continue with what you are doing now."

"You are trying to trick me."

"If you think somebody is doing something very wrong and you can't get him to stop by forbidding or scolding, and if instead you tell that person a truth the way I have told you a truth, do you then think it would be bad even if I were wrong? I have no proof, so it is possible that I am deceiving you, and if you don't try we'll never find out. But if you try, it will become apparent. And I know I am right. But you don't know it of course. If you are arguing with a person who has done something stupid, do you think it is wrong to tell that person a truth? You don't need to answer now, but think about it."

Then I showed him how that culture looks, and how *he* really is as a person. The gang he wanted belong to was very destructive. They were into drinking, fighting and stealing.

"Open your eyes and look around. Look carefully. Look at what they are doing. Look at what happened last Saturday in the park when one of them stole a car and ended up at the police station, and another was so drunk he became unconscious and ended up in the hospital. Look around. *Is* that really your culture? You can see how that culture looks. Use the inside of your skull and think. What is the status you want in that kind of group? The status you really want is to be with them, and what you want by being with them is to have fun together. You are after having fun, meeting girls, going to parties. And what they are doing without you is the exact opposite. Don't you see that they don't have much fun, only troubles, and they wind up in the hospital or jail, and the girls they meet are passed from one to the other? You can have status in that group with what you actually know and really feel. You have that in you. You are not totally lost and not blinded because if you were you wouldn't be bugging me every day. You are after something else."

"You are right, but it is damn difficult." He said. "I don't think I can do it. I have nothing to offer. I think they would just consider me a dork. I can't say the things *you* say. If I said it I would sound like a dork. When you say it sounds totally right, and I know it is right. It won't end well for them and not for me either. It will turn out bad for all of us. It's not possible to think like you do. It's not possible to talk like you do."

That's how our conversations used to end and that's how we carried on for a few years.

After some time he and I could look at the in-trend and see what parts he could adopt without putting himself in danger. He changed his style and still got his position in the group. Eventually he became a leader for youth projects in another county and has since helped innumerable youths who had been on the wrong road. Still today, he says if he had been left to himself he would have had no chance to make it.

I had a full-time job trying to understand what it meant to be a normal small-town person, how you should think and feel, how you should behave and dress, what interests you should have to be accepted, and how you should talk.

Slowly I absorbed the values of the material world and learned what was mandatory and what was optional. One basic rule was that you had to form a family: find a partner, get married, have children. This suited me fine. I had learned that you had to act a certain way to be attractive and that it would hopefully lead to marriage.

From the day I started working on having a communication field and being within someone else's atmosphere and knew how to behave, the world around me began to see me as normal and functional. Over the span of a few years I met many boys and eventually found one that was a good fit for me. He had a large surplus of love and was mentally very stable and capable. He took life as it came, played and assumed responsibility with an ease that people envied. He thought I was an exciting, unpredictable person who would never be boring or routine.

Suddenly I found myself in a lot of new social contexts, for example birthdays where I no longer was the Iris that everybody ignored and who sat under the table, but instead was the hostess who had to arrange the party for my husband. My husband had to teach me how to cater to others, treat them to cookies and cake, set the table, invite them to the table, but whether I did it according to his description or my own head, it still didn't become that sociable occasion where everybody could just come, relax together for a few hours and then go home.

There were many such parties and dates that I spoiled by creating uncomfortable situations. I knew how to follow convention and talk about neutral things. I didn't understand that there were only certain topics one could bring up, and that one could talk about them only in a certain way. Once when the cookie tray was being passed around, a guest came in late and excused himself by saying he had to do some preparations in the barn because he was sending some animals to slaughter. This socially quite acceptable information gave me the impulse to tell the story about how the butcher had once come to our farm a few days early and we had not had time to starve the hogs so that their guts would be empty. I described how they lifted out the stomach and guts and put them in a tub with water. And when I pressed out the contents –the guts were to be used as sausage skins – it squirted and sprayed so my uncle got a shower all over him. He looked like the pig had shit all over him. I thought this was a hilarious situation and laughed heartily, and concluded by saying: "It didn't actually smell like shit, more like offal." I noticed how quiet it got and nobody looked hungrily at the cakes and the tray was put down. Somebody said: "Nobody should talk like that when we're here to have a good time." I understood nothing, had no idea what it was you shouldn't talk about. Then my husband intervened: "You know, people think it was yucky and it's not the sort of thing to talk about when we are eating." Then he turned to the man that had excused himself and said: "So how many hogs are you sending to slaughter?" He answered, somebody else asked another question and with that the situation was saved. Personally I couldn't tell what the difference was between what they talked about and what I had talked about.

Eventually I learned when something occurred to me, to ask my husband: "Is this something you can talk about?" I often asked how he knew, how he could figure out why one thing was OK to talk about but not another, because that I couldn't understand. This he couldn't answer; he just said what I had heard a thousand times: "You just *know*" or "you understand it from the context".

My ability to see what people really meant, combined with my inability to see that they wanted to keep it secret, and that they sometimes didn't admit even to themselves how they actually felt, caused many uncomfortable situations. Friday nights, friends and neighbors used to gather at our place to talk and drink coffee. At one such occasion there was a woman who thought herself a very good dancer and assumed the prerogative of criticizing one after the other of the men in our group for being lousy dancers. What came out in the atmosphere was that the other women didn't agree they were bad dancers, and that the men thought it was just this woman who was a bad dancer. But according to the social convention, which I knew nothing about, they didn't say anything, just got uncomfortable, which I didn't pick up on either. And I didn't understand why they didn't say what they thought. So quite cluelessly I said to the woman: "But *you* constantly get your toes stepped on. You don't dance well at all." She got incredibly upset and accused me of maligning her falsely, and that I gave her a headache and now I had ruined several days for her. Then she got up theatrically and left the room. Even the bad-mouthed men got mad at me and said: "You can't say things like that." I didn't understand a thing.

When we were alone my husband explained to me that when you hear things like that, the best thing is to just let it pass, otherwise it gets uncomfortable for everyone concerned. He sometimes said he had had no idea that it was possible to ruin a social occasion in so many different ways as I could. Eventually he taught me how social events function. At first some people meet -- in a home, out on town or some other place --and then contact is established through a greeting ceremony. Then you begin talking about nothing and the topic itself is not important, but that the social game is started where you see each other, speak to each other, and let everybody be included. It's important that you don't talk about anything significant at this phase. This game continues until everybody is satisfied, and this can take from ten minutes to a couple of hours. After this there can be two different scenarios. Either somebody looks at his watch and says he has to go at which time there is an ending procedure where you say "So long" or "we'll call", or "See you later". Or it gets quiet for a minute and the focus on socializing disappears and instead some topic is raised that is interesting or current: politics, or religion, or whatever, which everyone has an opinion about and that everyone can share in. And the real conversation begins, which may become a discussion. The conversation is about some phenomenon, the discussion comes from the fact that people have differing opinions that they test against others' opinions. This continues until the topic is exhausted. Then a new topic may pop up or the group breaks up. And then the farewell ceremony starts, when one socializes again, plays the game and says "This was interesting" or "We'll return to this another time". And then everybody leaves.

What characterized my husband was that he did not have any symbiosis damage. His mother hadn't had the need for her children to satisfy her own needs. She was a strong woman who ran the whole farm alone. He was completely autonomous and lived the contented life of someone free from the yoke of being owned. Money was something you acquired in order to have fun. The car is a tin box which you can and should take care of because it serves a purpose. If he happened to put a dent in it his first comment was: "There are factories that do nothing but make cars, and they have to live also". After that he began to speculate at the secondary level about how we could get together the money, "resources", to be able to have the car fixed.

I had a child with him just before I turned eighteen. We still lived on the farm and in spite of my own lack of ability for close contact she was well provided for by him and the others in the house.

It is extremely important to distinguish between living in an autonomous connection with people and being completely without relationships. No human can handle being completely without relationships. She atrophies and succumbs, and then the only thing that can save her is symbiosis, to live through somebody else in order to share in connection again.

The life we lived after we got married was filled with relationships. The farm was crawling with people, both permanent residents and visitors. I had many opportunities to learn what happens in togetherness and in solitude, and this I busied myself with at every opportunity. For a long time I was not able to be alone. Every time I became alone my ability to think vanished. A bunch of irrational behaviors arose that were incomprehensible both from the outside and the inside.

Symbiosis and autonomy became important for me to understand in their deepest sense. Somebody who has lost contact with his womb-feeling −of being contented, of being secure, of getting all needs met without effort− that person becomes self- destructive, what we call mean or evil. To escape from this destructiveness it is necessary to reestablish the "womb-contact", but it has to happen on an immaterial level, since the person obviously can't return to the actual womb condition again. It is important to recall that everyone has been in that condition even if it is inaccessible, hidden in the past. We do have a memory of the womb-condition and it is possible through prime-thought work to get access to that memory again.

Over the years I have let some individuals who have lost their autonomy to enter into a healing symbiosis with me. To be able to do this I must not be the slightest dependent on them and I must allow them to react to all the pain and misery that is uncovered because of everything that has happened and been stored in them after they lost their autonomy.

Normal children who are born into normal human contact and never been subjected to violence or abuse, neglect or abandonment don't need any symbiosis, just normal human contact. If they get that they never succumb to jealousy, separation anxiety, destructive behavior or other dysfunctions.

I realized that this was an important basis for my understanding of life. I had lost the connection when I was three days old and become stuck in the solitariness of autism and not returned. On the other hand I had lived in an abundant connectedness and been fortunate to have people around me who allowed me to be in symbiosis with them. In that environment I wasn't forced to accommodate myself, instead I was allowed to adapt by letting my consciousness emerge and get grounded on its own time and terms. This uneven struggle took twenty-five years, instead of the normal seven to ten, and it started for me first when I was ten years old, an age when most people are already finished. As a consequence I gained much familiarity with the fundamental prerequisites for being human, being civilized and acculturated, and this familiarity I have since used in my practical everyday life.

When I worked as a cashier at the bath I met some of the municipality's representatives, among them a reform school superintendent. He came there and chatted with me a few times and wondered if I might be interested in being an instructor at the school. He felt that there was a need for someone to teach the youths about hair care and hygiene; he considered them so unkempt that normal people shunned them. Also, he knew that I had cared for quite a few children and adolescents who needed extra adult support since those youths had told him about me.

Without reflecting I said yes and started in the fall. The job fit me like a glove. For the first time I was asked existential questions that I could answer. I had the opportunity to develop and verbalize everything I had puzzled my way through. I was faced with new problems, young people who had suffered much abuse and who needed tangible help. I had to find the dysfunctional adults in order to help the children and adolescents. This involved visits to prisons, psychiatric hospitals, addict environments, and every possible aspect of society's underside. It involved a lot of negotiations with social authorities, guardians, and prison assistants. I realized that these kids couldn't be helped if you didn't help the ones they lived with.

This meant that I was involved in developing the at-home service which today is called "home therapist", participated in the development of neighborhood teams which eventually resulted in the field-assistant position in social welfare, was active in the work which led to block homes. There was also a lot of other youth projects involving music clubs, organized greasers and bikers, protest groups, DARE stop, that then turned into drug-free dances and drug-free culture. It was fifteen intensive years of work with adolescents and their environment, with schooling, home conditions, job, education and leisure time. It was all about a deep socialization of them in a constructive civilization without making them outsiders.

This work was about prevention. Those who were worst off got as much help as was available and it led to a great reduction in addicts, criminals, anti-socials, which would not have been the case if this strong tight protective net had not existed. It included a fairly small number of youths but it was the ones that needed it the most. Each of them could as an adult have destroyed so much for so many that it was worth every effort. For instance, preventing a youth with a lot of baggage from winding up an addict means one unscrupulous dealer less. Getting a youth into trade as a trainee so he gets a new basis for value in life means one criminal career less.

That aspect is especially hard to sell to the authorities since in retrospect you can only see a well functioning person and nobody can say what would have happened if he hadn't bet caught by the safety net. We who work in this field and see how those who fall outside the safety net derail, we know, but people in general don't, and especially not political decision-makers.

This led me into therapy. I worked as a therapist; I learned a series of therapeutic methods and I tried to find shortcuts to get through or around all the frightful stories those kids carried in them and were steered by.

A friend of mine called and read me the foreword to a book about near-death experiences that she had bought, *"We Experienced Death"* She thought the way of reasoning and describing in it reminded her of how I reasoned. I had not had any near-death experiences myself, but when I heard the foreword I thought it could have been written by me. The conclusion especially caught my attention:

Finally, people who have had a near-death experience but not had the possibility of describing it and discussing it with some knowledgeable person, can compare their experience with that of others and be freed of concerns that that they had experienced something abnormal.

And perhaps this book can communicate to them something which can't be shown to somebody who has not had such an experience herself, and which can only be vaguely described with human words: peace, clarity, wordless communication.

"...that they had experienced something abnormal ... wordless communication ..." Those words made me decide to write to the author of the foreword.

"And do you know where he lives?" she asked. "He is the head doctor at the hospital in your home town! His name is Göran Grip"

We became friends. Göran understood what I described, not just some fragments here and there, but he really understood, and he asked questions that nobody else had asked before. I had often asked such questions of others and now when Göran asked them of me I got an awareness of myself and also of the world and reality that I didn't have before. Before I had lived so much *in*, but now I could take a step back and say: This I am good at, this you can use me for. I had no idea that it was possible for me to find out what I was able to do.

The gold is in the mountain. I now was able to take the gold and make an ornament out of it. But the gold itself had not changed.

I told Göran about Rolf, who had no self-preservation instinct. He was six foot five and very strong, and every time he got enraged he beat somebody up. He had been in reform school and juvenile prison for assault and battery.

Göran: How could you see he lacked self-preservation instinct?

Iris:It looks entirely different. One who has that instinct, no matter how angry he gets, can see how it looks in front of him in reality. But I can see that when Rolf is angry there is a wall in front of him and he can't see anything, he just strikes out. I see that he strikes out because he can't see reality.

G: How do you see that?

I: I go Out and then it looks like a wall that keeps him from seeing reality and I see that he sees things coming at him that threaten him and that don't exist in reality.

G: How do you see that?

I: That I don't know, but I see it. I don't see it with my eyes and in images, but when I am Out I have a sense of what's happening inside him and what's controlling him. And I know exactly what I need to do.

G: What do you need to do then?

I: I know that I have to do what I did once in a threatening situation. I stepped in front of him, very close, and remained in Out, otherwise I couldn't have reached him. And I screamed at him: "Stop. Cease. I am stronger than you. You don't need to be afraid."

G: Hm. Interesting logic. He doesn't need to be afraid because you are stronger than him. And what happened with him when you said that?

I: I have never thought about that before. Yes, he became normal again.

G: What is that told you what you needed to do?

I: There is a lot of information, and it comes out of people, and you just look and you can see that information. And if you see a person that isn't functioning, you do what is necessary for him to function again.

G: Tell me about that information

I: If a person has a sad face and is crying it isn't necessarily certain that she is really sad. But when she is really sad, something numb comes out in the atmosphere and then I get the information that I am supposed to take it easy, that I should take it slowly, speak softly and carefully. When I do that, that person's atmosphere notices that she is understood. And then it is like there is a signal inside that person and then she can begin to cry for real and be precisely as sad as she really is. And then it passes when she is finished.

When Rolf had calmed down I asked him what happened when he got angry, did he see red? "No" he said, "it gets like a wall and I can't see anything else and then I punch myself free automatically." Exactly as I had seen.

After that time he asked me to help him with this problem because he realized that otherwise he'd be in jail for the rest of his life. For half a year I worked with him. Whenever I saw that he was on the verge of hitting someone I rushed forward and placed myself in front of him if possible and stopped him. It worked every time. Twice the police came and got me because they knew I could stop him.

One Saturday night half a year later, when there was a dance at Folkets Park he came bolting in, his face all beat up. He grabbed me and pushed me up against the wall and shouted: "It's your fault, you devil."

I said: "Put me down. What's happened?"

"Can't you see? I got beat up."

"I mean how did it happen?"

That's when I noticed a gleam in his eye and a slight smile on his mouth. And then he told me that a biker had said something that enraged him and then the wall had appeared as usual. But then my face appeared in front of him and dissolved the wall. And then he no longer had any strength to punch. And got thoroughly beat up: a fat lip, a black eye, a bloody nose. He was very satisfied. Because now he knew that he was free from his old reaction and that he now could control his actions. I don't know that he has hit a single person since then.

G: Do you have any example of seeing other people in this way?

I: Yes, several years ago I met Guy in a rehab for young addicts. He had just arrived and I was to have the first conversation with him. I saw that his filter between the dream world and the real world, the filter that allows you to tell the difference between dream and reality, that filter was thin and completely perforated. Occasional such perforations are present in most addicts but they usually close up after a while. But for Guy it was almost all holes. I saw that several times during the comedown after a high he had seen horror scenes involving his family and been gripped by reactions he couldn't control.

He said "I'll never stop doing drugs, that's something young people do and it is not harmful. It just you grownups that don't want us young people to have fun.

I answered: "With other young persons I usually let them have a few relapses until they discover the disadvantages with drugs themselves."

Then I told him about his perforated filter and that I could see that he had had many terror experiences.

"That you have no idea about." He said

"I only say what I see. And what I see is that you are just a hair away from psychosis and maybe lock-up for the rest of your life. So to you I say: It is over now. Not one more time. And I am thinking what can I do to help you?"

Then he let down his defenses and told me that early one morning after a high he had gone to kitchen to get something to drink and seen his father's decapitated head in the refrigerator. The eyes had stared directly at him. Afterwards he had shook with terror for hours. Another time he had seen his father's chopped off hand in the freezer, and he had experienced several such gruesome episodes. He was scared because I had seen this, but what shook him the most was that even before I told him what I saw he had seen that I saw it. And this made him take my words seriously. And he said what he needed was a goal to look forward to. I told him if he made it for a year without relapse I would take him to Greece for a week to go sailing. And after a difficult and dangerous year for him we went to Greece.

Göran, who had not been autistic, told me he was able to sense other people's feelings and intentions. Both as a child and as an adult he could, as he said, "reach into other people" and sense their feelings. He told me about how as a very small child he had reached into his father and detected that his father was jealous of him and his mother. And he described how he used his ability for example when he needed to anesthetize a frightened little girl who came with her frightened mother, and which he has described in his book *Allting finns.*

I had never talked with anyone else like this. I had talked about my immaterial world and my experiences many times, but up to now this had only given rise to disbelief or perplexed amazement, but nothing more. For me the immaterial reality was concrete and tangible, but when I told about it my listeners would respond with: "You are so clever", or "how did you come up with that?" or "that seems a little fishy. You can't rely on something like that, it could be as wrong as anything." What Göran did was to engage me in my experiences and ask questions from inside them, and that was revolutionary for me. Suddenly I realized that I knew something I didn't know I knew. I realized that my inner world, which I knew and which was secure for me was real. Göran and I talked on the same level, on the primary level, in the real world, and that gave me contact with my feeling, with my self-esteem. Earlier I had momentary contacts with my self-esteem as for example when I stopped Rolf, and knew I was doing the right thing. But this was the first time that I had contact with my self-feeling and shared it with another person. This was the first time I was talking with another person in the real reality. Fil and Emma had been in the real reality together with me but we had not conversed, it was they who had told me about their own reality. Exactly like me, Göran could distinguish between what was himself and what came from other people. He wrote as follows in *Allting finns*:

That I sensed other's feelings is not magic or mysticism. It isn't psychosis or identity mix-up.

And it is definitely not an illusion. Aside from the fact that it is inexplicable, it is very simple. It's like when you sit at the table and wonder if the tea pot is warm or cold. You reach out and touch it and then you know. It's the pot that is warm and it is I who feel the warmth. Before we knew about sense organs and the central nervous system this was just as inexplicable. And just as simple.

Göran wondered what I did instead of playing with other children. Then I told him about Slire and Skydde and our games. For me this was as self-evident as breathing, but Göran, who had had two near-death experiences, but no out-of-body experiences thought it was very fascinating, especially "buzz around the legs of the horse while it's walking" and "swallow-mommy". His questions and his fascination made me realize that my games in the real world with Slire and Skydde weren't as banal as playing hide and go seek.

Göran told me about the birth of his brother. He describes it as follows in his book *"Allting finns"*:

I told Iris about when my brother was born. I walked all the way back to the feeling of being three years old and how it felt while mom was in the hospital [...]

I told about my distress and my desperate longing for mommy. And the catastrophe when she finally came home and turned me away. [...]

Iris became disturbed while I was talking and I asked what the matter was. Had my story affected her so badly?

--I see an image she said in great agony and searched for the words. There is a block of ice and under the block is a baby, a little girl. She is almost dead but not quite because she is moving a little.

The dying child!

--What does that image mean?

Iris squirmed and went into the image. Her breath came in short painful gasps.

--Yes she finally said. Your mother's greatest wish was to have a girl. She had hoped that you would be a girl. And when she found out that your brother wasn't a girl either she became deeply depressed because she knew that was her last chance to have a daughter.

Then I remembered. Mom had told me that I should have been named Kerstin, and that was Lars supposed to be also. Then she bought a figurine in porcelain in the image of a girl reading a book and called it Kerstin.

I described for my aunt May my experiences when Lars was born. I didn't tell her what Iris had said. She was silent for a while. Then she said:

--Your mother's greatest wish was to have a girl. When Lars was born she was very disappointed and was depressed or several months and didn't have the energy to take care of you very well. She was very tired.

Suddenly I heard father's voice, categorical and determined. "Two children are enough. We shall not have more than two children." Lars was the last chance for a girl.

We talked about a lot of other things also. I told him that I couldn't write, was unable to spell correctly and was dyslexic. Göran asked if I knew how to type and then I told him I had learned to type in my class on business. "So you *know* how to type!" he said. "Then you'll have to type on my PC." This is how he describes it in *"Allting finns"*:

Iris told me that that she was word-blind and could only read slowly with great difficulty. This was presumably caused by a slight brain damage she explained casually. And this damage also made it difficult for her to learn how to operate appliances and machines, she added calmly and matter of fact.

Brain damage? Iris? I thought astounded. I looked at her. She was quick and intelligent and articulate and I couldn't discern any signs that she had brain damage. And her letters to me were not written by a dyslexic person that could barely read. They were lively and exciting and the language rippled like a spring brook. I was also surprised that she talked about her "brain damage" so blithely*. Hm.

To convince me of her dyslexia she showed me a paper on pedagogy that she had just written. When she handed me the paper I sensed that she had strong feelings of unease about it. The paper was really not good. It was strained and tedious and almost impossible to understand, in addition rife with spelling errors. But it didn't at all resemble the letters that I used to get from another friend who really was dyslexic and who wrote like a rake. And the spelling errors weren't of the right kind either. This had to be some completely different kind of word-blindness. I asked her to tell me the circumstances around the

——————— *foot note* ———————

*As a physician I had learned that people who talk about their injuries and handicaps in an unconcerned way may be subject to various kinds of defense mechanisms. But today, when I know Iris better than when I wrote *Allting finns* I have realized that the reason Iris talked so matter-of-factly about her brain damage was that she had really accepted the thought that she had a handicapping injury, notthat she was subject to some defense mechanism.

paper. She was studying pedagogy at the university and this was supposed to be double graded paper, she said. But her instructor was not satisfied with her writing. She had criticized both the style and the contents and consequently Iris had reformulated it over and over again.

While she was talking I sensed that she was scared of her female instructor, in fact she was terrified of her. Even when she sat here with me she became almost dumb-struck when she tried to talk about her. Not surprising she could not express herself in writing when she had such a terror in her.

Next time we met I decided to bet everything on one card.

--You are not dyslexic I asserted decisively.

--What? She said and looked at me concerned. What do you mean? It's obvious I am dyslexic. I can't read.

--No you are not dyslexic. I have friend who is dyslexic and she doesn't write like you.

--Yes, but...

--You are not dyslexic, I said and held her gaze. The person who wrote all these letters to me is not a dyslexic person. I held out the thick bundle of letters I had received from her.

--Yes, but those letters don't count. It is just me chatting with you.

--If you are word-blind because of brain damage you equally word-blind regardless of whom you are writing to. Your paper is in fact a complete mess, but it is not written by a word-blind person. The word-blind screw it up in a different way than you do.

I had caught her. She couldn't wriggle out of my arguments.

And when she accepted my argument I saw how the terror spread inside her. I was on the right track. Who gets scared when you take away from her handicap? Someone who uses it as a shield.

When she had recovered she said I was the first person who had not accepted her assertion that she was word-blind. But what was wrong with her then? That she had no clue of and I couldn't see what it might be either. One clue was her exaggerated fear of the instructor. But we didn't make any progress, and the conversation came to an end.

We sat silent for a while and my thoughts started to wander. I was thinking about my PC which I had now had for about half a year, and which I still found very entertaining. The word processing program I had used in doing the translation of We Experienced Death *still felt like a small miracle. Imagine, you placed the cursor in the middle of a sentence and typed a word and then the rest of text moved and made place for the new word. Astounding! I no longer needed to edit and rewrite and make complex notations to keep track of how I wanted to rearrange things in my texts.*

Iris sat there staring straight ahead with an empty look. I sensed that her inner process about the word-blindness had ceased. I suggested impulsively that I should show her how the word processor worked. She looked up surprised and wondered what the point would be.

Nothing special, I said. But we aren't doing anything else.

She sat down in the chair next to the PC, thinking I would give her a demonstration. When I asked her to sit at the PC she objected that she didn't understand such things. Balderdash! Just sit down and I'll tell you what to do.

I turned on the PC for her and empty screen with the blinking cursor lit up.

--Type a sentence I said. She put her fingers on the keyboard. looked at the screen and typed a sentence. Hi Iris, how are you? She did touch typing! She, who maintained that she was impractical and didn't know how to use machines! Hm.

I describe how you delete a word and type another. She did it. I described how you italicize a word. She did it.

After a while she had gone through all the basic commands and I discovered to my surprise that she learned very quickly. I needed to describe something once and she understood and remembered. And I could tell that she had no idea what was happening. She had an amused smile on her lips and her movements were light and quick. I sensed that she was unaware that she was busy doing one of the things that she stubbornly maintained she was unable to do. I had an idea.

--Now I want you to sort this list of words that you have just made.

--How do you do that? she asked cheerfully.

--It says here, I said casually and nonchalantly threw her the manual. She dove into the booklet and after skimming through the section on sorting she proceeded to do it, correctly on the first try. She looked at me with anticipation wanting more tasks to try.

--Do you know what you have just done?

--No she said, without a clue. What have I done?

Do you realize what you have been doing for the past half hour? I said with a touch of seriousness in my voice.

Her gaze brightened and she looked at me quizzically.

--What do you mean?

--You maintain that you have brain damage and that you can't read or operate machines. This PC is quite a complicated machine. Did you notice that I only needed to show you each thing once for you to learn it?

She looked at me surprised.

--Yes but ...she said and fell silent. She realized I was right.

--Of all the people I have shown this PC to, you are the one who learned it the quickest, I said and saw how the terror spread over her face. I drove in the last nail.

--And this sorting.

--What do you mean?

--Here the manual is a little unclear and I didn't understand what it said. I had to experiment a long while before I finally figured out what you have to do to sort a list of words. You read the manual yourself and did it correctly the first time without any help from me.

Red hectic roses blossomed on her cheeks and I saw her heart thumping in her chest. She was almost overwhelmed by fear. Now it was time to leave her in peace. I saw how the terror receded when she noticed that nothing dangerous was happening, and how it was replaced with astonishment and wonderment. She looked with her mouth half-open at the PC screen with the green text. Hi Iris, how are you? She looked at the open manual. She looked at the keyboard. She looked at me.

Her gaze became vacant when she went into herself. Slowly her face lit up with wonderment and quiet intensive joy when she – after all these years—began to achieve control of her talent. I had helped her abolish the brain damage.

The rest of the story Iris can tell in her own book.

Chaos erupted in me when Göran pointed out to me what I had done with the PC. Then I went Out inside me and I could see what he saw. And it wasn't only because he saw it; I saw it because it was in fact there. I saw my own capacity -- for the first time. This was the first time that I had any conception that I had some capacity, some talent. Everything I knew got tossed in the air and when it came down there was a new dimension in it: a consciousness of my own capacity. Everything was the same as before, but it was like a blossom had burst out, everything had become so beautiful. Earlier Father had said I had a talent for working with hair and I had seen that my customers at the salon were satisfied, but I had not myself *perceived* that I had any talent.

That experience changed my life. The entire image of myself in the world and in reality was totally changed. I got a self-confidence and self-respect that allowed me to happily affirm things in a way that hadn't been able to do before. I could affirm my knowing, and I saw that it was worth just as much as the scientific knowledge that I studied at the university, and that there wasn't any fundamental difference between knowing and scientific knowledge. And that gave an entirely different degree of self-esteem than I had before.

CHAPTER 8

Life today

Living with somebody with a disability is an art since the one who has it can't choose to not have it.

I understand that people want, or need, to have a private life but I don't know what it is. Working is what makes life meaningful for me. Not because of what I do, but because I have a role, a task, which means that somebody who needs help receives help from what I have to offer. Whoever gives me that task gives me the gift of knowing exactly what I need to do. Then I can make my internal lists and skip around among them, then I have an inner structure which enables me to be in the present and I don't have exist in a haze.

If nobody gives me a task I forget that others exist around me and then everything floats without direction and without substance. I end up in a type of feedback within myself. The outer world disappears and isolated thoughts spin around hundreds of times, for example: "It doesn't matter, because I've got no money." These thoughts actually come in English. It might also be a verse from a hit song, or a line from a film. As a child I called them crazy thoughts because I knew they had no meaning for me. While such a thought is buzzing around I am unaware of time and place, and when it stops of itself I may discover that an hour or six have passed. I have difficulty breaking the thought cycle myself, but sometimes I can by giving myself a task, for example to iron some clothes. When I have been ironing a while the thought disappears. Therefore I always keep a stack of un-ironed clothes available. Somebody coming to see me or the cell phone ringing can also break the cycle.

Until I was thirty-five years old it was always difficult for me to free myself of such obsessive thoughts. I don't know what anguish is other than as a description, but I believe the struggle I waged to free myself from such thoughts would be called anguish by normal people. Today my life is so well organized –I have many tasks and have minimized my alone-time—that I seldom end up in that state, and when I do I have a an easier time getting out of it than before.

Without substance describes the state I was in as a child. It was empty on the inside, nothingy and without feelings. Sometimes there were only motions, wandering aimlessly or spinning around or hands flapping or legs twitching. I did these things, or was compelled to do them, so I would know I existed; to experience my outside border, so I could be conscious of existing. The older I have become the more experience I have had, so now I can free myself from this state of obsessive thoughts and pour in life-substance instead. Then I find meaning and then I can let my mind spin around in some observation that I am trying to understand, for example something I have noticed about some person which doesn't seem to fit. That's how I have found what counts when nothing else counts. Once when an obsessive thought had been swirling around in my head for a long time I latched on to an observation I had made just before, when the lecturer at a management course had said: "It's important to trust other people." To free myself from the obsessive thought I turned the thought cycle to the word trust instead. If the world were static, if nothing was happening, you could rely on it. But the world isn't static, things are happening all the time, unpredictable, unforeseeable things and therefore you *can't* rely on the world and the people in the world. But I know that there *is* trust, that people do feel trusting, so it has to work a different way than by being able to rely on the *world*. I meet a person and don't know how she will react. *Her* I can't trust. However, I can trust that I will be able to handle whatever this person can possibly subject me to; I can trust my own ability to handle the world. The trust lies within oneself and is not, as the lecturer and many others believe, dependent on others, whom one "can trust".

When I cleared up for myself in this way what trust was, and had tested my insight on others and found it sound, the atmosphere around the concept trust changed for good and its old appearance vanished for all time.

If I were to describe to myself, in words that I myself understand, the process I described here about my struggling with the concept trust I could say:

What I "see" when someone says something is how it looks in the immaterial, and then I connect it. Then it can swirl around

*until it becomes a swoop and then it is clear. Then both worlds
disappear and it becomes apparent what it is.*

These are words and formulations that may not be
understandable to an outsider, but it is exactly how I describe it
to myself, and I understand exactly what I mean.

To have a husband and children, a core family, and live in
it, and be able to be as contented with it as others are, that
did not work. I grew up with many people around me and had
an atmosphere that constantly changed and where there never
was an empty atmosphere, even at night, and it got terribly
difficult for me with only one person, who besides only wanted
to relax and didn't need any contribution from me, It was more
like I was a bother. As I grew up there was always somebody
who needed something, not least of all me, so consequently
there was nothing that is called private.

To live in a pair relation doesn't work well for me since I don't
have the ability to constantly   zoom in on my partner's needs
and meet them. My ex-husband was superb at being available
and giving me all the space in the world so that I would have a
chance to learn everything that was so difficult and impossible
for me. He is such a loving person, with such a large surplus
that it sufficed for both of us, and for me that would have been
enough. He put up with all my peculiarities and liked to be with
me for twenty-five years, but then he needed something else,
and that I can understand. Deep inside he was hoping that my
capacity for harmony would awaken some time, but it didn't,
and then he felt that he was turning bitter. I didn't want this to

happen, because he is such a fine person. I wanted sincerely that he should have it good and be happy. We got divorced and I believe he is happy today.

All the ones I had been involved with and who had needed me and that I had cared for, my biological child, my foster children, my adolescents in the Youth Home, the families I had helped, the projects I had in the county etc, they all now stood on their own two feet. Nobody needed me that desperately anymore, and I could raise my gaze and look around. Then I wanted to get something for myself. I wanted to study at the university. Sure, I had studied earlier, but then it had been isolated topics on the side when I was working and was taking care of people who needed me.

I was planning to study to become a high school teacher. I had worked as teacher in child-care education and I had done the same at an agricultural school, I had worked at several adult education schools from time to time when I was needed and I liked very much to convey all that I had stored in my mind. I realized that there was something special that you needed to understand, or understand it in a special way to be accepted as a teacher. It wasn't enough that you instructed and the students learned what the syllabus specified, it also had to be pedagogically correct. I didn't know what that was but I planned to find out.

I used to think that the most accomplished people on earth are the ones in the university because they knew so much about everything, right? But I discovered that they didn't have any clue either about the natural, the primary, that which counts when nothing else counts, and I got exceedingly slight response to things that caught my interest. Still, I learned a lot of other things and met many fun persons so it was quite rewarding anyway. In addition I got to guide several of my lecturers.

There was one lecturer whose teaching was superb, but I saw that he constantly came into conflict with his students. I saw that he "blurred", that he constantly disparaged himself, questioned what he had just said, which frequently was fantastically good. This caused the students to disbelieve him, actually didn't hear what he said, and constantly contradicted him. It became a kind of war which he tried to win by making the students lose, and this led to him being disregarded by the students and the superb contents got lost.

After one lecture which had been fantastic, but which everyone left with a bad feeling, and none of the contents, I went up to him and described for him exactly what was happening between him and the students, and said that if he was willing I could help him solve the conflict inside him which caused this external conflict.

He accepted, and after half a year he had detected his own negative strategies, and thereby was able to change them. After that he received the recognition for the characteristics I had ascribed to him, both from students and colleagues.

This spread via the grapevine and then several other lecturers discovered they had issues they carried around which they asked me to help them with. That's how my consulting career started.

The reason I started to study in Uppsala was that one of my

youths lived there and he needed me during the period when the application was due so I figured I might as well apply there as anywhere else. I entered a two-subject teacher training program in religion and child-and-youth studies. I soon realized that what we were to study the first two years I already knew, and more thoroughly than my instructors, which gave me an idea of how little they knew at the university.

Since it was a long commute from Stockholm I rented a studio apartment in Uppsala and was about to live alone for the first time in my life. It was difficult and I discovered that it was impossible to read or do anything else productive when there was nobody else's atmosphere in the apartment.

I went to the local middle school and got a job as a special ed teacher for a group of six and seventh graders that didn't fit in their large classes, and had been huge problems there. One had Aspergers, one was deeply depressed, one was a delinquent, one had suicidal tendencies, one constantly cut classes, and one had ADHD.

It was a very enjoyable time and I found different solutions for getting these kids to come to class and listen to my lectures.

The boy with Aspergers had no capacity for empathy and could not understand that other people got upset or wounded or insulted by what he did. I told him how he functioned inside and he recognized this and accepted it. And then I explained how it was for other people, and that was a whole new world for him that he had no clue about. This understanding didn't change much in his behavior, but it made him able to own up to what he had done and acknowledge that it was dumb, or say: "I don't know how to act." That way he became more acceptable both to himself and to those around him.

The delinquent and the boy with Aspergers were friends, but the delinquent carried on in his usual style and often said stupid things. Once he said: "Go and hang yourself" and the boy with Aspergers disappeared. I heard a noise from the bathroom and found him there standing on the toilet seat with something tied around his neck. "What are you doing?" I said. "I was supposed to hang myself" he answered. I got the delinquent and showed him the effect his words had had. "Can you see that he takes after all the bad things you do and say?" Yes, that he did. And then I asked him to not show his bad behavior because it could hurt his buddy. With that he began to change his language and also stopped fighting.

Of the boy who was severely depressed I asked: "Is there something in your life that makes your life bearable?" "Music" he answered, and then I allowed him to bring his Freestyle player and listen to music during the lessons, with the ear phones a little to the side so he could hear the lectures.

The boy with ADHD had a lot of energy and zero ability to concentrate, and could never sit still. He was constantly running around in the class-room and mumbled and made noises, disturbing the others. I got the idea that if I let him ride around on a unicycle in the class-room it required so much energy and concentration to keep his balance that he could stay collected, and he learned to both read and write thanks to this trick.

The kid who was always cutting class got the assignment to make sure that the girl with suicidal tendencies did not kill herself, and thereby he was compelled to be in class every day.

To the girl with suicidal tendencies I said that I would tell the class about her problem, and she could be present then if she wanted to, but she didn't have to. She sat in front, closest to the door when I told the class and asked them to take care of her. They let her join in their games, and the guy that cut classes was above all the one who made sure that she was included.

One afternoon when I went for my walk I went past the motocross track where my students used to compete. I caught sight of something pink on top of a crest right next to the track and went closer. It was the suicidal girl that they had placed there so she would be included. She sat crouched with her chin on her knees. When I returned from my walk an hour later she was still there in the same position.

She kept her passivity and depression, but her fixation on suicide disappeared eventually and life stopped being dreadful for her and became nothingness, which was better.

I talked in class about communication, about doing good things, but it got no resonance from the kids. "Nobody would believe it if one of us did something good", they said. "We might as well smash some windows, because everybody thinks that we are the ones who are responsible for everything." Then I asked them if they wanted to challenge this and if they were prepared to try it. Four of the boys went along with it.

I described for them how dress, looks and behavior influence how others perceive us. If you imagine yourselves in a dark suit with leather shoes, do you think they would perceive you the same way as when you come in dirty jeans and t-shirts? Then we played with their own prejudices about people who were nicely dressed.

They accepted the challenge and we went out shopping, buying suits and shoes for them at second-hand stores.

Then we set a date.

On that day they came to school at six am. I cut their hair and blow dried it, and they ironed their shirts, pressed their suits, and polished their shoes to a high shine. They dressed, and then I had them stand in front of two big mirrors I had brought to practice smiling, shaking hands and bowing. At first they didn't do so good, but they learned.

The teachers usually arrived at the school at a quarter to eight, and then three of the boys stood by the main entrance and waited for them. The fourth had not dared to go down there but was standing all dressed up with me and the other two students in our class-room and watched. The boys greeted the teachers, offered their hands and asked if there was anything they could help with. They held the door open, and one of them helped with a bicycle lock, but otherwise the teachers, whom I had not clued in, were suspicious and guessed that there was some kind of mischief cooking. I had warned the boys ahead of time that they would get such reactions. They spent the entire morning in the hallways and the recess room, and whenever they saw an adult they went up to them and opened doors or carried a bag.

The afternoon was devoted to reviewing the day's

experiences in our class-room. The boys almost died laughing when they described all the surprised and suspicious reactions they had seen during the day.

In the evening a teacher's meeting was called where I was invited to explain what I was up to. I told them that these youths felt judged beforehand, that they felt that it was useless to behave because they would get the blame for everything anyway. Then I had challenged them, I said, to try and see if they got another reaction if they changed their appearance and behavior. I said there was no hidden motive in this but that the intention was open: to bring about an engagement instead of a judgment.

Most teachers thought this was a fantastic initiative. At first they had reacted with suspicion, but then they noticed that it felt heart warming, and many of them realized that these boys also had positive sides.

Next day they repeated the same thing and then they got a different reception. They were appreciated and politely treated by the teachers and received nice comments, and when they came to see me in the afternoon they were touched by the nice reception they had gotten. I explained to them that they could continue receiving this nice reception even when they were dressed in jeans and t-shirt.

It was the most fun class that I have ever had.

I had them for three years, and when they graduated from ninth grade they appreciated that they had changed their behavior in this way.

These youths enriched my life by visiting with me in the

evenings also. Now I was needed again. I had the privilege of being of service to others and being used. It was bright inside me again and I escaped struggling with my obsessions and repetitions.

Thanks to this class my private life was again blended with what is called work. For me there is no such distinction. I do what I do, and part of it I get paid for, and that's what others call work. I live life and have my worth and it doesn't depend on whether I am private or official. Life for me is to establish what exists naturally for other people, relationships and communication between people. Unless I can bring this about my life gets barren and soulless.

One day a friend whom I worked with in summertime called. He thought we should start this commune that we had dreamt about for so long. Lovely, he came and filled my one-room apartment. Then there was another boy who also worked summers with us and he also wanted to join the commune. He came – lovely. Then there was a boy we had met one summer, who understood something we weren't quite clear on ourselves – he came and so we were three youths and I in a one-room apartment.

Life was rich again, rich in people and relationships, many persons who needed contact and I got to be needed. We moved into a big apartment together and my youths got partners and our existence was full of life and substance in a superb way. Then came children and that was even more fantastic, to have a bunch of toddlers around us, what richness!

I lived alone in the sense that I was not in a pair relationship, but otherwise I was not alone. I lived communally with two families with three children each and this meant that I was stimulated into contact continuously and that was great. I love people, especially children, so living like this fit me like a glove. To be able to participate in the children's growth and be allowed to contribute my insight and knowledge both to parents and children is a great privilege.

After a lecture that I gave on communication Lennart came up to me. He thought that what I had said was valuable, in fact unique, even if he couldn't quite put his finger on what it was. He thought it was important that others should share it and offered to help me organize it. Thanks to him I got an assignment to establish a development program in a big company for women in leadership positions. They learned about male and female language so that they could gain greater respect from the men and feel better about themselves. Both the men and the women in the company were satisfied and several women succeeded later in breaking through the glass ceiling. When the man who had engaged me in this assignment later became treasurer in a municipality he engaged me in staff development groups and women's projects there.

In another big company I worked with a group with such great internal conflicts that almost no work got done. With my help they succeeded in resolving the conflicts and gained the respect of their superiors for their work. They were so satisfied that they still contact me when they feel that new problems are brewing.

In several schools I conducted workshops in communications.

In three adult education schools I tutored a group of prospective social pedagogues.

At a conference at the Arstahemmet in 1987 I described my views on communication and one of the participants, who was director of a therapy-study home in Järna and who had tried at least four different instructors, decided that it was my concept he wanted to adopt. My work with him grew eventually into work with the entire Haga foundation, which works with clients with communication difficulties that no other institutions can handle. There I began mentoring the staff, a role which I still have today.

Thus, the avalanche was started and today, almost twenty years later, I am booked two years in advance , not just in Sweden but also in Norway, Germany, Russia, Lithuania, Estonia, Italy, and Albania.

Unfortunately I have only been able to experience feelings in glimpses and with a lot of hard work. I know what it is to live with feelings and through feelings, and what a richness it is but also what a burden. I live intensely to keep from losing my awareness control – this need that I all the time have to have a conversation inside myself to keep from losing it. This is a hard job but it is completely private and few people see me doing it. Occasionally somebody has a glimpse of what it is like to have a disability but most lose it quickly when I switch inside and meet them.

If for example I am about to travel somewhere, on the road to an assignment, or if I am home alone, it may happen that I lose my awareness control, and then there may come a lot of impulses -- I'll do the wash, I'll do some ironing – but none of them remains long enough to make me do something. Then I go into a complete jumble, the relationship world disappears and I don't know if I have said goodbye and said where I am going, and I don't notice if I am hungry or thirsty or need to use the bathroom. When I finally sit on the train or the bus and suddenly hear a voice or a phone ringing, or when somebody comes to talk to me I return to the relationship world, and then I can hear my stomach rumble and understand that I am hungry, and become aware of my bodily needs and can attend to them.

I never disappear from the relationship world like that when I am on an assignment, only when I am by myself.

In our commune we had long talked about finding a platform where we could live and support ourselves together. We contacted the Summer-child agency in Stockholm and were given the position of running a children's summer camp on a homestead operated by the summer-child agency. Suddenly we had a camp. Thirty-four children in each three-week group and three groups each summer.

It was a wonderful time: having everyone present and also having a common assignment. Working as the camp-leader was ideal for me, having everyone near and dear, and seeing them at all hours of the day, in addition being allowed to be responsible for structuring the work, handling conflicts among the children and among ourselves, and other problems. How could anyone have it better? In my private world it was as close to paradise as it was possible to be.

Most of the children from Stockholm came from low-income

families, where both parents worked through the summer and were not able to do much together with the kids.

The old idea with the summer camps was that children could come out in the country and participate in country life; they would work with cooking, cleaning and washing, take part in harvest work and such, in other words emphasizing the concept of duty. Our idea was to eliminate the duties for the children and that we grown-ups would do what we most enjoyed and draw the kids into it. Thus the camp became shaped by the interests of the grown-ups, such as theater, role-play, music and song, adventurous hikes, and exciting great-games that could last days and where nobody won or lost. The important thing was that we were happy with what we were doing, that we didn't have any definite goal orientation or predetermined result in mind, and we didn't create any competitive situations. We purchased as few things as possible and fabricated ourselves much of what we needed.

We had very few rules for the children: they could not go swimming without an adult, they could not climb the fire escapes, and they had to be in their room after 11 pm. And we had no punishments.

One evening when we had a teenage group we discovered that four girls had snuck into one of the boys rooms via the fire escape. We addressed this issue, had a conversation with the girls as we usually did when somebody broke the rules, and sent them to bed. And that was that. We thought.

Two days later two of the girls came and asked why they hadn't been punished. I answered:

"We are not based on distrust; we have confidence that we can talk our way to a good solution. And it works very well. Therefore we have no reason to administer punishments."

"But couldn't we be punished anyway?"

"Why do you want to be punished?"

"Yes, because if we are punished we get rid of our guilty conscience and we can do it again."

I discussed this with the other grownups and we decided that for this once we would hand out some punishments. A suitable punishment was that each of the four girls would have to go out and pick one liter of blueberries, which we would then use to make blueberry pie.

Next morning we had a meeting and then I brought up that four girls had been out running around and that the punishment was they had to pick blueberries. I knew only who two of the girls were so I said: "You, who were out running around, raise your hand." Ten hands came up in the air. I said: "But it was only four girls who were out. Why did the rest of you raise your hands?"

One of the girls said: "We thought we could take out our punishment in advance."

We had a ten-year old Stockholm boy, in effect a street child, who was a mascot in the underworld, and was often used by pushers as a go-between and keeping track of plain-clothes policemen, for which he received food, and sometimes clothes in return. His immature mother was incapable of being a mother and had no money for food, and his father was nowhere.

He was overjoyed when he came to camp. He got food, got to be in a secure environment, there were grownups who cared, he got to do a lot of fun things, and above all he didn't need to be scared, which he normally was otherwise. The day his group was set to return we could not find him. His buddy told me that he had said he wasn't going back to Stockholm but planned to stay here with us. We went searching but finally we had to send the bus away, two hours late, without him.

Two days later the second group of the summer kids came, and then suddenly there he was standing there among the new kids. We didn't make a big deal of it, just counted him in with the others. We called the mother, who was desperate, because she couldn't afford to pay for another stay, and then we let him be a stowaway and let stay the whole summer.

Afterwards he stayed with us every summer—the whole summer—and when he turned sixteen and couldn't attend camp anymore, he decided unilaterally that he would work as a trainee with us. After two years of that I made him a leader.

Today he is an enormously competent young man who arranges adventure activities for the public and for companies.

The years went by. Some in the commune got jobs in different places and left. Another one got divorced and thereby got another home. The commune changed successively and eventually we were four singles with children who lived together. Every summer we reconnected at camp.

The camp activity was closed after eleven summers and the property was put up for sale. One of my commune mates, who had been a camp trainee before, bought it and we continued to gather there in the summertime. Later there was another camp-child who got married and bought the place and moved there and invited me to move there. This I did happily. It was the first time in my life that I could say "at home" and know what it meant. I got to live in a small granary, a wonderful little log house which had an atmosphere all its own. I had the opportunity to write my books with a man that I shared the communal life with. It was fantastic to sit in the same room with someone who has such an atmosphere that I don't lose myself, but am able to focus on my writing several hours at a time. This was another private period of the greatest importance for me.

One day a neighbor came, who is the partner of one of my old camp leaders, and said he would build an "in-law house" for me. He was going to take down an old barn and build an extension around it to make me a small house. Thank you, thank you! Can one be more privileged than to spend one's old age in a courtyard, an old-lady-place, with one's friends around? For me it is almost incomprehensible that it is possible to receive something like that. And ...

All of a sudden my foster-daughter shows up and moves here. What a favor! And ...

Then it didn't take long before my biological daughter, who has lived in Canada for twenty years, came back home and moved into a small croft.

If somebody had told me that these things would happen I would have thought they were insane. But they *have* happened. Now I have my near and dear right in the neighborhood and I have good and frequent contact with most of the people I have lived with communally for the past twenty years.

To receive impulses and maintain contact with people I arrange meetings a few times per year. I sometimes go to a spa with the women who have worked with me in the camp, and there we sit in the Jacuzzi and talk. It is very pleasant and enjoyable. A group of women living in Stockholm I see a few times per year and we go out to a restaurant and sit and talk. Some of them still celebrate birthdays and then I am invited. When I turned fifty I had birthday parties in three places in Sweden so that everyone who wished would have the opportunity to celebrate with me, and I did the same when I turned sixty. Whenever I visit Umeå there is always a get-together, and when I visit Järna I can bring guests home to a friend that I used to live with, and she does and cares for me so I have it fantastically good.

I have photo-albums which I use to connect me to the ordinary world, pictures of the most important people in my calendar, pictures in my PC, so I can look and remember. I have about three hundred names and telephone numbers in my cell phone, and my email and regular address books are all filled up.

One day I sat down and figured out how many people I have had regular contact with during the year and found that it was almost a thousand people. For the most part it is other people who make contact with me. It's people from many different countries and each relationship has its own story. My network is exciting and fun and it intersects in interesting patterns now and then.

Somebody came from Norway and met a man in my network and married him and had children with him.

Somebody came from Germany and introduced himself to my mother who lives in Värmland, and that led to us organizing a project there.

I met a young girl who was attending a school where I instructed. She made a strong connection with me since she had grown up on an agricultural commune in Uruguay which was a lot like my childhood home. Through her I met her mother, and she arranged for a group of ten people to visit this commune in Uruguay. There we made contacts which led to one of the children in the commune coming to Sweden and for a long time attended the school where I had met the young girl.

The son in the family where I used to live when I worked in St Petersburg followed me to Sweden and worked as a trainee in a camp. He got to know some of those working at the camp and they later went to St Petersburg and participated in his work with retarded people.

One guy who came along on one of my Greek weeks for personal development met an Albanian woman there whom he eventually married and took with him to Sweden. She has in turn arranged trips to Albania with Swedes and Albanians, where they work with personal development.

If somebody were to ask me how it's possible to have personal relationships with so many people I would answer that it is a privilege, that it is not burdensome, and that since I never store up anything inside there is always room. I don't understand how it could be too much. Everybody is different and nobody can be compared so it is only a matter of one and one and one.

Somebody wonders how I have time. I work almost every day all year, and at the same time I socialize with a bunch of people, and write books and travel with groups hither and dither. There is a secret, and that is that I don't sleep very much. I don't need more than four hours of sleep per night, plus an hour for practice, programming and enjoyment after I wake up. I have no problem with insomnia since I am always peppy when I wake up, and if I get tired during the day I can always take a nap whenever I have a moment free. I can sleep on a rug on the floor, in the car or bus or train or the plane. The worst part is that I snore, so when I sleep in public I often get told I can't sleep.

I have zero need for relaxation. For me "relaxation" leads to emptiness, obsession and repetitions, so I try to stay "on" at all times. This means that when I recount what I do in a day other people get tired just from listening to it. Some who are with me a few days feel that they need as many days of rest afterwards because it is so intense. I am never stressed but follow my to do lists, and they are made up with margins so it never gets too tight.

From time to time I can still lose myself, usually when no alternative listed in my head has worked. Then I get confused and wander aimlessly around until somebody speaks to me. Then it lets go and I can orient myself. Nowadays this happens at most twice per year.

To feel no emotions and not be able to use feelings to understand different situations, this I am entirely reconciled with. I know I have to use other ways, ways that are awkward and subject to error. But I have learned that the ways I use allow me to get a lot of contact and feelings from others, which I need. What I also gain is that I am never bored. I am busy full-time trying to interpret and understand what is the key in different situations, what tacit agreements people have and what is counted as normal, and so forth.

In many situations I am an off-beat element and this causes me to receive the attention that I need. I was at a school where I had just concluded a mentoring session. In the dining room two parents were talking with some teachers about their son, who was a problem student, and they asked me to join them. They talked about the boy in a way that I don't understand and can't participate in. One of the parents said:

"He is so difficult and creates so much trouble, and ruins it for the rest of us. We have locked him up, grounded him, deprived him of TV, but nothing helps. We don't know what to do."

One of the teachers said: "Yes he is completely hopeless in class also. He hides the other kids' boots, provokes everyone and twists and turns everything others say."

One of the other teachers turned to me and said: "What has he done that you have seen or heard?"

That kind of question is completely impossible for me to answer. Not that I don't understand what they are saying, and not that I haven't seen and heard what the boy has done. But their way of talking about him was full of values and judgments, and I didn't know what they expected me to say, because I can't talk that way, I couldn't speak judgmentally about their son.

It's not that I want to avoid talking that way, but much more basic, that I am *not able* to talk that way, that I *don't have* any valuations. I don't see the boy's behavior as a problem but as an expression for communication. He is *saying* something with his behavior, and the only way to talk about it is to try to figure out what he means. But these people were talking about the boy as if he was a problem entirely outside of them. And the minute the problem lies out there, outside of them, they have to change the world to make it better. But that isn't possible. For me the boy is the way he is, he has the difficulties he has and that's all there is to that. Children don't change just because you tell them to. When the environment changes they change too. That is their only way.

So instead of answering the question I said: "What problem do *you* as a person, as a unique individual, have with the boy having the issues he has?"

He at once moved the problem out to the boy again: "Why, the boy misbehaves so badly!"

"In what way does that impact *you*? How does it affect *you*?"

He moved the problem to the boy one more time: "But, you shouldn't behave that way."

"That is true, you shouldn't behave that way, but he does behave that way, and then we must make sure that our frustration and irritation don't reinforce his negative behavior. The only way *we* can help is to make sure that *we* don't have a problem with his problem. So I think we should talk about our problems with his behavior."

Then the mother told us what she had been like when she

was a child and was a problem for those around her and was criticized but that she didn't know what to do with that input because she was not aware of her own behavior. Then the others began telling about situations in their childhoods where the adults had judged them and punished them, and that given them no other opportunity to change than be passive and accommodating and scared. All at once they began to chime in and outdo each other with stories about their own bad behavior. They started laughing and the grim mood was as blown away.

I asked: "Based on what you have related, what would have helped in your situation?"

The father said: "What would have helped me would be that somebody told me what I could do and not just what I *couldn't* do. By myself I couldn't come up with something I could do to make it better."

One of the teachers said: "Yes, if somebody had non-judgmentally asked: what do you want to accomplish with what you are doing? Do you get that result with what you are doing? That would have helped me, because it would have got me to see the consequences of what I was doing."

Another of the teachers said: "Yes, *that* could be the right way to talk about this to help the boy." The mother said: "It is always so great when you join us Iris, because you always say something that gets me thinking differently, and suddenly I notice that my problems aren't as insoluble as I thought; that there are things I can do."

Me being an unusual element for others also causes information to come out in the atmosphere that makes it possible for me to know things which I think are common knowledge, but which turn out to be unique and sometimes secret – even for the one I am speaking with. In this way I often assume special meaning which lets me see myself in a mirror and learn something about who I am. I was talking with a woman who had problems with her parents. Her parents didn't talk with each other, they irritated each other, and she found it unbearable to visit and be together with them. She didn't take either side but felt that they were both birds of a feather. She said to me: "I would like to ask you for help, but I don't know what I need help with."

"Just start talking, it usually comes out what the issue is" I answered. She continued to talk about the problem and described three episodes.

While she was talking, as usual a lot of information from her body came out in the atmosphere. As usual this information appeared to me as an awareness of what she was talking about. I saw that her mother and father had a bad atmosphere between them, that they took every opportunity to wound each other. But when the father went to his other family he left this whole way behind. In the other family he was very intimate, very present. There were children there, and that's where he lived. That's what the real life was for him.

When I saw that I interrupted and said: "Wait a moment! Do you find it odd that there is such a bad atmosphere in your family with the double life your father lives?"

She turned white as a sheet. "What double life, what do you mean?"

"You just described his double life."

"No *that* I have never said. He doesn't have a double life!"

I thought to myself: Ah, these repressions, I miss those constantly. I sat there without saying anything more.

She sat silent for long time, in chaos, in a spin. After a long while she said: "Oh! Then everything makes sense. Then I understand in a whole new way why he gets so weird and unnatural, towards me also. And why I constantly end up taking my mothers side, which I don't like, because I think she is just as idiotic as he is in what's happening."

She asked me to tell her what I had seen.

"It looks like your father has a second family, and that there are children involved, maybe not his own, but there may be children that are his also.

She thanked me and said that this she would find out about.

About half a year later I met her again. Then she told me she had gone to see her father at the other family. When she got there he told her the whole story. He had two children in this family, and there were three other kids, and he had had this new family for seven years.

What I have learned from such episodes is that when a person talks with me about something that is a problem for her and has trust in me, then her body becomes so secure and relaxed that it conveys this information, which I capture. What I sometimes miss then is that the person herself is not always aware of what her body is telling me, which comes out in the atmosphere.

And while I have this ability when I have a task, when I

am "on", I am completely unaware of how people around me feel and what's happening around me when am not "on". I never *sense* how another person feels, I can only read it in the atmosphere, which I can't do if I am not "on".

Then I am indifferent to how they feel, then they are just somebody in the crowd. But the moment I get a task, it may be a question or a request for something, this state is dispelled, and then I can see how this person's atmosphere looks, and I know from experience what different problem-atmospheres look like. First I see the person's own atmosphere. Then I see how it works, what color and shape it has, if it is ragged, if it hangs together, if it is too compact, if it is too close or too far away. I know what such things mean, and it is in this way I can see if she is sad or angry or apathetic or suicidal. I use this information when I talk to the person and when she answers it comes out in the atmosphere what the problem is about. Not so that it ends up between us but rather behind me as background information.

That I have this ability can be confusing for others, because they think I always do it and therefore can tell how they feel, but I don't at all, and it can lead to disappointment and anger. I have to actively make sure that the cramp releases so I can turn "on".

I love my calendar. It is full at least two years in advance. The more there is in it, the freer I am. When people see my calendar and imagine that it is theirs they feel a noose around their neck and feel like all their time and independence is being consumed and disappears. Most people often have a need for unplanned, unstructured time. For me it is the opposite. When I see a word in the calendar about what will happen, what assignment I have, whom I will meet or where I will travel, at least one year in advance, then I become completely free, then there is order in the atmosphere, which allows my inner, my imagination, can open to: "How will that be?: Who will be there? What will it be about? What needs will the people have?"

Somebody asks: don't you get obsessive thoughts when you have filled your calendar this way?" For me the full calendar gives me impulses that make my whole inner self get that small added contribution that I can't get from myself. I get impulses to think and that makes the world come to me and become distinct. If I don't have it I find myself in a bubble which is so small that I don't hear or see or understand anything, and it is *then* that there are obsessions and repetitiveness, not when I have the calendar filled.

Before, I lived only in the present, in the moment, and what had been and what was going to be didn't exist for me in any real way, at most maybe as some pictures, a description, or a bunch of words that were not associated with me but were just a fact, something dead. It caused a lot of my life to be a time-less and place-less recycling and it was then that obsessions and stereotypy came in.

Now I have learned how to bring out memories from past things to the present and relive them, and this is very enjoyable. I know how to think about things planned in the future and bring even that to the present and fantasize about that. I know that the primary meaning of life is to feel alive.

This I can't do, but I know that I am alive, that I exist, and this I am happy about. I also know what value is and that the only value we have as humans is to exist. I exist, and that I can be entirely content with.

I know that when I am able to connect what I call Iris with what I call my self, the knowledge of life's value is actualized. Then the idea of the primary, that which prevails when nothing else prevails, becomes very clear as well as the idea of the secondary, that which begins and ends. And then I have access to all the information, both in the real world and the ordinary world. And, as I understand it, this is what people are searching for in the spiritual, although many people look for it in the wrong places. They think what they seek is something outside themselves and don't understand that it is a *state*, something one can enter within oneself. They mistakenly think that they need to do something in order to attain what they are seeking, not that they just need to remove what's in the way. They also don't know that what they are seeking isn't some permanent condition but something that you now and then happen upon. It is glimpses of joy. And these glimpses lend their color to everything else so they are valuable however short they may be.

Their value is related to the fact that I am alive, that I have a life which starts someplace and only goes in one direction and then ends. When I die, this value doesn't exist anymore. But that doesn't mean that I myself don't exist anymore: what has been gathered together and become me and has had experiences is repeated and exists in the atmosphere. And there are other people who take it in since we have the paradoxical characteristic that we are both perfected and incomplete. The mortal part of us makes it possible for the atmosphere to develop. The atmosphere can't evolve unless there is something that is alive; is born and dies. And this is what gives life value, that we change the atmosphere. Every life that is lived, even that of an aborted fetus, affects the atmosphere and brings something to it. And this is something you do whether you want to or not, and it has nothing to do with how bad or good you are.

Because of that it is incumbent upon us to not judge and blame other people. To prevent what is destructive is OK, but to punish others is to make yourself God, and that is impossible.

I play with words and meaning. Words are my tools and they enrich my life a lot. I am careful with words and seldom say things from habit. I stand before a person and capture some knowledge in the atmosphere about that person; I play with it and put a word to it. For example "power". He uses power instead of intimacy. If I said that word to him directly it wouldn't have any meaning for him.

In this way I don't use the word "power" as in a rut, but every time I use that word or any other word, it is new for me, and then it becomes a living force, a live being. I think that's what John meant when he said: "In the beginning was the Word, and the Word was with God, and the word was God."

I have learned from all my flaws and from those of others as well. I have learned to fix things that I have gotten wrong, that which can be fixed. The rest I have just learned from. I notice many misconceptions in myself and others and I do the work that is needed to correct them and try to free myself from ossified judgments inside me.

Such as what my mother always said: "You will never amount to anything." I repeated those words to myself and for a long time it kept me from even trying to see if I could handle some task or another that somebody put in front of me. But after Father said: "Don't say that. You can't know if she will amount to something", I started to wonder what I could become and what I could not become. In that way my mother's words gradually lost their power and the prejudgment crumbled.

When I was upset because I could never keep from making other people mad or taking offense my father said: "Iris, we all have the need for others, it's not only you, and everybody can't be resisting at the same time, so there will always be somebody that responds to you, so continue searching, even if it looks hopeless." This I have done and I know today that he was right. That's what much of my private life consists of: looking for those who for the moment are accessible, and this is exciting.

My security also comes from the fact there is a person who I know unconditionally is always there for me and engages with me, and that is Göran. His friendship has been the most stable base I have, which has always been there in the turbo of my life. With him I have always been able to talk, or come and be silent, or see a film together, or sit by his side with the PC, or drink a cup of tea. He usually exists inside me as company, and when I met him, my inner loneliness I had always had, which had worried me and been uncomfortable, gradually disappeared.

I also have other friends, but they come and go in my life,

even if they are life-long friends and 100% valuable. It is as if Göran is inside the cramp and the other friends are outside the cramp.

One time I was struck by the fact Göran had so many books and so many films and I asked if he had read all the books and seen all the films. "yes" he said, "almost all." I thought this must be fantastic, because I had read very little and skimmed through most of I had read. Then he said: "Think instead about everything you have done during that time and you won't feel envious any more." I did that and then I realized that comparisons are worthless, that they only lead to somebody being up and somebody down, pride and fall. Then I also realized that a mortal sin is not something you do to others, it's something you do to yourself, and then others lose by it also.

From my relationship with Göran I have understood what real friendship is, that it is life-long and doesn't vanish because you make an error, mess up, fail to understand how or when to be in contact. Real friendship exists, and there is no between time, no matter how long between times. I have also learned that it is the most private thing there is and that there is no prescribed template. No-one except you knows if it is a real friendship you have. It may also be that it is a one-sided friendship and that doesn't matter, it is also good, because it such a richness to really know that you have a person who is your friend. I believe our friendship is mutual, I believe that Göran appreciates me and I believe he knows I appreciate him. He is the kind don't have say too much, he understands anyway. He is able to bring out his feelings in a completely different way than I, but I know that he also struggles with things in his life.

All my other friends also exist and I am spinning a network that lives and grows. It is my private life and it contains people, people, people. Since I was twelve and understood completely that the human is something different than animal life, I have devoted myself to trying to understand it and I realize that the more I understand the more I realize that there is much more that is unfathomed and that that is a richness beyond all limits.

I also see that the paradigm shift that has taken place from industrial thinking to communications thinking means that the times are catching up with me. The youth understand in an entirely different way than grownups my way of perceiving the world, and for them the hang-up of wanting to be better than others and richer than others is not highly rated. For them it is about quality of life, i.e. having inner contentment.

In school today, as in almost every institution, they move in the other direction: children with distracting behavior are expected to adapt to normal constraints instead of the adults trying to understand the behavior and what its message is. If the child with the behavior is met with curiosity and interest, and if one talks with her without a bunch of values and diagnoses in the way, she can tell you what it actually is about. And then there is the possibility for cooperation that that gives her the possibility of solving the problem or healing or development. There my knowledge can be helpful, primarily by mentoring of those who work with other people and who are interested in their own development, instead of being good at changing and accommodating their clients according to going professional norms, which is to put a band aid on an abscess.

That's what my next book will be about.

People I meet today can't understand that I have had the problems I have. You simply can't be as well functioning as I am now if you have had the kinds of problems I have described the thinking is.

I have had a fabulous luck in life. I have been cared for exactly in the manner I have needed. It has allowed my damaged ingredients to be healed, and I have had sufficient strength to go through or around all obstacles, all walls and all dead ends I have run into.

There is a wonderful paradox in life. On the one hand, there is a deficiency, on the other it causes a treasure to emerge which you wouldn't have known about if the deficiency hadn't been there. Life certainly is strange and fantastic.

CHAPTER 9

Frequently asked questions about autism

What do you do as a parent when your autistic child faces something it must do and which is not negotiable, such as going to school each day? What do you do to get the child to go along without its feeling threatened?

The most important thing is to reconcile yourself to the situation and junk all expectations that things will work "normally". When you have accomplished that and there is no longer a dream in the way between you and the child, and in your communication with him you have taken the first step. Then if you have the focus inside yourself, you can play with the thought "What's the way I can to be happy today however it goes?" When you play with that thought you free yourself from the belief that time is of the essence. And you get into the playful thought that you have all the time in the world, in the next five minutes.

In that is the freedom for the child to just be present in getting up, putting on the outer clothes, and following you to the car. So long as the child perceives that you have all the time in the world and are happy and contented inside yourself there is nothing for the child to struggle against. Then it is possible for the child to unreflectively and happily go along with what is happening. The child doesn't need to accommodate itself but just does what the adult wants because that's the only thing there is.

The way it was for me was that when the grownups got to the state inside that they just *were* in the daily routine, without charge and without putting demands on me, then I could easily fit in with what was to happen. The hard part for the grownup was to control herself and not rush ahead and think of the result ahead of time, because as soon as she stopped being *present* in the situation my whole body objected and then I was forced to protest, resist or cling to something.

What should you do about all the compulsive behaviors that children with autism engage in?

The compulsion comes from the child having a need it can't interpret. What happens is that the child, instead of attending to the need, retreats into something secure because it is known and can be repeated. From the child's position this is a communication which says: "I have a need". The child doesn't say what the need it is because it doesn't know; only "I have a need". And for the child to relieve the burden it is your task to recognize the situation and think: "Now it is up to me to think of what need it could be that the child has." And just thinking that thought and being in the here and now often causes the pressure to let go in the child, and then it is a matter of guessing what need it concerns.

When the pressure is relieved and you are present in the situation it can happen that the child becomes aware of what the need is or at least so that it comes out in the atmosphere so to speak. If you are then present with curiosity or wonder you often get a glimpse of which need is involved. Then it is important that you don't miss that glimpse, but stay in it and play together with the child with your inkling or idea. Often it will turn out to be correct, even if you never could have *thought* what it was.

It may be as simple as that the child is too warm, but of itself doesn't think of removing its jacket. It just feels the over-heating and wants to be rid of it, but that feeling doesn't lead to an association with "take off the jacket". But if you make yourself present in the here and now, and make yourself curious it may happen that you suddenly see: "But you have so many clothes on. We'd better take your jacket off."

Sometimes compulsive behavior erupts when the child can't feel its own body, and only feels nothingness. What the child needs then is that you wrestle with it, lay it down on the floor and roll around, touch the child, hold it, wrap your arms around it, but without hoping that you will get a hug, because then there will just be a tantrum. Or you can start to sing.

When we autistics detect that there is no limit for us we get anxious if nobody takes control and starts to steer us. Then the cramp releases and it becomes pleasant again.

Why is it so difficult for an autistic person to communicate and answer in a normal way?

The reason is that the child doesn't know there is any other way to be than the way she is. The child finds herself in a foreign country where she doesn't understand the language that everybody else speaks. She views the world solely as things which surround her but which do not have anything to do with her.

When I was ten and saw that one person could say something that another person could understand, and the other person could reply with something that the first one understood, then I discovered a different reality that I hadn't known about before. I saw that it existed but I had no idea how to have that kind of interaction with another person. What I did then was to practice by looking at myself in the mirror until I saw myself, until the state I was in changed to an interaction with myself; my appearance vanished, what I looked at vanished, and it was like something completely different was between me and the mirror image. And then my whole self-image was transformed. To start with this lasted only for a short while and then I returned to my normal way of seeing. But I had seen that the other reality existed, and I could see that the grownups were in it almost continuously. Also, I realized that I had always been separated from it. But when I was in the other state, in the real world, I was no longer separated from myself and from others.

The child that has this communication difficulty fails to develop the natural communication and compensates for it in its own way. It turns out that most such children have similar ways to express themselves and that *is* communication, but it is not easy for the people around them to understand. If they accept in their mind that it *is* communication, it is possible to achieve accord and understanding.

What can you do as a parent to achieve
communication with you autistic child?

The problem for most people is that they want the child to adapt and communicate in *their* way, and that is an impossibility for an autistic child. It doesn't have the emotional basis required for communicating on somebody else's terms, therefore the communication becomes one-way. If you realize this you open yourself to the possibility of real communication and development, both for you and for your child.

The conditions for the natural development of communications with the autistic child are the short moments when it for a millisecond makes contact with you or some other person. In that contact the child gets imprinted by the other's communication. That's why the child's development gets so jerky, because for most of the time it doesn't have real contact with somebody else.

The difficulty for you is that it is so hard to constantly be wholly present, because you react to all the rejections from the child.

*What should I do as an adult to not let my feeling of
rejection inhibit me in communicating with the child?*

First of all it is important that you become aware of what
you do yourself. That you acknowledge the pain you feel when
you try to engage the child and you experience rejection. It is
important that you conclude that pain is harmless: "It hurts
and is unpleasant, but it is not harmful, so I can bear it." It is
important that you free yourself from the preconceptions that it
isn't supposed to feel that way, that it isn't supposed to happen
that the child rejects you.

When you feel into that pain and admit that it exists you are
in a kind of openness within yourself, and you are vulnerable,
and you have that contact with yourself which may make it
possible for the child to have a moment of contact with you.

Secondly, you should try to look at it as a challenge, and
remember that that, in ninety-seven cases of a hundred there
won't be contact. That's just how it is, there's no need to attach
any importance to it. Adopt the attitude ahead of time that
that it doesn't matter if there is contact or not, just let it be
free and easy, so it will be neither successful nor unsuccessful,
neither better nor worse. "I make myself available for contact,
and whatever happens happens." Make sure that you don't try
to control what will happen because the least little attempt at
control makes the contact unattainable.

Thirdly, it is about you realizing that you are privileged to be
put against the wall with things so pointed that you can't hide
from your own hang-ups and rituals, and that you achieve an

awareness of yourself that life normally does not force on you otherwise. According to the experts, this is the best stimulus for preventing senility.

When you can appreciate your own difficulties with communication it will inspire a joy in you that greatly reduces the tendency to depression and promotes bodily well-being like nothing else. This was in great measure the secret to my father's attitude, that he could not imagine a better life than to be needed, and to meet the challenges in being forced to come up with a lot of things to make progress with me.

What do you do to let an autistic child become independent?

There is a misconception in the way people think about independence. An autistic person is totally independent, completely his or her own person, but has no self- preservation instinct. That is undeveloped. When you as a parent think of the child becoming independent you think of him or her being able to wash, clean, and do dishes, i.e. handle ADL (Activities of Daily Living). To develop this is the is the most difficult task for a person who cannot be imprinted by what other people do, who cannot adopt it or emotionally imitate it.

We autistics don't suffer from this lack of independence, the way normal people would. For us it is precisely this dependence on others which compensates for our non-communication because it entails others doing something to us, for us, and together with us. And that is the only type of connection we can participate in. For us there is no urge or ambition to take this on in order to be independent. And this is where the uneven struggle originates: our surroundings want us to be externally well functioning, but for us this would only leads to inner isolation.

That's why it is the wrong order to try to make the child ADL-wise well functioning in the hope that it will become independent and communicative. That's the misconception. Only when an autistic person succeeds in achieving communication with others so that a natural connection emerges, then first is that person interested in handling ADL.

It is not possible to make the child externally well functioning and then wait for communication to develop. The communication must come first, and only after that can the autistic person begin to practice being externally well functioning.

This is usually difficult for a parent to understand. We autistics can only be as well functioning externally as our ability to communicate permits. This is perhaps best seen in those who have Aspergers syndrome, a mild form of autism. They can be fully aware of what is needed but still not be able to accomplish it with routines in daily life, but often need help with cleaning, clothes, and such.

We eventually learn as parents to communicate with our children but then we get in situations with other people and we run into problems we so often don't know how to deal with. For example we know how to arrange things around our child so it can play and be content and have it pleasant. But then we

need to leave her in school or the day-care and then we have to
explain to the staff what they need to do, and they often resent
it because they are the experts and know themselves what to
do. And then we see how the child has tantrums and reverts in
development. How do we handle this? How can we as parents
talk with the staff without them feeling insulted or denigrated?

The first thing is to explain that this is a child with an
unusual method of communication. Try to explain it to the staff
approximately as follows:

It is important to think roughly the same way as when
dealing with someone who is blind or deaf or disabled, i.e.
to think practically: this child needs this special arrangement
because it has this disability.

Try to talk to the staff about this until they abandon their
attempts to normalize the child. The problem for the child is
not that it isn't together with the others; the problem is that
it is unable to communicate with the others. Therefore, it isn't
possible to just put the child in a group, it needs a bridge.
What constitutes that bridge is individual and the staff needs
all the information from the parents about exactly this child's
characteristics and behaviors and what they mean.

If the staff can listen to this and really learn from it, the child
will recognize in the staff what it knows from its parents, and
then it will have a real possibility to participate in the group.

If that works, what do you then do when you go into a store
and the child tries to orient itself in its way and the people are

disturbed by it?

What I experienced many times when my father took me with him in different situations where people were unaware of my behaviors was that he quickly informed them about it: "I have a child with me who has some unusual behaviors. But it is completely harmless. Just ignore it and it passes after a while."

What brings out the worst behaviors in autistic children is that other people get scared of an unusual behavior and react with an urge to correct the child or do something about it. This causes the child to either be delighted and behave even worse to get more attention, or get scared or convulsive and have more negative behaviors. I use to call this the "Don't-spill-on-the-tablecloth" syndrome. When you are dealing with children, and they are allowed to be within themselves without being scared or anxious, they often behave perfectly and handle themselves fine. But the moment somebody says "Don't spill on the tablecloth" a kind of tension comes over the child and the tendency to spill is eighty times greater. We autistics are subjected to this situation all too frequently and this leads to our behavior being worse than it could have been.

As a parent it is important that you say to yourself: "There is no point in me being anxious or worried about that kind of situation occurring, but I count on it happening. Probably there will be a situation which is like previous situations. Or else, a completely new situation arises. In either case I gain experience in the art of tackling difficult situations with an unusual child. Plus, I see it as a challenge, as something interesting, as something that the others involved can have some benefit from. Even if they don't think that right now, I know that's how it is."

The Russian parents I have worked with for many years say that what has been invaluable for them is their habit of meeting once a month to discuss all these perfectly impossible situations they have experienced with their children in public. There they relate for each other the dramatics they have been involved in, which has allowed them to learn from both their own and others' situations, consequently they can tackle almost everything they encounter.

So I recommend that parent with unusual children form networks with four to six children where they meet regularly.

How do you think about school?

When you have come so far that it is no longer a problem to take the child away from home and take her to school, and it works OK to leave the child with the teachers and other students, then the difficult problem arrives. We who have communication difficulties can't accommodate ourselves to learning the traditional way. We may be as intelligent as anybody, but we still can't use that intelligence in the traditional way.

What you as a parent need to know is that most children with autism don't have a problem learning what is taught in school. However, we can't give responses and tell what we know in the way it was taught. If you as a parent dare to have confidence that you child is fully capable of learning what the school is teaching without you needing proof, then your child will be fine in a normal school.

Today there is something called facilitated communication and with that method grown-ups with autism have learned how to express themselves and communicate, and then they have said that they were very sorry that they were not able attend regular school as children but were put in special classes, often together with retarded children. There they could learn only the most basic things at an elementary level, and they feel they didn't get a general education. They feel that they have been made to keep training their body to express something they knew but couldn't express.

Therefore the same thing as when you put the child in day care holds true, that you as the parent need to help the teachers understand that they should not underrate the child's intelligence, which is like that of other children, but that the difference is that this child can't communicate. During the school years it is important hat you become aware of the normal course of development so that you put the child in situations where it gets the same experiences as other children of that age, but that you don't expect that it will lead to the child learning to function in those situations. It is enormously important that the child have the experience of such situations. Because the moment it is possible the child will apply the knowledge it has received, even if it may take many years before it happens.

What you as a parent have to discard is the hope that your child will *become* something and instead learn that the child *is* the person he is and make sure he gets the help he needs. We who have communication difficulties need extended arms; we always need help with the thing we can't do by ourselves, and that is not spoiling us, it is a necessity. Most parent have a guilty conscience because the think they are spoiling their children, but that is not the case.

How as a parent do you handle that the child has become a teenager and is beginning to be interested in the opposite sex?

It is important to remember that the physical and sexual development is not in the least impacted by autism. The longing for a partner and the want of a partner and the ignorance of how to deal with sexual feelings means that there is a huge area which is very important for the parents to think through.

First you have to think back to yourself when you entered puberty and until you were grown up and got it figured out. Just thinking back on yourself, your own experience, helps you abstain from a lot of value judgments between you and your autistic child. Every time you want the child to change a behavior which is unacceptable in society, particularly this is so important. It doesn't work to moralize, what's needed is to give very clear directives about how and when this young person can use his/her sexuality.

How to approach and show interest for the opposite sex is something that the child needs to learn in very concrete terms. Here is an example. However strong feelings one has for another person what is expected is to greet the person politely, shake hands and not pay any attention to all the feelings one gets on the inside. Or you may tell a person you want to hug her but then back off and let her respond or reject. You say it and then do nothing, then it is up to the other one to do something.

This whole pair-relation development needs to happen in very small steps, and you have to teach your child in a very concrete and detailed way. It is something that we autistics have the ability to learn because there is such a powerful motivation. And make sure that you as a parent don't waste that opportunity and try to slide past the discomfort. Use the time well when the child is so motivated.

Then there is a period when the teenager has a great need to free himself from his extended arms. It doesn't matter how much or how little he is able to handle. He still gets an enormous urge to free himself from all those who constrains him and above all from everything that represents the old. This is caused by two factors: one is that the child is constantly pulled back by his environment and can't get out of the old. The other is that those who know all the routines and rituals and know precisely how to act as his extended arms, they don't see the new, they don't see the change.

Both of those factors become very great obstacles for the teenager's development. At this time when this liberation becomes an issue it is a good idea to arrange an entirely new place to live such as boarding school, his own apartment or a commune. What is needed is a milieu where the child can keep the contact with the parents but also leave that contact and have another world parallel with the home world.

It is enormously important to not focus on the effect of the disability on this liberation but on the natural urge to be free, to be grown up.

Of all the questions that I get this is the most central one.

Why is it so difficult to accept that your child isn't like others?
Why does it feel harder to have an autistic child than to
have one who is blind, or deaf, or disabled?

If a child is retarded, or paralyzed, or has some other visible physical handicap it is something the parents sooner or later come to accept, that's nature and nothing can change it. They realize it is some thing they have to live with and find a good way to handle it.

But the autistic child is constantly playing hide-and-seek. In some areas it functions adequately and in others it is completely hopeless. This cat-and-mouse game makes the experience for the parents extremely frustrating.

Another reason is that an autistic child may one day know something as perfectly as if he has done it his whole life, and the next day that knowledge is completely gone. For the parents this doesn't compute, and the uneven behavior constantly nourishes the parents' hopes that it will be possible to get the child to function normally. They may also come to suspect that from the child's side it is a game of defiance or a strategy for disobedience and troublemaking.

An autistic child always taunts the expected, the natural. The natural is to be in connection and contact, and an autistic child is not. The autistic child thereby also mocks reciprocity, that all relationship is give and take. The autistic child is either in nothingness or only in taking. It does not give.

The parents' hopes that the child will function naturally are constantly mocked. They constantly swing between hope and despair and it never gets to where it makes sense. What characterizes autism is the communications lock and the shifting between good functioning and non-functioning.

Someone who lives with an autistic person needs to scrap her expectations and instead learn to constantly ask herself: "what is it that applies now?"

Why do autistic children have so many tantrums?
How should a grownup handle these outbursts?

One reason an autistic child often has tantrums is that she doesn't perceive her body and herself as being one and the same, that the body has any significance. The child sees how other people function in communication and how they think and feel and react since these exist as information in the atmosphere. The child thinks that she communicates the same way as other people. She doesn't experience her own behaviors as strange or unusual or destructive. She is used to them and therefore she gets very upset when her surroundings react negatively to her behavior instead of to what she is trying to communicate. Then the child feels run over and misunderstood.

If, for example, the child isn't allowed to tap the table with her fingers, or spin around, or keep humming she gets agitated and then the cramp sets in. It's as if a normal person asks another person something and he says: "stop frowning" instead of answering the question. The autistic child often has great patience with such off-topic communication but eventually it snaps and then the outburst starts.

The child is often misunderstood. The grown-ups have bad timing: things are happening too slow or too fast. Frustration is stored in the body of the child just as in others. And when the child eventually comes into a situation with a real connection it immediately gets the impulse to unload the stored frustration, and then it often comes in the form of an outburst. Then it's important that the grownup doesn't try to stop the outburst or manipulate it away, but just makes sure the child doesn't get hurt by it.

After a healthy outburst like that the child is much more communicative. Therefore it is important for the parent to take a break from his or her tasks during the outburst and just be in connection with the child, because then it has the opportunity to free itself of its frustration and be healed. If you just continue with your activities the outburst won't be complete and healing, but leave remnants that have to come out later.

Another cause of outbursts is situations when the child feels insecure because the external reality is not secure and familiar. It may be a question of too much change in the routines and rituals or that new people enter the picture. If the external reality gets so chaotic that the child can't orient itself her possibility for internal movement gets so small that she becomes anxious which triggers the impulses for an outburst. Such outbursts need to be treated entirely differently than the previous type.

The grownup needs to do something to reestablish the external security. It may mean closing a door or bring out a stuffed animal or singing a familiar song. In other words, focus on something that can be a bridge to an orientation in the environment for the child. The outburst calms down as soon as the external security returns.

But if you don't know what causes the tantrum?
What do you do then?

It is important that you don't start controlling the child. Don't do anything, just stop and observe the child. See first if there is any danger involved because then, of course, you have to intervene immediately. But if there is no danger you have plenty of time to think about what intuitive impulses you are getting. Often when the child has an outburst there is some information of what the child needs right then and it is up to you as a parent to read it.

If you stay calm and just observe the child you will get ideas about what the need is. Maybe just for you to be present. Maybe you just need to put your hand on the child's hand. Or that you need to speak calmly about everyday things or about the coming day. Or that you describe for the child what you think happened: "Sometimes we have anger inside us and it wants to come out", or "Sometime we get very unhappy about something." When you say those things you need to allow your own consciousness and your own body to feel how it is to be sad or angry or glad, so that your own emotion in some way emerges from yourself and comes out in the atmosphere, hopefully something of the feeling the child has which it can capture.

Then the outburst often changes. It subsides and the child ends up in her feeling instead of in the outburst. The autistic child is to a certain degree like an infant. It cries when something feels wrong, but it doesn't know what's wrong. By talking about what feeling it might be that is in the child which has caused the outburst you can help the child find that feeling, and then the outburst stops and the child ends up in the feeling instead, and thereby in communication.

What do you do if a tantrum happens in a store where everything is different and unpredictable and you have to make sure the child doesn't steal or break something?

The first thing is that when you walk into a store you decide for yourself: "OK, what will happen will happen." If you hope it will go well, it won't because that hope destroys the external security for the child. But if you have the attitude that what will be will be, you can release the child and let it orient itself, let it touch things, smell them, feel them and turn them over. Most of the time nothing is damaged. The child is doing this to build its security in a new and strange world. If you give yourself time to observe this without doing anything you will notice when the child is finished with it, and then you can shop under normal conditions. It's that timing which is important.

If the tantrum happens in the checkout line, what do I do then?

Outbursts in the checkout line are caused by several factors. One is that the grown-ups are tense, observing and distant and then the external environment gets insecure. The parent is already prepared for an outburst, which reveals that she had hoped things would go well this time. And this hope is the triggering factor. That's why it is important to constantly maintain the attitude that what will be will be. Then you are present in a way which allows you to influence the atmosphere around the child so that it minimizes the need for an outburst.

Another reason for an outburst in the checkout line is that after a while in the store the child has had time to orient itself and gained some security. When the child notices that it is time to leave the store it feels uncomfortable because a new change is impending, and the outburst is against that: "now, when I finally feel at home we have go out again."

It is a problem for the child to be in the store and get oriented and it is a problem to leave the store. But it is important that you not let this prevent you from taking the child with you to the store, because the child derives great benefit from doing this: going into something strange, get oriented, break off from the familiar, and go out again. Often there are too few changes for autistic persons because the parents find it troublesome since changes lead to outbursts. But the child doesn't suffer any ill effects from it.

How can I get my autistic child to be toilet trained? Pooping works o.k., this we have a routine for. After breakfast I put him on the toilet and then he sits there until he has done what he is supposed to. But tinkling is much harder since it is needed several times per day. You can't put the kid on the toilet and say "tinkle now!" How do you get him to feel by himself that he needs to go to the toilet?

This immaturity is at about the level of a normal one to two year old. What the autistic child needs is lots of tactile stimulation. Touch the child all over his body, pull on arms and legs, bend and stretch them in a pleasant way. The more you work with this the easier it is for the body to mature in this function. It is OK to begin this stimulation so long as the child is younger than 15. If you do this pleasant body stimulation several times per day it will lead to stimulation of the signals for the tinkle and pooping urge.

What's important to remember is that this is a pedagogic question. It is not a behavior pattern modification that is required. It is the sensory stimulation in the body that leads to maturing.

Is there any way I help my child begin to talk. I know that he understands everything and that he really can speak, but it is like he doesn't get to around to doing it.

Very often when a child doesn't speak it is because there are no impulses between the consciousness and the speech organs. What you can do is to put the child on your lap, put your cheek against the child's cheek and you both look at the same thing. You say "The suuuunnnn. The suuuunnnn shiiiinnnes. Oooohhh preeettttyyy suuuunnnn." If you make yourself conscious of the coupling between your consciousness and your speech organ, it may give an impulse for the child to make that coupling. In some children the preconditions for this coupling is missing, but in some it exists and it is these that can be stimulated to begin speaking.